CW00922521

The Seven Stone Path

An Everyday Journey to Wisdom

Peter Bolland

"A brilliant synthesis of wisdom drawn from the world's great philosophies and spiritual traditions. Truly a great book—a magnum opus."

— Joan Borysenko, PhD, author of *Minding the Body, Mending the Mind*

"This remarkable book will change lives."

— Richard Louv, author of *Our Wild Calling* and *Last Child in the Woods*

BALBOA.PRESS
A DIVISION OF HAY HOUSE

Balboa Press books may be ordered through booksellers or by contacting:

Balboa Press
A Division of Hay House
1663 Liberty Drive
Bloomington, IN 47403
www.balboapress.com
844-682-1282

Print information available on the last page.

ISBN: 979-8-7652-4011-3 (sc)
ISBN: 979-8-7652-4013-7 (hc)
ISBN: 979-8-7652-4012-0 (e)

Library of Congress Control Number: 2023904323

Balboa Press rev. date: 08/10/2023

Praise for *The Seven Stone Path*

If you've ever wondered, "What is enlightenment," and if so, "How do I get there?" Peter Bolland has laid out a universal path for you, paved by seven sacred stones. We all want the same thing: love, freedom, and happiness. In this comprehensive volume, a brilliant synthesis of wisdom drawn from the world's great philosophies and spiritual traditions, you hold the means to awakening. Go to it! Truly a great book – a magnum opus. I hope it becomes an enduring classic.

Joan Borysenko, Ph.D.
Author of *Minding the Body, Mending the Mind*

"This remarkable book will change lives. Peter Bolland is the rare wise man who would never claim that title, because he knows that the wisest people are the ones who say, 'I don't know.' With great humility, he offers a shared road through humankind's spiritual beliefs, a road that takes us home."

Richard Louv
Author of *Our Wild Calling* and *Last Child in the Woods*

In this remarkable book, a gifted and compassionate teacher gives readers a guide to access the wisdom that is within all of us. By following the Seven Stone Path that Peter Bolland paves for us, he allows us to awaken our inner wisdom through the teachings of ancient systems, and in a way that applies to us in this moment in time. This beautifully laid out path ties together teachings from various wisdom traditions as the foundation, and then teaches us how to bring them into action so that we can live our best and most awakened lives.

Sheila Patel, MD
Medical Director, Chopra Global

Life is large, unpredictable, and messy. We are small, and brief, and highly biodegradable. How then are we to live? How are we to make meaning, and live deeply and fully with open hearts and minds? In *The Seven Stone Path* Peter Bolland skillfully weaves together the inquiry and insights of philosophical traditions, world religions, and the great mystics. He offers us real guidance on ways to contemplate our own small lives in light of what we know and the vastness of the Mystery that lives beyond all of our ideas. *The Seven Stone Path* offers us guidance and whets our appetite for deeply joyful living.

Oriah "Mountain Dreamer" House
Author of *The Invitation*

In your hands you are holding something more like a treasure chest whose every surface is adorned with pearls of wisdom, than simply a book made of paper, glue, and ink. Written with the skill and soul of a poet, the depth of a philosopher, the openness of an eager student, and the mastery of an accomplished teacher, *The Seven Stone Path* will guide you into a deep and rewarding journey of self-discovery. A journey that simply cannot leave you where it first finds you.

Wendy Craig-Purcell
Spiritual Director and Founder of The Unity Center, San Diego, and author of *Ask Yourself This*

It might come across as faint praise to call *The Seven Stone Path* "philosophy 101" but as a fellow author who has always striven to make the esoteric understandable and enchanting, I have met more than my match. This is truly a lovely book; not just because of the wealth of information, experience, knowledge and wisdom (demonstrated by an author who actually understands the differences between those four) but also because it is beautifully written. Peter, you are the love that binds the moon and the stars together to the very depths of your soul – the kind of love that, when necessary, doesn't take prisoners.

Maggy Whitehouse
Author, broadcaster, mystic, and maverick priest

Peter Bolland is an enigma. A regular guy with remarkable insight, Peter explores this life with an aplomb that both challenges and inspires. *The Seven Stone Path* embraces

Plato's belief that wisdom is more lived than understood, and truth is revealed less through books and equations and more through the breeze gently rippling your curtains. Read this book, have a cup of tea, walk outside, and let the sun warm your face. Take a deep breath and smile. You will be closer to finding your own path.

Chip Franklin, comedian, radio host at KGO San Francisco

The Seven Stone Path:

An Everyday Journey to Wisdom

Contents

Introduction: The Beginning of Wisdom

Wonder is the dawn of wisdom. To be steadily and consistently wondering is *sadhana* (spiritual practice).
—*Nisargadatta Maharaj*[1]

The Seven Stone Path

This is a book about wisdom. Not my wisdom, but the universal wisdom that wells up through the soil of the world's spiritual and philosophical traditions. When we search beneath the surface inflections of time, language, and culture, a small number of universal concepts and practices emerge. When we get past the doctrinal debates, we notice a deep and rich commonality that transcends all temporal, cultural, geographical, and ideological borders. I am not the first person to notice this. This truth is as old as philosophy itself.

After teaching philosophy, religion, and mythology to college students for many years, leading bright and curious young people through the vast storehouses of the collective wisdom of humankind, an unmistakable realization began to take shape. Behind all the endless diversity and complexity of the world's wisdom traditions lay a deceptively simple set of insights and suggestions. If we slow down, step back, and deepen our attention, seven key ideas come into view. If we learned to embody these ideas, our lives would change for the better.

These seven ideas constitute a transformational process that effectively moves us through our own evolution from earlier stages characterized by dependency, fear, and ego protection to later stages characterized by freedom, compassion, and joy. In other words, if we follow the seven stone path, we will emerge from the cave of conditioned consciousness a little wiser, a little freer, and a lot happier.

The seven ideas are acceptance, surrender, engagement, allowance, enjoyment, love, and integration. The goal of this book is to broaden our understanding of these crucial ideas and root them deeply into our everyday lives.

This book is not about the acquisition of theoretical knowledge. We're already overwhelmed with information and ideas. What we need is a map that leads us out of our problem-enamored minds and toward the home we have always longed for—the realization of our own best lives. This book could be that map.

An Everyday Journey to Wisdom

Moving toward wisdom is not a once-in-a-while thing; it's an everyday journey. It is a process deeply rooted in innumerable insights, shaped by countless choices, realized in action, and nourished by the voices of those who came before us and those who walk alongside us. Buoyed by the wisdom of others, we sail toward the harbor of our own transcendent realization.

Moving toward wisdom is not an esoteric practice reserved only for specialists and insiders. Cultivating wisdom, like breathing, is an innate, natural process available to everyone. Wisdom cannot be transferred from one person to another. Instead, it is drawn out of us by questions, challenges, and our own unavoidable suffering. The best teachers are never concerned with content delivery. What they really want to do is shake us awake from the dream of unconsciousness.

What Is Wisdom?

How can we seek wisdom until we have some sense of what it is? Can you look for something you cannot describe and don't understand? If we don't know what wisdom looks like, how will we recognize it when it begins to emerge?

For many years I've been asking my students, "What is the difference between wisdom and knowledge?" It is always a rich and rewarding discussion. At first it seems simple to distinguish the two, but then as often happens in philosophy, the well-drawn boundaries between different concepts become diaphanous in the light of dawning awareness. In the beginning, knowledge seems to be about facts and ideas you can get from books and teachers, whereas wisdom seems to come from experience. But then we realize that the reverse is also true—knowledge can come from experience, and wisdom can come from books or teachers.

Let's start again.

Upon deeper reflection, we realize that knowledge is often disembodied from behavior or action whereas wisdom manifests itself in behaviors and actions. In other words, knowledge seems purely conceptual, whereas wisdom bridges the conceptual and the actual. Wisdom is not just having the right ideas. Wisdom changes us. Wisdom isn't something you know. It's something you do.

In traditional Greek philosophy knowledge is divided into two categories, theoretical and practical. Theoretical knowledge is knowledge about how and why things work the way they do. One could have theoretical knowledge about the causes of the American Civil War or the life cycle of the Chinook salmon. Practical knowledge, in contrast, is knowledge of how to do things, like bake a cake or perform heart surgery. What if wisdom has components of both of these modes of knowing, the theoretical and the practical? What if wisdom is the result of being able to put into practice the perennial principles of the world's wisdom traditions and teachings?

As we look at the way wisdom is understood around the world and throughout history, it seems that the best definition is this: Wisdom is the art of living well. It is not a specific doctrine or theology, nor is it a rigid prescription of specific behaviors and actions. Wisdom is a way of being in the world that results in a deeply satisfying life of purpose, love, effectiveness, freedom, and joy.

What Would a Wise Person Be Like?

One way of approaching the question of wisdom is to envision a wise person. What would a wise person be like? How would you describe their qualities? How does a wise person show up in the world?

Would a wise person be locked into a rigid and fixed thinking pattern, or would they be open-minded and flexible?

Would a wise person be anxious, worried, and fearful, or would they be calm, serene, and optimistic?

Would a wise person be continually disgruntled, disappointed, and dissatisfied, forever craving more, or would they be joyful and satisfied?

Would a wise person be timid, indecisive, and tentative; hamstrung by self-doubt or, worse, self-loathing? Or would they be quietly confident and self-accepting?

Would a wise person be self-absorbed, locked into victim consciousness, and obsessed with scarcity, or would they be generous and selfless?

Would a wise person be stuck in the past, reliving memories of prior glory and trauma? Would they be caught up in worry about possible future problems? Or would they be fully present and available in this moment?

Would a wise person be rigidly controlling and deeply rooted in the consciousness of fear and anxiety, or would they be fluidly disciplined and masterful, embodying the consciousness of co-creation and cooperation?

Would a wise person be humorless, dour, somber, and serious, or would they be playful?

From these and other questions, a portrait begins to emerge from the depths of our own experience. We know this person because deep down inside, we are this person. When we put the characteristics of a wise person together into one descriptive passage, do we recognize our own best selves?

A wise person is open-minded and flexible; calm, serene and optimistic; joyful and satisfied; quietly confident and self-accepting; generous and selfless; fully present and available in this moment; fluidly disciplined and masterful, deeply rooted in the consciousness of co-creation and cooperation; playful.

By envisioning a wise person, we move much closer toward an understanding of what wisdom is. And when we have a clearer idea of what wisdom is, we have a better chance of recognizing it when it begins to well up through the cracks in our own lives. Search your heart. Is it not true that cultivating and realizing these qualities is one of our deepest dreams? Do we not yearn for wisdom? Do we not long to break free of our old limiting ideas and move into a life of simplicity, clarity, insight, ease, purpose, and love? Wouldn't we all like to be this person?

The Beginning of Wisdom

Wisdom begins with a very simple shift any of us can do right now with no special preparation, training, or strained exertion. Wisdom begins with an honest admission of ignorance.

The best preparation for wisdom is a condition of deep and genuine humility. For many people, even this simple step is too challenging. Many of us are so invested in our current worldview, our current collection of carefully constructed concepts, opinions, and perceptions, that giving them up sounds dangerous, like a short, steep drop into madness. Abandoning our hard-won concepts and understandings feels like failure.

Buddha pointed out that in our unenlightened consciousness, we are attached to our opinions, most of them secondhand, and our egos become so interwoven with our conditioning that when our ideas are threatened, it feels as if our very being is under attack. This cognitive illusion is the source of untold suffering, both on the personal and global level. According to Buddha, wisdom begins with letting go.

Confucius is blunt: "When you know a thing, to recognize that you know it, and when you do not know a thing, to recognize that you do not know it. That is knowledge."[2] If your head is full of false opinions, half-baked notions, prejudices, rumors, inaccuracies, and pride-based assumptions, there is simply no room for the truth. Wouldn't it be better to know nothing than to believe a raft of lies? Twentieth-century Hindu teacher Nisargadatta Maharaj put it this way: "The very admission 'I am ignorant' is the dawn of knowledge. An ignorant man is ignorant of his own ignorance.... To know that you do not know and do not understand is true knowledge, the knowledge of a humble heart."[3]

The most famous and influential story illustrating this curious dynamic is the story of Socrates, told by Plato in the fourth century BCE. In many ways, Socrates is the most important philosopher in the Western tradition. It is Socrates who sets the tone for all the philosophy to follow. To appropriate Voltaire's famous remark about God, if Socrates did not exist, it would be necessary to invent him.

Socrates wrote nothing, but his student Plato thankfully felt no such compunctions. Plato wrote a lot. To this day, his dialogues constitute the hallowed canon of Western philosophy and are essential reading for every lover of wisdom who followed. After Socrates's death, Plato used him as the central character in nearly all of his dialogues, etching an indelible portrait of a man singularly devoted to the love of learning and the pursuit of wisdom. For twenty-four centuries, philosophy students have had their first glimpse of the noble pursuit of wisdom through the eyes of Plato's beloved teacher Socrates.

Socrates was executed by the Athenian court for the crime of corrupting the young and worshipping the gods whom the state did not worship. Those hardly sound like death penalty charges, and historians disagree about the real motivation for the prosecution. In any event, one of the most lasting results of the trial is Plato's rendering of Socrates's defense, or *apologia*, in which Socrates attempts to explain to the jury how he gained his notorious reputation for being arrogant, iconoclastic, caustic, and ultimately treasonous to the values of Athenian culture.

Facing a large and boisterous jury, Socrates tried to explain how he was drawn into the philosophic life. It all began at the Oracle at Delphi.

Socrates's friend Chaerephon had visited the Oracle and asked the resident priestess if there was "…anyone wiser than Socrates. The priestess replied that there was no one."[4] Chaerephon rushed back to Athens to deliver the wonderful news. Instead of feeling honored and flattered, Socrates was horrified. The Oracle's words threw him into a crisis. He knew he wasn't the wisest man in Athens, yet the gods don't lie. This irreconcilable paradox drove him like a lash.

Socrates set out to disprove the Oracle. It seemed to be the only reasonable thing to do. He tracked down every wise person in Athens in order to interview them and lay bare his own intellectual inferiority, thereby disproving the Oracle. But something went wrong. As he dialogued with every wise person he could find, he came to a startling realization: they were just as ignorant as he was. But it was worse than that. Not only were they just as ignorant as he was, but also they suffered from an even deeper malady: they were utterly unaware of their ignorance. They really thought they were wise even though they were not. Socrates, in contrast, was completely conscious of his own ignorance.

It began to dawn on Socrates that the only advantage he had over these so-called wise people was that he was humble enough to admit his limitations—he was aware of his ignorance, whereas they were not aware of theirs. Socrates's simple admission made him the wisest man in Athens by default.

The portrait of wisdom that emerges from Plato's *Apologia* is a surprising one. Wisdom, it turns out, is not a body of knowledge or information, or even a carefully constructed edifice of well-informed opinions. Wisdom is a condition of consciousness characterized by humility, openness, willingness, fluidity, and formlessness.

Wisdom is content-free.

At first it is difficult for the mind, in its normal way of thinking, to make sense of this. There is nothing to hold on to. How can wisdom be so empty? Of course, the search for wisdom doesn't end here; this is only the beginning. But without this crucial first step—the admission of ignorance—none of the subsequent steps are possible. In his courageous and costly quest for wisdom, Socrates had stumbled onto the most important philosophical statement ever made: "I don't know."

Wisdom as an Admission of Ignorance

"The Dao that can be told is not the eternal Dao."[5] So begins the essential wisdom classic *Dao De Jing*, compiled in China twenty-five centuries ago. From Plato to Jesus, from Buddha to Einstein, from Yoda to the Wizard of Oz, sages through the ages agree. The ultimate mystery of existence cannot be told, explained, or defined—it can only be pointed to with parables, analogies, and metaphors. The willingness to acknowledge our limitations, specifically the limitation of the intellect to fully apprehend reality, is a perennial principle found throughout the world's wisdom traditions. The Qur'an famously lists the ninety-nine names of God. But the Sufis know that the truest name is the one hundredth—silence. The Upanishads of ancient India claim that ultimate reality is beyond all thoughts and forms; no tongue can touch it, no word can soil it. We can only say what it is not. Buddhist philosophy affirms this fundamental emptiness by defining ultimate reality as *shunyata*, or the void, a realm of being beyond even the concept of being. Again and again, this theme confronts the seeker of wisdom. What you seek cannot be grasped by the conceptual mind nor adequately expressed by language. Zen Buddhism reminds us that even our most eloquent words and brilliant concepts are merely fingers pointing at the moon. No one can hold the moon in her hand, let alone put it in her pocket.

Plato taught that the highest form of wisdom lay beyond the reach of the rational mind. *Noesis*, or pure, intuitive awareness, was beyond the reach of concepts and language. Careful thinking at the conceptual level is an essential preliminary step, but reason and logic must be left behind at the gate to the final stage. The second-century Indian philosopher Nagarjuna taught the same thing. For Nagarjuna, transcendent knowledge is of an entirely different order than ordinary knowledge. Ordinary knowledge is comprised solely of names and forms, whereas transcendent knowledge exists in a realm beyond boundaries and limitations. In one of the Buddha's most famous sermons, he simply held up a flower and didn't say a word. By his enigmatic smile, the disciple Kashyapa indicated that he understood, securing his place as Buddha's successor.

Wisdom then must recognize this fundamental paradox: that intellectual, rational thought and its handmaiden language are essential tools in the pursuit of wisdom, yet they cannot carry us all the way. At some point in our journey, we must climb out of the ship that brought us into the harbor and walk the final mile home.

That is why wisdom is fundamentally incommunicable. It must be experienced at the level of being, not understood at the level of mind.

That doesn't mean that there is any shortage of people willing to reduce the ineffable Source to a concept, doctrine, or dogma. But any definitive statement about the ultimate mystery of existence belies its own incompletion, its own inadequacy. As Laozi pointed out in chapter fifty-six of the *Dao De Jing*, "Those who know don't talk. Those who talk don't know."[6]

And here is the final irony. The wise person often appears foolish to those still enamored with language and concepts. "Don't cast your pearls before swine,"[7] Jesus cautioned his disciples. Most people will not recognize wisdom when they see it, and in their confusion they will probably destroy it, just as pigs mistake pearls for food and crush them with their powerful jaws. Again and again we have seen the essential, fundamental insights of the great spiritual and philosophical traditions of the world misconstrued and misapplied, often with horrifying results.

So we have a choice. Do we attach ourselves to rigid ideologies and defend them to the death, attacking anything and everything that threatens our portrait of the mystery? Or do we leave the mystery undefined and allow a wide variety of portraits to coexist? The way we answer this question affects our personal well-being, our relationships, and ultimately our very survival.

Wisdom as a Way of Being

In a Zen story, two monks were walking to a distant monastery when they came upon a swollen stream. There they noticed a beautiful geisha trying to cross through the dangerous, rushing water. The older monk approached her, bowed, and then lifted her into his arms and carried her across the stream.

After he set her down on the other side, he returned to his younger companion, who had a look of deep consternation on his face. Out of respect, the young monk said nothing, although he clearly wanted to.

Later that evening, when the two monks arrived at their destination and were preparing to go to sleep, the young monk could no longer contain himself.

"How could you do that?" he shouted, "How could you touch that woman? We are monks, we have taken vows, we have sworn never to touch women, and you just threw it all away—all your years of training, all your sacrifice. How could you?"

The old monk paused. "I set her down by the river," he said. "Why are you still carrying her?"

The young monk was of course technically correct. Monks are not supposed to touch women. The young monk knew the rules and recited them perfectly. But in his fundamentalism, he lost sight of the essential core of Buddhist teaching: compassionate action. His slavery to the letter of the law blinded him to the spirit of the teachings: to selflessly serve the needs of others. His literalism dehumanized him and led to his dehumanization of others. He looked upon the woman as a category, a stereotype, a courtesan, a projection of his own inner turmoil—in a word, a problem.

The old monk simply saw an opportunity for kindness.

Attachment to doctrines and their distorted misapplication is the shadow side of religion and philosophy. Buddha, Jesus, and countless others came to shed light. But the sad fact is the brighter the light, the harsher the shadows. Race hatred and murderous terrorism are the bitter fruit of the same tree that yields our loftiest visions of a compassionate world that works for everyone.

Because wisdom is a way of being in the world and not an intellectual construct, we needn't rigidly cleave to one ideology or another. Whatever ultimate reality is, it transcends all concepts. So we can relax. Socrates showed us that. "...[T]ruth," said Krishnamurti, "is a pathless land."[8]

But to avoid walking in circles, it helps to have a map.

Fortunately for us, countless teachers throughout the ages have left behind their best attempts to explain the journey from ignorance to wisdom. There is no shortage of great religious and philosophical literature. The secrets of the ages are hidden in plain sight.

Philosophy as Therapy

One of the most pressing reasons for writing this book is the sadness I feel that philosophy—the theory and practice of wise living—has been sequestered away from everyday people, cloaked in an impenetrable shroud of linguistic abstraction, and held hostage in the ivory tower of professional academia. I wanted to be a part of a larger movement of people who are working to bring philosophy, the longing for wisdom, back down to the ground.

The fundamental character of the philosophical project shifted in the last hundred years. Perhaps emboldened by the growing influence of the social sciences and rapid progress in the fields of biology, astronomy, and physics, philosophy began to refashion itself as a "science." The twentieth century brought a new wave of empirical rigor to the pursuit of wisdom, and the ancient model of philosophy as a healing modality fell out of fashion. For Plato and others in the ancient world, philosophy was primarily *therapeia*, a healing, a way of restoring human beings to a state of equilibrium and well-being. In contrast, twentieth century philosophy turned increasingly to the business of linguistic analysis and the mechanics of cognition itself; interesting and well-intentioned to be sure, but ultimately disconnected from the very people who needed it most. The language of philosophy became a secret code taught only in graduate schools to a tiny number of specialists. The central question of the philosophical project shifted from "What is truth?" to "What do people mean by the word *truth*?" Like cats chasing their tails, philosophers were left with little to do but endlessly analyze their own cognitive processes.

The rest of us stopped caring.

Philosophy lost touch with everyday people. With this book, I hope to reacquaint these two long-lost friends.

Walking the Seven Stone Path

As my students and I spent thousands of hours discussing life, death, and everything in between with the great books and philosophers as our guides, certain common themes began to emerge.

This is a book about those common themes.

These seven ideas—acceptance, surrender, engagement, allowance, enjoyment, love, and integration—have a vibrant, living relationship with one another. This is not yet another to-do list for the weary seeker. Instead, this is an unfolding spiral of life choices and modes of consciousness that are readily available to all. No arduous preparation, special training, or long apprenticeship is required. What I am offering is a simple and down-to-earth way of looking at old ideas that have been taught, and ignored, for thousands of years. The seven stone path is an opportunity to deepen our understanding and move closer toward a lived realization of wisdom right in the midst of our ordinary lives.

How to Use This Book

The seven stones are seven stages of one continuous awakening process. Each stage emerges from the previous stage like a blossom from a bud, and each stage in turn gives birth to the following stage. Just as the apple seed contains the tree to come, so too the first stage of acceptance contains all the subsequent stages. And as we move through the process, earlier stages never really go away. The first stage, acceptance, is taken up into the second stage, surrender. Both acceptance and surrender inform the third stage of engagement, and so on. In this way, the seven stages of the seven stone path are entirely interdependent.

We will, however, consider them one by one.

Each chapter will end with a guided meditation, an opportunity to allow the work to sink down deep into the stillness of our awareness, beneath the mind and its incessant thought stream. That way, each of the seven ideas or modes of consciousness will be available to us as we move through the remaining stages, as well as through all of the challenges of our lives.

Let's not be coy. We are not merely curious. The purpose of studying wisdom is not to collect theories or increase our conceptual knowledge. We are not studying wisdom in order to become more clever, erudite, or sophisticated. This isn't a game—this is our life. Nor are we trying to overcome some long-held inferiority complex or increase our self-importance. We are studying wisdom for one reason and one reason alone. We want to awaken from the dream of unconsciousness, we want to break free of ignorance and fear, and we want to emerge from the struggle into the bright light of our own significance. We are not studying wisdom in order to know what wisdom is. We are studying wisdom in order to become wise.

Not-knowing is true knowledge. Presuming to know is a disease.

—Laozi, *Dao De Jing*, 71

The First Stone

Chapter 1

Wisdom as Acceptance

The Master dwells in reality and lets all illusions go.
—Laozi, *Dao De Jing,* 38

What the Buddha Said

Legend has it that as the Buddha lay dying, he left his grieving monks one last piece of advice: "Remember this," he said, "all forms are impermanent."

It seems that his lifelong students—ardent, committed, disciplined practitioners of the dharma—still needed one last reminder. That shows how difficult this idea is to really understand, let alone embody. No matter how hard we try, we can't seem to let go of our expectations of how things should be. We cling to forms and suffer when they dissolve. And what are forms? All physical things are forms. So are thoughts, concepts, and ideas. A bicycle is a form. The moon is a form. The flight path of a bird is a form. The thought *I am hungry* is a form. Our concept of beauty is a form. Everything in existence is a form. And the fundamental characteristic of forms is that they arise and fade; they come into being and go out of being. But for some reason, we seem to be genetically hardwired to ignore this essential fact. It never fails. When something comes to an end, our default reaction is shock and sadness. In order to begin moving closer to wisdom, we have to start here.

The Wisdom of Acceptance

Wisdom begins with acceptance of what is.

At the end of his masterpiece *Walden*, Henry David Thoreau wrote, "I went to the woods because I wished to live deliberately, to front only the essential facts of life, and see if I could not learn what it had to teach, and not, when I came to die, discover that I had not lived."[9] Rising up out of intellectual complacency, cultural conditioning, and the phenomenon of denial is a necessary first step on the path to wisdom. If we don't somehow scratch our way down to the essential facts, and more importantly make peace with them, wisdom will forever elude us.

We spend an enormous amount of energy struggling against and resisting the elemental conditions of existence. We're upset because it's raining. We wanted it to be sunny today. Then the sun came out, and it got too hot. We wanted it to be just a little cooler. There is no end to our capacity to manufacture disappointment from the raw materials around us.

This same dynamic shapes our human relationships as well. *Why does she have to be that way? Why is he always doing that? Can you believe the way that guy is driving?* Resistance to what is dogs our every step.

We are perpetually frustrated by the ever-present gap between our desires and reality. People don't act the way they're supposed to. Events unfold with little or no consideration for our plans. The things we want are forever out of reach. The things we have aren't good enough. Wisdom demands that we uncover the mechanics of this ubiquitous phenomenon. We can't go on like this.

Wishing that a stone was a diamond, and resenting the stone for not being a diamond, is the height of foolishness. It is also a surefire shortcut to suffering and misery. In addition, this petulant error robs us of the opportunity to experience the simple beauty of the stone just as it is. Caught in the pathology of craving, we fall blind to the bounty right in front of us. It's a lose-lose situation.

When the fog of craving lifts and we see only the stone—miraculous and radiant in its own natural beauty—we experience for ourselves how much the consciousness of non-acceptance costs us. It costs us everything.

The Four Noble Truths

As we'll see, many ancient philosophies advocate the wisdom of acceptance, but none as thoroughly or effectively as Buddhism. Through his own experiments with truth, Siddhartha Gautama gained increasing insight into the nature of reality, the nature of consciousness, and the cause of suffering. As he taught throughout India in the fifth century BCE, he came to be known as the Buddha—literally, the awakened one. Out of the depth of his own realizations, he saw that human experience is characterized by a few deceptively simple ideas. He expressed them as the Four Noble Truths.

The first Noble Truth states that suffering is a part of life. Normal, unenlightened consciousness dwells in a near-constant state of disappointment, frustration, and dissatisfaction. Occasional moments of joy wash over us, but we soon return to our habitual state: uneasiness or dis-ease. A more modern word for it would be anxiety. According to the Buddha, life as it is normally lived is fundamentally characterized by suffering and dissatisfaction. It is imperative, therefore, that we discover both the root cause of this malady as well as the cure.

The second Noble Truth is the hub of the wheel of the entire Buddhist project. It is the rather startling claim that our dissatisfaction is rooted in our own errant thinking. Suffering, the Buddha claims, is caused by egoic craving, clinging, and attachment. Our unhappiness is caused not by outer events and circumstances, but by our stubborn unwillingness to accept them. This is both bad and good news. It's bad news because it's embarrassing to learn that we are the principle cause of our own suffering. But it's good news because now that we know the problem is within our own mind, we can do something about it.

In the third Noble Truth, Buddha shows us with impeccable logic that suffering can be relieved by softening our attachments and expectations. Instead of seeing the world through the lens of our incessant cravings and demands, we can embody the wisdom of acceptance and experience immediate relief from suffering and dissatisfaction. Easier said than done. How do we do this? The answer is the fourth Noble Truth.

The fourth Noble Truth is the Noble Eightfold Path, eight suggestions for how to change the way we think, act, speak, work, and meditate. By practicing the Eightfold Path, we reduce our self-centeredness, which in turn reduces our suffering. Born in his own awakening process and shared simply as suggestions, not dogma, the Eightfold Path draws us out of the rut of our unconsciousness by changing the way we think, act, and interact. To employ the central metaphor of Buddhism, practicing the Eightfold Path draws us out of our unconsciousness and shifts us toward awakening.

The Noble Eightfold Path

The Noble Eightfold Path is the action step of the Four Noble Truths. Incorporating these new behaviors and new ways of thinking into our lives would soften the hold our fearful minds have on us, moving us away from dissatisfaction and toward a way of being in the world that embodies freedom and joy. But the Buddha was not a prophet, nor did he demand ideological loyalty. He was simply a scientist employing an empirical (experience-based) and pragmatic (results-oriented) methodology and sharing the results of his fruitful self-inquiry with anyone who was interested. As a teacher, he cautioned us not to simply accept these ideas on faith—or worse, on authority—but rather to test these ideas in the light of our own experience, the way he did. "Be lamps unto yourselves," he often said. Here are his eight specific suggestions.

1. **Right View.** Without clarity about the nature of suffering and the method of release, little progress can be made. Here, at the beginning of the process, it is important that we be brutally honest with ourselves about our complicity in our own unhappiness. Without drama or self-loathing, we must pull the latch, look under the hood, and see with clear eyes the engine of our own suffering and dissatisfaction.
2. **Right Intention.** No process of transformation can begin without setting an intention. As in drug or alcohol addiction, recovery cannot begin until the addict decides for themselves to abandon their self-destruction and move toward healing. So too, in this process, we must resolve to cultivate the willingness to follow suggestions and move toward well-being and wisdom. If you don't want to, you don't want to, and there isn't much anybody can do about it. Only you can decide. No one can decide for you.
3. **Right Speech.** Words concretize thoughts. When we speak, we turn thoughts into physical waves that move through the atmosphere and give shape to everything around us. Through speech we define the world for ourselves—for better, or often for worse. With this step we commit to using language impeccably, truthfully, mindfully, and compassionately.
4. **Right Action.** Buddha knew that in any process of awakening, we must attend to the quality and timbre of

our actions. What we do is who we are. In this step, we vow to mold our actions into accord with our moral values, committing ourselves to the non-harm of ourselves and others as much as possible.

5. **Right Livelihood.** Naturally, right action also entails the manner in which we make money. Life requires that we engage with one another in an exchange of goods and services. We all have bills to pay and work to do. Our economic exchanges are a perfect arena in which to practice our spiritual principles. We should earn a living in a way that honors ourselves and others. Profiting from cruelty and suffering harms others and ultimately ourselves.
6. **Right Effort.** This step is the simple observation that if you want to make changes, you have to get to work. But don't overdo it. The right amount of effort is a middle ground between doing nothing and trying to do everything. Sensible moderation married with steadfast commitment is the best way forward on any path, even the path toward wisdom-embodiment.
7. **Right Mindfulness**. In many ways, right mindfulness is the linchpin of the entire Eightfold Path. Everything begins and ends in thought. Thoughts give rise to words, words give rise to actions, actions repeated become habits, and habits construct character. Mindfulness also means focusing our awareness on the present moment. Our habitual tendency is to tune out and drift away on a river of thought. Again and again we flee from present moment

awareness to hide behind a screen of well-worn opinions and presumptions. As a gardener tends the soil to generate a fruitful harvest, the truth-seeker tends the mind to yield a harvest of wisdom and joy. The gift of a sound mind requires careful maintenance, gentle courage, unwavering constancy, and heartfelt compassion. Right mindfulness means cultivating the habit of gently monitoring and shaping mental content knowing that thoughts are seeds which give rise to everything we say, everything we do, everything we are, and everything we become. Our life is indeed the product of our mind.

8. **Right Meditation.** It is difficult to overestimate the importance of meditation, not only in the Buddhist project but in any journey toward wisdom. Meditation is the art and science of sitting still and slipping beneath the thought-waves of the mind. In meditation we learn how to shift our attention from thoughts to the field of awareness beneath the thought stream. We are not our thoughts; we are that vast stillness from which thoughts arise and to which they return. In the world's wisdom traditions this inner depth goes by many names: Atman, soul, Inner Christ, Buddha consciousness, spirit. It doesn't matter what you call it or how you define it—it eludes words and concepts. It is a reality to be experienced, not conceptualized. When you begin practicing meditation, you experience this shift for yourself, and once you do, you have established a foundation upon which to build a whole new way of being in the world. All of the inestimable benefits of meditation grow

from this one insight. Regarding meditation, thirteenth-century Japanese Zen master Dogen wrote, "Don't doubt its possibilities because of the simplicity of its method. If you can't find the truth right where you are, where else do you think you will find it?"[10]

Like a physician diagnosing a symptom (suffering and dissatisfaction) and uncovering its cause (egoic craving and attachment), Buddha offers the Noble Eightfold Path as a prescription, a course of action that will relieve the symptom by reducing its cause. How well it works depends entirely on the patient's willingness to follow doctor's orders. Are we ready and willing to let go of our comfortably familiar role as long-suffering victims and cultivate the courage to embrace our emerging vitality? It all begins with a shift into the consciousness of acceptance.

Flapping My Arms

One day while working on the Four Noble Truths with one of my world religions classes, a student told a story that stopped me in my tracks. It was one of those joyful moments when, as a teacher, you realize that not only is deep conceptual learning taking place in the minds of your students, but even more importantly, a spark from an ancient wisdom tradition suddenly caught fire in the tinder of their personal lives. A distant abstraction had in an instant become an immediate and concrete experience. In education, that's the jackpot. In the classroom, you try every day to create moments like this. Sometimes it even happens.

Steve was twenty-two, bright, gregarious, athletic, and paralyzed from the waist down. Four years earlier at the age of eighteen he was hit by a drunk driver and severely injured. As a surfer, water polo player, and runner, he was devastated by the news that because of irreversible spinal damage, he would never again have the use of his legs. He had to learn how to navigate the world in a wheelchair. It was all the little things that really got to him—the way he couldn't reach anything on the higher shelves in the kitchen, and how the whole house had to be reordered. And how the same ubiquitous curbs he had skateboarded over a million times now became insurmountable barriers a hundred feet high.

He talked about how for the first year, he sat in his room feeling sorry for himself, tortured by all of the things he would never be able to do. Shock gave way to anger and despair.

Everything seemed hopeless. He was grieving the loss of a life.

Then he said he realized something. Yes, he had lost a lot, but he hadn't lost everything. He still had his mind and the capacity to dream, envision, and realize great things. He still had his heart and his love for his family and friends. He still had his powerful arms and his back and his ambition and spirit and the will to blend all of these gifts and energies into a purposeful life of creativity and service. He decided to take back his joy.

Then he asked me a question.

"Mr. Bolland," he said, "do you wake up in the morning and cry because you can't flap your arms and fly to work?"

"No."

"Do you go to the beach and feel sorry for yourself because you can't jump in the ocean, hold your breath, and swim underwater all the way to Catalina Island?"

"No."

"We all have physical limitations," he said, "and we accept them. I just had some new limitations to get used to. It could be worse—I could be dead. But I'm not. I made the adjustment and got back into my life."

You could have heard a pin drop in that room. Eyes were shining. No one was looking at their phone.

For Steve, there was a huge and vitally important distinction between pain and suffering, a distinction most of us fail to make. Pain is a part of there being a world at all. If you're alive, you're going to experience pain (see the First Noble Truth). Dropping a rock on your foot is going to hurt, not because you're egoically craving anything, but simply because you have a nervous system and pain receptors in your feet. Suffering, in contrast, is a mental condition, the decision to cling to and find one's identity in some past pain event. As Steve's story so eloquently shows, pain is inevitable, but suffering is optional.

Most of us think happiness is a future state that will magically arise only after all of our desires, demands, and expectations have been met. Apparently not. Happiness is a decision. We choose happiness in spite of the favorable or unfavorable conditions in which we find ourselves. "Most folks are about as happy as they make their minds up to be," said Abraham Lincoln. This is the wisdom of acceptance.

The prominent twentieth-century spiritual teacher Krishnamurti taught all over the world, quite often in the shade of a grove of oak trees near his home in Ojai, California. Author and nonduality teacher Jim Dreaver was there one afternoon in 1977. At one point during the lecture, Krishnamurti, who rarely spoke about himself or his process, paused and asked the audience, "Do you want to know what my secret is?" In Dreaver's account, the entire audience leaned in. This was the moment they'd all been waiting for—the master was about to reveal his secret. "You see," he said, "I don't mind what happens."[11]

In the *Dao De Jing* Laozi writes, "The master gives himself up to whatever the moment brings."[12] My student Steve had attained a level of mastery through his own deeply painful confrontation with suffering. And by sharing his story, he awakened an entire room of sleeping people to the beautiful possibilities that lay dormant in their own difficult lives.

Steve's story points out how odd it is that we are somehow perfectly accepting of our current limitations—the fact that we cannot flap our arms and fly—yet when one of our abilities is lost, we are thrown into anger and despair. Buddha was right. Suffering and dissatisfaction have little to do with external circumstances. Instead, they have everything to do with the way we respond to and think about our circumstances. In Buddhism, this diseased and destructive mental habit, this capacity to manufacture unhappiness out of thin air, is known as attachment.

Attachment

Attachment comes in many shapes and sizes. We form attachments to our favorite foods, our favorite songs, our favorite jeans. Our very identity becomes interwoven with these objects and experiences. That's simple enough. But on a subtler and more invasive level, we also become attached to ideas and concepts. We identify ourselves with our theories, opinions, and judgments about the world. In fact, attaching to and defending a particular worldview is one of the primary ways our ego shores up its own importance. Our idea of the world forms a shroud through which we can no longer see the world as it is. Our idea of the world replaces a direct experience of reality itself, the reality that exists independent to and outside of the realm of thought. Countless examples from the world's philosophical traditions make this point again and again, from Plato's *Allegory of the Cave* to the Hindu concept of maya. For Buddha, the primary cause of suffering is the fact that our illusory sense of self is woven deeply into the fabric of a limited set of perceptions, thoughts, and opinions constructed by the ego. When those perceptions and beliefs are shown to be false, as they inevitably are, our ego responds as if under attack. This form of attachment is far more destructive than the simple sadness one feels when the ice cream is gone.

Understanding attachment as the primary cause of suffering becomes easier when we consider our relationship to the concepts of past and future. What we call the past is really just a selection of partial and distorted memories. Only a tiny fraction of what we actually experience ever makes it into long-term memory where it can be recalled as the past. What we call the past is a neurological event, a memory that occurs in this now-moment. In the final analysis, there is no such thing as the past. The past is a thought you're having in the present moment. And if that weren't bad enough, consider the future, or rather our idea of the future. Here, we don't even have any neurological events to cling too, only wild guesses and self-serving projections. We have absolutely no idea what's going to happen next. If the past is a heavily edited, deeply redacted, and thoroughly untrustworthy movie, then the future is an entire warehouse of unexposed film. We got nothing.

When Albert Einstein learned of the death of his longtime collaborator and closest friend Michele Besso, he sat down to write a letter to Besso's family. "Now he has departed from this strange world a little ahead of me," Einstein wrote. "That means nothing. People like us, who believe in physics, know that the distinction between past, present and future is only a stubbornly persistent illusion."[13] Einstein died thirty-three days later.

When we realize that the past and the future are simply thought-events that occur only in this present moment, the only thing left is now. And as we reflect on these ideas, we gain a greater appreciation for how insidiously destructive the process of attachment is. The deeper we indulge in our attachments to the past and the future, the further we recede from the only reality that actually exists—the here and now.

Nirvana

In Buddhism, the opposite of suffering and dissatisfaction is known as nirvana. Nirvana is a Sanskrit word that literally means no wind or no breath. Nirvana is a one-word poem that evokes the stillness and serenity that remains after all agitation has subsided.

Imagine a lake during a storm. The wind is howling, and the water is churning. Now imagine the wind dying down and the surface of the lake becoming still. As the water grows calm, the sediment stirred up by the waves begins to settle to the bottom. Soon the surface of the lake is as flat as a mirror, and the depths are crystal clear. As you look into the water, you see both the pebbles on the bottom and the sky's reflection on the surface. Clarity and insight are only possible when there is stillness.

Nirvana is a state of being characterized by lucidity, insight, and vision. Nirvana means the tranquility that remains when the flames of craving and fear are extinguished. Nirvana is not a future event, nor is it a place. Nirvana is not a cosmic reward bestowed upon us by a deity for good behavior (although that idea will arise in later forms of devotional Buddhism). In the teachings of the Buddha, nirvana is an ever-present reality that the agitated mind blocks out. The serenity of our original wisdom can be recovered if we learn to be still and slip into the consciousness of acceptance.

Nirvana also means to blow out or extinguish, as in blow out a candle. In this sense, nirvana means extinguishing the two primary conditions of unenlightened consciousness, desire and aversion.

Our minds are fundamentally occupied with the maintenance of two lists. One is a list of all things we want, and the other is a list of all things we don't want. One part of our mind compiles and fuels a running list of cravings: *I want a sandwich. I want a cup of coffee. I want her to like me. I want the sun to come out. I want some new shoes. I wish people were good drivers like me. I wish the people I work with did things the way I think they should be done. I wish my body looked different. I want a new car. I want world peace.* Another part of our mind compiles and fuels a running list of aversions: *I don't want anchovies on my pizza. I don't want a computer virus. I don't want telemarketers to call me. I don't want to be unpopular or disliked. I wish it would stop raining. I don't want to catch a cold. I don't want cancer. I hate this traffic jam. I don't want to run out of gas or break down. I hate this song on the radio. I don't want anyone I love to ever die.*

To complicate matters, these two lists are often intertwined. *I wish I had more money so I could afford a new car, because I don't like this old car. People would be more impressed with me, and I would feel better about myself and what I've achieved if I drove a nice new car, preferably German. And I want people to like me more because if they liked me more, I could probably get a better job, make more money, and get an even better car.* As you can see, we make ourselves crazy. Does anyone really believe that wisdom, joy, and happiness lie down this road?

Life as it is normally lived is one long, continuous preoccupation with these two lists, our desires and our aversions.

We invest enormous time and energy into their maintenance and then call that our "life." For many people, life is about keeping the bad stuff away and pulling the good stuff toward us. That's it. *Here are all the things we want. Here are all the things we don't want. Let's struggle and strain to control it all as best we can.*

There is an alternative to this madness.

Close your eyes and imagine for a moment what it would feel like—what it would *really* feel like deep down inside—if both lists suddenly vanished. There is nothing you want. There is nothing you need. And there is nothing you fear, nothing you are struggling against. All craving and resistance has dissolved. You are in the consciousness of deep acceptance. Suddenly all worry and anxiety fall away replaced by a vibrant sense of gratitude. Now that you are no longer trying to control everything, a deep peace washes over you and the world. Other people, situations, your own mercurial emotions—all of it is permeated by a subtle, beautiful, organizing intelligence. You no longer have to run the world. For once, you feel completely at home in your own skin. Now you know why the Buddha had that little smile on his face all the time.

By now your mind is probably racing ahead, resisting, arguing, and in other ways cleverly amassing reasons why this will never work. "Why on earth would I want to accept cruelty, thoughtlessness, poverty, disease, or injustice?" Good question. Of course, wisdom means being an agent of positive change in the world. But all our efforts to change the world are futile if not grounded in a fundamentally positive, optimistic, and accepting consciousness. In order to be effective agents of change in the world, we must first change ourselves. Without a powerful internal shift, all our attempts to improve the world are simply clever, sophisticated manifestations of the same old cravings and fears that got us into this mess in the first place. Any attempt to change outer circumstances without this deep internal shift may produce temporary results and the appearance of justice, but like a mirage, it has no depth and is doomed to fail.

When we move out of the need to control circumstances, events, and people, we slip into the consciousness of acceptance. And from this base, we are able to see more clearly and move more effectively into right action. No longer clouded and confused by conflicting fears and cravings, we are open to universal intelligence and know what the next right step is. No longer attached to a particular portrait of the future nor beholden to a fading image of the past, we stand firm in this now moment fully present in our own lives. Nonattachment, acceptance, nirvana—whatever you want to call it, it is not a spacey, detached, apathetic stance. Quite the opposite. In the consciousness of acceptance, we are finally able to engage with the world as it actually is, no longer caught in the fog of our own projections.

The Kingdom of Heaven

Jesus may be many things to many people, but one thing's for sure: he challenged his students to radically reorder their moral lives and shift their consciousness from self-interest to universal loving-kindness. He referred to this shift as entering the kingdom of heaven.

If we place Jesus, for a moment anyway, outside the two-thousand-year-old mainstream of Christian orthodoxy and see him instead as simply another in a long line of wisdom teachers, we catch a startling glimpse of a master in action tirelessly and creatively seeking ways to provoke his students into experiencing a depth-reality he clearly already embodied.

Like the Daoist philosophers Laozi and Zhuangzi, Jesus taught almost exclusively through metaphors, similes, and parables. He used language to prod, provoke, and pry open our slammed-shut minds that are conditioned by ego, fear, and illusions of separateness. And the central metaphor Jesus employed was the kingdom of heaven.

The kingdom of heaven or the kingdom of God was a common Jewish concept in Jesus's time. Jesus was a master at drawing phrases from the common vernacular and employing them in new and creative ways. For some, the kingdom of heaven was a physical kingdom—the overthrowing of Roman rule and the reestablishment of the kingdom of Israel. As Christian thought evolved in the centuries after Jesus, the kingdom of heaven became an afterlife reward for those obedient to Church doctrines. Jesus, however, seemed to use the image of the kingdom to indicate a new way of thinking and being in the world right here, right now. When asked about the kingdom of heaven, in the Gospel of Thomas Jesus replied, "What you look for has come, only you do not know it".[14] In the Gospel of Luke, he says, "The kingdom of God does not come with your careful observation, nor will people say, 'Here it is,' or 'There it is,' because the kingdom of God is within you."[15] In these and many other passages, Jesus portrays the kingdom of God not as a physical place or a future event but as an ever-present reality to which we are generally blind.

Both Buddha's metaphor of sleep and Jesus's metaphor of blindness point to our fundamental unconsciousness, a lack of awareness of our true nature. We mistakenly identify with our egos, our bodies, our ideologies, and our tribes, unaware of our underlying unity with the divine and with each other. In the Qur'an Allah tells humanity that he is "closer to them than their jugular vein."[16] Awakening to the reality of our own Buddha nature is an inward process, not an outward journey. We always carry it with us. "Not one of your steps leads away from it,"[17] said Dogen, the twelfth-century Zen master. And for Jesus, "the kingdom of Heaven is at hand."[18]

If all of this is true, then what concrete, specific advice do these wisdom teachers offer as a means of opening the door to the kingdom of God? Clearly, a change has to occur within us—a shift in our thinking. We have to release our death grip on certain self-definitions and move instead into open-ended awareness of the depth of our true nature. The first step in this process is to move out of the consciousness of fear and scarcity and move into the consciousness of acceptance and abundance. As Jesus said in the Gospel of Matthew,

> Therefore I tell you, do not worry about your life … Look at the birds of the air; they do not sow or reap or stow away in barns, and yet your heavenly Father feeds

> them. Are you not much more valuable than they? Who of you by worrying can add a single hour to his life? And why do you worry about clothes? See how the lilies of the field grow. They do not labor or spin. Yet I tell you that not even Solomon in all his splendor was dressed like one of these.[19]

By letting go of the need to control everything—a dangerous game characterized by worry, fear, and continual failure—we leave ourselves open to the opportunity to experience a boundless serenity founded on a deep and lasting alliance with the ground of being within us. Jesus called this divine inner reality the Father, a rather personal reference to the God of Abraham. Muhammad called it Allah, Arabic for *the God.* Laozi called it Dao, an impersonal, ineffable first principle. Buddha, in contrast, didn't call it anything at all—he tried only to lead us to a direct and immediate experience of it, knowing that when we experience it within ourselves, it won't need a name.

In the consciousness of acceptance, not only of the fact that the waiter forgot to bring you a spoon for your soup again but also of the reality of your own sacred nature, every other so-called problem in your life begins to lose its hold. Life stops being about chasing money, health, love, and happiness, and we begin to see that we already have all of these things, and more, in abundance. "Seek first his kingdom," said Jesus, "and all these things will be given to you as well."[20] Instead of looking for fulfillment in the outer world of forms, make the internal shift instead and be granted new eyes with which to see the world. When we change our thinking, the whole world changes. No one says it better than Laozi in the *Dao De Jing*: "Be content with what you have; rejoice in the way things are. When you realize there is nothing lacking, the whole world belongs to you."[21]

Stoicism

In the first century after Jesus, a Roman school of philosophy called Stoicism gained prominence and wormed its way into the woodwork of Western thought. With its emphasis on cultivating inner strength in the face of adversity, Stoicism offers a surprisingly relevant set of solutions to the perennial problems of modern life. For two thousand years, being called stoic has been high praise indeed.

In a word, Stoicism counsels acceptance. What makes this all the more remarkable is that Epictetus, Stoicism's most valuable voice, was a slave whose leg was permanently disabled by his master during torture. Later in life, after earning his freedom, Epictetus became a teacher, awakening his students to the possibility that happiness was an internal condition over which we exert sole dominion. None of his writings survive, but his lectures and lessons were preserved by his devoted student Flavius Arrian and have come down to us in two collections, *Discourses* and *Manual*. Sharon Lebell's rendering of Epictetus, under the title *The Art of Living,* is an excellent place to start. It's the first book I mention whenever someone asks me to recommend a great philosophy book.

Epictetus taught that no matter what is happening around us, we always have a choice in how to respond. Epictetus learned this on the torture rack. His agony set him free. He considered this one of the greatest gifts of his tormentor. "The trials we endure," he later said, "introduce us to our strengths."[22]

A hundred years after Epictetus and on the other end of the socioeconomic spectrum, Roman Emperor Marcus Aurelius also found the tenets of Stoicism particularly useful as he weathered the storms of loneliness, deceit, war, treachery, and the other trappings of leadership. Late at night in his tent along the banks of the Danube River while on a military campaign far from home, Marcus Aurelius composed one of Stoicism's most enduring classics, *Meditations.* Never intended for publication, *Meditations* was a personal journal, a fact that perhaps accounts for its unvarnished honesty and unflinching introspection. Though separated by rank and station, both Epictetus and Marcus Aurelius share the lived experience and bedrock conviction that though we exert little control over other people or events around us, we can always find solace in our inner strength and freedom—the freedom to realize happiness simply by shifting our thinking. And as always, it begins with acceptance of what is.

"Nothing happens to anyone that he can't endure," wrote Marcus Aurelius. "Then what should we work for? Only this: proper understanding; unselfish action; truthful speech. A resolve to accept whatever happens as necessary and familiar."[23] And what does Aurelius mean by "proper understanding?" This:

> To welcome with affection what is sent by fate. Not to stain or disturb the spirit within him with a mess of false beliefs. Instead, to preserve it faithfully, by calmly obeying God – saying nothing untrue, doing nothing unjust. And if the others don't acknowledge it – this life lived with simplicity, humility, cheerfulness – he doesn't resent them for it, and isn't deterred from following the road where it leads: to the end of life. An end to be approached in purity, in serenity, in acceptance, in peaceful unity with what must be.[24]

Marcus Aurelius was a great student of philosophy, reading everything he could get his hands on, especially Plato and Epictetus. He counted Epictetus as one his greatest influences. It's easy to see why. A century before Emperor Marcus Aurelius, the former Roman slave Epictetus wrote,

> Circumstances do not rise to meet our expectations. Events happen as they do. People behave as they are. Embrace what you actually get. Open your eyes: see things for what they really are, thereby sparing yourself the pain of false attachments and avoidable devastation…When something happens, the only thing in your power is your attitude toward it; you can either accept it or resent it.[25]

Like Buddha and Jesus before him, Epictetus brings us back to the foundation of the edifice of wisdom – the power of thought to shape all reality. Another great admirer of the Stoics, Ralph Waldo Emerson put it this way: "We know that the ancestor of every action is a thought."[26]

By choosing acceptance, you free yourself from the prison of your own opinions and move instead into an immediate experience of what is. From this unencumbered stance, you are better able to discern, feel, and ultimately act in ways that benefit you and others.

The first task in Stoicism is to make the crucial distinction between the things we can control and the things we cannot. Most of our suffering comes from our stubborn unwillingness to carefully and consistently differentiate between these two categories. What are the things we cannot control? We cannot control events, or the thoughts and actions of other people. Influence, sometimes. Control, never. We cannot control the weather, the price of gold, or which horse crosses the finish line first. We cannot control our genetics, our body types, or our fundamental personalities. We are left with a simple choice: accept these events and conditions or live in perpetual misery.

What can we control? We can control our thoughts and actions. We can control how we respond to the events and circumstances around us. We are always free to think and feel any way we wish.

Easier said than done? Certainly. The difficulty of accomplishing this task, however, in no way diminishes its value. This is the central, load-bearing column of our overall mental, physical, and spiritual well-being. We are the authors of our own experience; the extent to which we deny this truth determines the breadth and depth of our unhappiness.

The worldwide recovery movement got its start in the mid-twentieth century in a group called Alcoholics Anonymous.

Since then, various twelve-step programs have blossomed in every country and in every language to help people break free from compulsive, destructive behaviors. At the heart of every twelve-step recovery program is the serenity prayer, authored by Protestant theologian Reinhold Niebuhr: "God, grant me serenity to accept the things I cannot change, courage to change the things I can, and wisdom to know the difference."[27] It is Stoicism distilled into twenty-four words.

Serenity

In the curious paradox of seeking to change while accepting what is, we find the endless play of the polarities of life—yet another mystery of reality we simply have to accept. Even our own nature as confounding, conflicted, and imperfect beings is to be accepted, not resisted and condemned. Spiritual and philosophical growth is bedeviled with this vexing problem: how to simultaneously pursue transformation while unequivocally accepting and loving who we are today. How do we acknowledge our shortcomings while avoiding the trap of self-condemnation?

Compassion, humility, and a vibrant sense of humor go a long way. Self-acceptance is essential. Desiring to be something we're not is just another destructive ego craving whose only fruit is suffering. "Even the wise act within the limitations of their own nature,"[28] said Krishna in the Bhagavad Gita. The wise learn how to distinguish between natural yearning and pathological craving. The tree doesn't agonize over its inner urge to grow new leaves and branches. As it grows, it is simply cooperating with its own nature. We too must cooperate with the emergence of our authentic selves. In this way, we move confidently from the field of acceptance into the field of action. Serenity is not inactivity. Cultivating inner stillness is the prerequisite of all great achievement. Whether in the struggle to accept our own inner contradictions or square the puzzling paradoxes of the world, we must see past appearances and recognize the deeper layers of the underlying symmetry of the world.

In 1899, Rudyard Kipling's young daughter Josephine suddenly died. Two years later, partly to preserve his own sanity as well as offer solace and encouragement to his young family, he sat down to write the powerfully inspirational poem "If" to his twelve-year-old son John. It's all about perseverance in the face of life's changing fortunes. How could he have known that John would be lost a few years later on a World War I battlefield?

Kipling's inspirational words eventually found their way into an inscription over the player's entrance to Centre Court at the Wimbledon tennis facility. Whether in real battle or in the nonlethal battle of the athletic court, Kipling's rendering of the Stoic exhortation rings clear: "If you meet with triumph and disaster … treat those two imposters just the same."[29]

You have to admit nature is a little rough, even cruel, with all this constant killing. Either you're eating or you're the food. There is no third alternative. Individual forms are short-lived. But beneath the surface lies a deep harmony. The

Stoics call that underlying harmony the *logos*, the order and structure of the world. Whether you call it Dao or Nature, or personify and deify it as God, there is a deep intelligence, an organizing principle already at work. Cooperation with this principle is the central suggestion of wisdom traditions the world over.

"Learn the will of Nature," counseled Epictetus. "Follow the Dao," said Laozi. "Put first the Kingdom of Heaven and all else will be given to you," said Jesus. Without the practice of deep and conscious acceptance, the door to serenity remains forever closed to us. Without acceptance, we lose our shot at serenity and live instead in constant dis-ease. "…[L]ife and nature are governed by laws that we can't change," said Epictetus. "The quicker we accept this, the more tranquil we can be."[30] Of course we want our loved ones to live forever. But one by one, they will fall. Even our own death is the will of nature. What choice do we have but to say yes?

Saying Yes

The next time you walk in the rain, pay attention. Do you tense up, hunch over, and scurry away, trying in vain to hide from the rain? Does tensing up and resenting the rain in any way keep you dry? Instead, try something different. Breathe deeply. Relax. Stand up straight.

Soften your shoulders. Look ahead. Instead of fighting the rain, say yes to it. With this simple shift in awareness, the rain is transformed from an annoying inconvenience into a beautiful, miraculous, and ultimately nourishing experience. Saying yes changes everything.

When you relax and accept the rain, you feel all the stress and tension leaving your body. Suddenly you notice how delicious the air tastes. The sound of the rain on the sidewalk makes you smile. You feel the trees silently celebrating their sudden good fortune. When you stop resisting, you become fully present to the simple, beautiful perfection of this moment. Saying yes is the key that opens every gift.

You just have to laugh when you realize that you create most of the stress and anxiety in your life simply by not accepting what is.

The Bhagavad Gita

One of the most lasting and powerful expressions of the wisdom of acceptance in all sacred literature is found in the Indian masterpiece the Bhagavad Gita. Written around the time of Christ, the Bhagavad Gita is an allegorical tale set on a battlefield where two armies are about to engage. As the story opens, our hero, the warrior prince Arjuna, is reluctant. His dharma, or duty, is to lead his army into battle and confront an evil enemy, but there's a problem. He realizes that he knows a lot of the soldiers he is about to face. In fact, on both sides of the battlefield he sees friends, teachers, cousins, uncles—in a word, humanity. As he struggles with moral ambivalence, fear, uncertainty, and confusion, his chariot driver and boyhood friend, Krishna, draws him into an inquiry that unfolds throughout the remaining chapters of the book. Their conversation touches on a wide range of philosophical and spiritual subjects, but in the end Krishna has one core message for Arjuna: *Say yes.*

The philosophy of the Bhagavad Gita and the earlier Upanishads is known as Vedanta, a word meaning the end or culmination of the Vedas. Both the Bhagavad Gita and the Upanishads are extensions of the ancient Vedas, the first written expression of the Hindu worldview now at least three thousand years old, and some say much older. Whether or not one subscribes to the tenets of Vedanta, the Gita represents a stunning illustration of the wisdom of acceptance. Mohandas Gandhi carried a copy of chapter two of the Gita (along with chapters five, six, and seven of the Gospel of Matthew, also known as the Sermon on the Mount) with him at all times. He read both passages every morning, drawing guidance, sustenance, and strength from these bracing examples of the power of the consciousness of acceptance.

By the end of chapter one, Arjuna has collapsed in a crumpled heap, unable even to lift his beloved bow, Gandiva. His revulsion at the thought of battle might be considered a commendable stroke of pacifism. Krishna, however, doesn't see it that way. He acknowledges Arjuna's compassion and respects his emotional honesty, but in chapter two Krishna tells Arjuna to get up and fight.

There are two fundamental facts that Krishna sets out to teach Arjuna. The first is the changeless oneness of all Being at the deepest level, despite the surface appearance of the world as a transient field of becoming and fading away. Therefore death, from this perspective, isn't real. Death or dissolution happens to forms, but not to the Formless Source that we are at core. As Eckhart Tolle writes in *Stillness Speaks*, "Death is not the opposite of life. Life has no opposite. The opposite of death is birth."[31] In other words, death and birth cycle endlessly like a wheel, while life remains unaffected. Life, as a totality, has no beginning or end. Individual forms may come and go, but that which is real was never born and can never die—it is eternal and therefore changeless. At core, we are identical with this unborn and undying reality. Beneath the layers of the body, the sense organs, the mind, and even the unconscious is the Atman, the Universal Self. The Self is not our individual personality or ego. There is only one Atman or Self in which we all share. The Self is changeless awareness, universally present within all sentient beings, both transcendent and immanent. Krishna calls it the "Inner Witness" to all of the outer events of our lives, including the ceaseless workings of our mind with all its cherished concepts, judgments, and opinions. Attachment to individual thoughts, sensations, and forms, therefore, is ignorance. Only when we understand our true nature as the living presence of the one divine reality can we truly understand what right action means. Acceptance of our own inherent divinity is step one.

The second fundamental fact Krishna explains is that given this context, Arjuna has a very important job to do, as do we all. Our lives are anything but insignificant. We are manifestations of eternal God-consciousness in the field of time, and as such we participate in the sacred work of the universe. Our work *is* the sacred work of the universe. Each of us has a dharma, a divine purpose or duty to realize. This is not to be construed as a determined fate or a specific task or job description. Instead, dharma means that in a very real sense, our lives are not our own—they are not private pleasure cruises free of any and all obligation and responsibility. Rather, our lives are opportunities to live in accord with our deeper purpose, and that is in fact where our joy lies. It is Arjuna's dharma, as a warrior prince, to lead the battle against evil and protect goodness in the world.

As a work of literature, the Bhagavad Gita is of course subject to a variety of interpretations. For some it seems to authorize violence. For others, like Gandhi, it is a sprawling metaphor for the struggle within us all—the struggle against our own venal and destructive instincts and a return to our sacred purpose. Finding the courage to face what needs facing is a skill born only out of the conscious acceptance of who and what we really are, and of the transitory nature of all forms. Without this fundamental, underlying awareness, moving forward into wisdom is simply not possible. Whether or not one accepts the precepts of Vedanta philosophy, the Bhagavad Gita offers a compelling vision of a path to wisdom built on awareness, intellectual honesty, spiritual humility, personal responsibility, and deep acceptance of the conditions in which we find ourselves.

We'll return to the story of Arjuna and Krishna in chapter three of this book, when we take up the wisdom of engagement.

Acceptance Is Not Indifference

As we reflect on the concepts of nonattachment and acceptance, a confusion arises: If I accept cruelty, thoughtlessness, vulgarity, violence, and injustice, am I not in fact condoning and perpetuating these horrors? How can we accept these things? Aren't we supposed to work tirelessly to erase these nightmares? It is crucial that we consider these questions to clarify what we precisely mean by acceptance.

Acceptance does not mean indifference, apathy, avoidance, denial, or inaction. Instead, cultivating the consciousness of acceptance means moving willingly into a field of pure possibility, unhindered by rigid conceptual frameworks, arbitrary personal preferences, or lifeless limitations. If anything, the consciousness of acceptance is an ideal starting point for deeply engaged, effective, and compassionate action. Despite its content-free nature and apparent fluidity, the consciousness of acceptance is simply the best foundation for the construction of wisdom and compassion, as well as the realization of a joyful and fully actualized life. As we will see, all of the other stones or stages of wisdom will emerge from the wisdom of acceptance.

As we continue to reflect on the nature of acceptance, the portrait that emerges is of a condition of consciousness where all resistance to reality has been relinquished and replaced by a clear-eyed awareness that no matter what my intentions are for what comes next, I must begin in the here and now. Resentment, frustration, anger, and denial only inhibit my ability to respond powerfully by moving forward and participating in the cocreation of my intentions. As Carl Jung wrote, “We cannot change anything until we accept it. Condemnation does not liberate, it oppresses.” In fact, when I do not practice acceptance, I am practicing a kind of oppression. “I am the oppressor of the person I condemn, not his friend and fellow-sufferer.” In order to help someone, we “must be able to accept him as he is. And he can do this in reality only when he has already seen and accepted himself as he is.”[32] Until I learn to let people be who they are (instead of who I think they should be), and until I learn to accept myself in my current condition, and the circumstances in which I find myself, I will be forever stuck in a prison of my own thinking, chained by resentment, powerless to act, doomed only to react, never seeing the world as it is but seeing only a projection of my own opinions, expectations, disappointments, judgments, and demands. In other words, I’ll be utterly miserable. Without acceptance, we will never know freedom.

A Wise Person

A wise person accepts current conditions without resentment or anger.

A wise person accepts the things they cannot change.

A wise person accepts other people as they are without projecting their expectations onto them.

A wise person accepts themselves as they are today, at this particular stage of their evolution.

A wise person accepts and moves willingly into the next moment, no matter what it brings.

A wise person embodies the knowledge that beneath the surface, the world is in harmony with itself, and things are proceeding in accord with fate, nature, God, or divine intelligence.

A wise person knows that the consciousness of acceptance is not a reclusive retreat from the challenges of the world, but a peaceful foundation upon which we can build clarity, compassionate service, and conscious engagement.

Closing Meditation

I want to end this chapter, and every chapter of this book, with a closing meditation, an opportunity to allow these ideas to sink deeper into our awareness, beyond the conceptual mind.

If you are listening to this, I invite you now to close your eyes. If you are reading, then soften your gaze. Take a deep breath in and then exhale. Do it again. Relax your face and allow your body to go into a state of alert relaxation.

Imagine that you are sitting on the bank of a slow-moving river. You are breathing deeply and evenly, relaxing into the peacefulness of your surroundings. An occasional leaf or twig floats slowly by on the surface of the river. Imagine now a smooth, round river stone, the stone of acceptance, sinking slowly down through the water and coming to rest on the soft, sandy bottom. See the stone there on the bottom, in the silence, deep beneath the flowing water. Like your consciousness, the river keeps moving, carrying with it thoughts of all kinds—what you should be doing instead of this, the sensation of being hungry or tired or thirsty or bored or excited, remembrances of past experiences, anticipations of future experiences. All those thoughts travel on the surface of the river, but your attention is deep below, with the stone of acceptance. As you go forward into the rest of your day, the rest of the week, you know that you carry with you this stone, this seed of consciousness, this source of awareness, and that you can call on it at any time.

Whenever life confronts you with a challenge, and it will, you have a choice. You can return to habitual and recurring patterns of resistance, resentment, and the impulse to control, or you can practice the consciousness of acceptance. You can experiment with the possibility that through the practice of acceptance, you will more smoothly and effectively move through the challenges you face. As you test this possibility in the light of your own experience, you will come to know the wisdom shared by so many ancient traditions and teachers—through the practice of deep acceptance you open a door through which your own sacred intelligence can begin to emerge, a way of knowing and a way of being far more authentic than the mechanisms of our busy minds and our carefully constructed and well-defended personas. By sitting quietly with the consciousness of acceptance, we begin to open up to the possibility of moving beyond our usual mode of fear-based reactivity and into a grace-filled serenity that bears its own unmistakable authority. We will know that this is the beginning of a process that will draw us closer to an authentic way of being in the world, a way of being free from the ego and its incessant demands and continual failures. We cannot stop the river. We aren't even going to try.

We accept that the river will flow and we feel a deep peace welling up within and around us as we begin to rise up through the water and return to the surface, knowing that with this newfound awareness we can walk forward into this next moment more effectively, more compassionately, more willingly, more powerfully, and more fully alive than we've felt in years.

When you're ready, open your eyes and bring your attention back to your breath, breathing deeply and evenly, allowing your body to feel the flow of its natural rhythms. Feel the gratitude that has largely eclipsed the anxiety. Say yes to that too.

The consciousness of acceptance is within you now, in your core, ready to bring its healing power to bear whenever resistance, resentment, or anxiety arises. The first step is in place. From this solid footing, we are ready to move onto the next six stages of wisdom.

The awakened heart loves the world as it is, not just as it could be.

—Adyashanti, *The End of Your World*[33]

Be content with what you have; rejoice in the way things are. When you realize there is nothing lacking, the whole world belongs to you.

—Laozi, *Dao De Jing*, 44

The Second Stone

Chapter 2

Wisdom as Surrender

The Master gives himself up to
whatever the moment brings.
—Laozi, *Dao De Jing*, 50

Falling In

Acceptance means acknowledging there is a river. Surrender means falling in.

The consciousness of surrender is a natural outgrowth of the consciousness of acceptance. As we saw in the introduction, the stages of the seven stone path are really one integrated process where each stone is interconnected with all of the others; none of the stones stand alone. They are bound together into one evolutionary progression. The second stone, surrender, is inherently informed by its source, acceptance, just as a pear blossom is an expression of its source, the bud. And deep within the blossom lie all of the future stages: the fruit, the seeds, and the unseen orchards those seeds contain, each stage only a moment in an endless unfolding. The continuum of wisdom does not divide neatly into discreet and wholly separate chunks—we are simply saying it does in order to understand wisdom better, just as we call one hour eight o'clock and another hour nine o'clock, knowing full well that the eternal presence of this now moment knows nothing of hours.

What we mean by surrender, then, is a deepening into the consciousness of acceptance. Acceptance is an intellectual or cognitive shift. Surrender is body, mind, and soul.

Flying

There was a time many years ago when I did not enjoy flying at all. I would dread the experience—the hours of claustrophobia, crammed into a long metal tube with hundreds of strangers, hurtling through space at distressing speeds miles above the earth's surface with no chance of escape. Being six feet three inches tall didn't help. Having my knees pressed against the seat in front of me only exacerbated the hopeless feeling of being trapped. Then one day, I let go.

As I grew older, I finally internalized all of the beautiful words I had been reading and teaching for years. It dawned on me that nothing was gained by struggling against the conditions in which I found myself. Laozi's wisdom from the *Dao De Jing* suddenly sprang to life: "The Master gives himself to whatever the moment brings."[34] As soon as I made this shift, I was astonished to discover how easy flying was. Now I don't merely tolerate it—I love it. External conditions didn't change.

Everything remained as it was before—everything but me. I began showing up differently. Instead of fighting, I surrendered.

Undefeated

When we think of surrender, we think of defeat, and defeat means failure. If surrender is failure, then how can it be a good thing? Before we can move into the wisdom of surrender, we have to clear up this confusion.

We grew up struggling. We spent our whole lives learning to master new and difficult tasks, from tying our shoes to passing exams. Nothing is easy. No one hands you anything on a platter. Mountains don't lower themselves to let you pass, and violins don't play themselves. We have to fight for all of it. Never surrender, we're told.

In the next chapter, "Wisdom as Engagement," we'll take up the essential role that energetic and well-directed action plays in the construction and maintenance of a good life. But for now, let's examine the still, silent core of right action. "The Master sees things as they are, without trying to control them," says Laozi in the *Dao De Jing*. "She lets them go their own way, and resides at the center of the circle."[35] Just as every hurricane has an eye at its center—a place of utter calm and stillness—so too right action has at its core the consciousness of acceptance and surrender. As Krishna tells Arjuna in the Bhagavad Gita, "The wise see that there is action in the midst of inaction, and inaction in the midst of action."[36] Our challenge, then, is to awaken to the stillness within us and deeply root our being there.

We have learned that striving, fighting, and struggling are necessary to face challenges, overcome obstacles, and achieve mastery. Now let's give equal time to an opposite and equally true idea: nothing is gained without surrender.

Struggling and straining against things we cannot change only weakens us. Futile agitation, anxiety, and resentment rob us of our tranquility, happiness, and power. Being strapped into an airplane seat at fifteen thousand feet is a good time to relinquish the illusion of control. Surrender is a powerful decision that frees us from the turmoil of our fears and desires. Surrender as empowerment—who saw that coming? When we surrender, we are far from defeated. Surrender is victory.

Breathe into It

When I first began practicing yoga, like every other beginner, I was surprised by how challenging it was. From outside the window, yoga looked like the easiest class at the gym. But on the floor, stretching past all boundaries, legs and arms twisted into a pretzel, it hits you. Why are first impressions so often wrong?

I'll never forget the advice my yoga teacher gave me. I was stretching into a new pose, frustrated by how much resistance was flaring up in my legs and knees. "Breathe into it," she said. "Slow down and imagine that you are breathing directly into and through that place of resistance." In my argumentative mind, a silent objection immediately arose. *You don't breathe with your hips and your knees. You breathe with your lungs. What is she talking about?* But I tried it anyway. I surrendered. Suddenly the tightness relaxed, and with each exhalation I sank deeper into the pose.

Prana is Sanskrit for "breath." It also means "life force" or "vital energy." *Breathing into it* allowed this primal energy to flow into the constricted area and open channels that exertion and strain closed down.

You cannot clench and claw your way into flexibility and effectiveness. You have to allow it. When I stopped trying to fight and force my way into deeper poses, I discovered that by unclenching my muscles, I achieved far more. Once again, surrendering accomplished what struggling could not.

We Have Met the Enemy

In the dubious narrative we tell ourselves—that nothing good comes without a fight—we imagine there to be an enemy. The enemy goes by many names: poverty, ignorance, disease, powerful others, disempowerment. But what if the narrative is flawed? What if beneath our simple-minded characterization of life as a war there lies a deeper, less convenient truth that evolution, growth, and emergence, whether of an individual organism, a culture, or an entire universe, is necessarily messy, painful, and littered with dissolving forms? Loss is a part of there being a world at all. That fact does not make the world our enemy. Perhaps the enemy is our own misconception, born in the ego's illusion of separateness. We have met the enemy, and it is us.

If all is one, then the struggle disappears. In the world's wisdom traditions, especially in the teachings of the mystics, we find a challenging alternative to the standard dualistic portrait of life as a battle between good and evil. As Jesus counseled his students to "turn the other cheek" and "resist not evil," he was asserting the ancient insight that we are already at one with the Good; we don't have to create it from scratch with our ingenuity, cleverness, and sweat. Instead, what is required is deep-tissue surrender and cooperation. "For my yoke is easy," said Jesus, "and my burden is light."[37] Straining to control everything is, in stark contrast, a painfully difficult yoke to bear.

In order for us to move into this deep and vibrant surrender, we have to give up the fight. Until our sense of separateness dies, we will never experience the liberation and power of surrender. In the Gospel of John, Jesus wove another memorable metaphor ideally suited for his agricultural audience: "Unless a kernel of wheat falls to the ground and dies, it remains only a single seed. But if it dies it produces many seeds."[38] If our lives are to bear any fruit, we too must die to the illusion of egoic control and forever relinquish the notion that we are separate from the all-knowing universe.

Of course we have intentions. Of course we make plans. Of course we long for justice, freedom, and joy—and rightly so. Without some vision of the life we want to create, we squander opportunities and waste resources. But we know that a loose hand on the reins is best. "We must be willing to let go of the life we planned," said Joseph Campbell, "so as to have the life that is waiting for us." Reflecting on our lives up to this point, we see how true this is, how only in those moments when we trusted and let go of control did the right people, the right books, the right events, and the right gifts come into our lives. Sometimes surrender is voluntary. Sometimes it is forced upon us. In any case, surrender shifts us into a deeper state of connection with the source from which we and all things come, freeing us to realize our authentic life beyond the wildest imaginings of our worried minds. Jesus surrendered. Buddha surrendered. We say we admire these and many other teachers, yet surrender still seems like defeat to us. We fear it. This perhaps is the last remnant of the battle—to realize there is no battle. "The condition of an enlightened mind," said Alan Redpath, "is a surrendered heart." Wisdom, enlightenment, awakening, the kingdom of heaven, nirvana—whatever we call it, it will forever elude us until we somehow learn to surrender. Surrender is not yet another hard-earned achievement. It is the end of the consciousness of achievement. We are already there. Taking off the painful yoke of egoic control, moving into a state of deep cooperation, dying to our false sense of separateness, breathing into it—these are the shifts that move us deeper into the soil out of which our best, most fully realized lives will grow.

Surrender to What?

What are we surrendering to? God?

For many people, God is a conscious entity, the sacred creator of all things, the author of morality, and the giver of laws.

Some religions teach that this God is beyond the material world and beyond the fabric of space and time, yet he is somehow engaged with it, guiding it, responsible for its sustenance and its purpose. Developing and maintaining a relationship with this transcendent God is the work of many religious people the world over, especially in the world's two biggest religions, Christianity and Islam.

For many other people, God is an idea that has grown tired, worn out by centuries of mindless repetition, misuse, and misappropriation. For some, simply the sound of the word *God* evokes eye-rolling frustration, sighs of fatigue, yawns of indifference, or outright hostility. There may well be a mystery at the core of existence—a transcendent source that cannot be defined and contained by empirical science—but personifying it and giving it human characteristics is for many people the height of foolishness. Assuming God to be a powerful man in the sky is textbook anthropomorphism. "If horses and cows had gods," quipped the ancient Greek poet Xenophanes, "they would look like horses and cows." In patriarchal societies, God is a man. In matriarchal societies, God is a woman. Freud was right in this sense at least: we project onto the heavens our own sense of human power and our own deep needs. The distant, angry, judgmental father; the compassionate, nurturing mother—we make God into whatever we need him or her to be.

The idea of God, therefore, is problematic. Deeply significant to many, tired and worn to many others, the word *God* is spread so thin it seems to have lost all meaning. When German philosopher Friedrich Nietzsche's famously declared,

"God is dead," it was not the demise of our transcendent deity that Nietzsche was lamenting—it was the loss of meaning that the idea of God afforded. The idea of God, once so central in Western civilization, a sun around which all the planets of our conceptual framework orbited, had faded away. It wasn't Nietzsche's fault; he was just the messenger, describing what he saw in the decadent, nihilistic European culture of the nineteenth century. Whatever the transcendent source of the universe was, our concept of that source had simply worn out and fallen apart. We no longer share a simple, centralized, codifying concept of God. We have shattered into a thousand conflicting visions. The center cannot hold. "God is dead," wrote Nietzsche. "He remains dead. And we have killed him."[39]

Despite all of these problems, the word *God* is still a useful placeholder for most people. God signifies the organizing principle of the universe, personified or not. As such, God becomes synonymous with nature, law, spirit, truth, and many familiar terms from the world's wisdom traditions like logos, Dao, and Brahman. Once the need for personification and anthropomorphizing is outgrown, we are left with a useful concept that wears many hats with dignity and aplomb.

Paul McCartney tells the story that when he wrote the song "Yesterday," he awoke with the melody playing in his head, but the words had not yet taken shape. In the place of "yesterday," he sang "scrambled eggs," as in, "Scrambled eggs, la da da da da da, da da da, da da da da da da da da da, oh da da da, da scrambled eggs." "Scrambled eggs" was a placeholder. As we all know, "Yesterday" has nothing to do with scrambled eggs.

Like the phrase "scrambled eggs" in McCartney's songwriting process, the God-word serves as a placeholder in our process of coming to terms with ultimate reality.

Joseph Campbell carved a path out of this thicket of confusion. As a scholar of mythology and religion, he made a career out of the study of the world's dizzying pantheons and religious systems. Campbell argued that any idea of God is like a mask that is initially useful but ultimately destructive. At first, the mask shows us where to look; it gives us a point of reference, a place around which we can gather. The mask often resembles our own face, making the beginnings of a relationship easier. But in the end, Campbell laments, we get stuck with the mask and fail to look behind it.

The inspiration for the mask is drawn from two places: our physical environment, and our unexamined assumptions about power. For the Navajo of the American Southwest, gods are coyotes and ravens. For the Polynesians, gods are sea turtles and dolphins. The local environment provides the raw material. And in patriarchal societies where men have power, God is a male, whereas in matriarchal societies the Goddess prevails. We project onto the heavens our own provincial notions of power. A culture's God-masks tells us much more about its own values than it does about the nameless, transcendent reality they claim to convey.

We forget that we made the mask. We begin to mistake the mask for the hidden reality behind it. Worse still, we ridicule, condemn, and sometimes even kill those who utilize different masks. If we wish to know God, Campbell asserts, we must lift off the mask. In other words, our concept of God is the final obstacle between us and God. If you want to *know* God, you have to forget everything you know *about* God.

In an old Hindu story, a student asks his guru, "How many gods are there?" "330,000", said the old teacher.

Realizing this number was a little unwieldy, the student asked again.

"But among those," the student asked, "which are the really important ones? How many are there really?"

"Thirty-three thousand," said the teacher.

"Okay, but among those, how many are there really?"

"Three thousand three hundred."

"All right, but of those, how many should I worship? How many are there really?"

"Three hundred thirty."

"But among those, which are the most important? How many are they?"

"Thirty-three."

"Yes, but of those, how many are there really?

"Three."

"Okay, but of those three, how many are there really?"

"One," said the teacher.

"One?" asked the student, "If there is only one, then why did you tell me there were 330,000?"

"Those are simply the names of the many powers of the One."

This story stirs up a powerful paradox. Is Hinduism polytheistic with many gods, or monotheistic with only one god? The answer is it's both. The religious and philosophical traditions of India lay bare the futility of trying to conceptualize God. When the infinite mystery of transcendent reality is dragged down into the realm of conceptual thought, it shatters into a thousand pieces. Masks are clear enough, but when we lift off the mask, what remains is a mystery that transcends all labels and definitions.

"The Dao that can be told is not the eternal Dao," wrote Laozi in the opening line of the *Dao De Jing*. If the ineffable source of the universe is beyond all thoughts and concepts, then of course we cannot talk about it. Even our elaborate metaphysics and theologies are masks. Our best ideas about the transcendent are only fingers pointing at the moon, and only an idiot would mistake a finger for the moon.

Zhuangzi is another Daoist philosopher wary of language's ability to encapsulate and convey wisdom. Like Jesus, Zhuangzi was a master of analogies. Here he makes his point simply and clearly, especially to his pre-industrial, agrarian, third century BCE Chinese audience:

> The purpose of a fish trap is to catch fish, and when the fish are caught the trap is forgotten. The purpose of a rabbit snare is to catch rabbits. When the rabbits are caught the snare is forgotten. The purpose of words is to convey ideas. When the ideas are grasped the words are forgotten. Where can I find the man who has forgotten words? He is the one I would like to talk to.[40]

The understanding that ultimate reality is ineffable, that is, cannot be expressed with words and concepts, is a universal theme shared throughout the world's wisdom traditions. At the top of Plato's metaphysical hierarchy is the Form of the Good, beyond the reach of language and thought, knowable only through direct experience. In the Vedanta philosophy of India, Brahman, the ultimate source of all things including the gods, is beyond all thoughts and forms.

In the mystical traditions of Judaism, Christianity, and Islam we find the same insight, that the God that can be named is only a signpost pointing the way toward the true God, utterly transcendent yet imminently knowable. In Buddhism, most pointedly in its Zen expression, mental constructions hinder more than help our transformation from limited, conditioned beings into awakened beings. In the *Dao De Jing*, Laozi's favorite word for Dao is the "nameless."

If Brahman, the ground of being, cannot be named or contained in a concept, where can we find it? In Vedanta, Brahman is simply the name of the nameless source from which all matter, energy, and consciousness arise. Within sentient beings like us, it is called Atman, or the Self. Deep beneath the layers of the body, the sense organs, the mind, and the subconscious mind lies the reality of Atman or the Self, what Krishna in the Bhagavad Gita called the inner witness. This is why the Upanishads simply report that all is one.

We don't realize our oneness because we are caught by an intricate and beautiful play of sensations and thought-forms that fool us into thinking we are separate egos in separate bodies, in conflict with one another. In Hinduism, this illusory play of forms is known as *maya*, or illusion. Overcoming maya and seeing the underlying unity of all things is the goal of the various spiritual paths or yogas of Hinduism. Buddha called awakening from the dream of separateness nirvana. Jesus called it the kingdom of heaven. Jesus claimed unity with God when he said, "I am in the Father, and … the Father is in me."[41] This, in the eyes of the Pharisees and Sadducees, the religious authorities of Jerusalem, was blasphemy.

Blasphemy means claiming for oneself the characteristics of God. For the Pharisees and Sadducees, God could not be found within oneself but only through the proper observance of rituals overseen by priests in the Temple. Jesus, like mystics the world over, threatened the established religious order by showing us that we are all united with the divine ground of being: "The Kingdom of Heaven is within you."[42] After his death, Jesus himself became the focal point of a new and vigorous religious establishment, Christianity, which championed the idea that Jesus was the sole incarnation of God, a miraculous being who required worship and obedience. Slowly, the loving vision Jesus had of our interconnectedness and identity in God, of our inherent goodness and inner divinity, transformed into a theological doctrine built on the inherent evil of man and the need for salvation brought about solely by the Church and its priests. As with all revolutions, when the dust had settled, the new boss looked a lot like the old boss.

One possibility, then, is this: What if we surrendered our concepts and theologies? What if we let go of our carefully constructed ideologies? What if we released our need to be right? What if we let words and concepts slip back into their rightful roles as tools designed to deepen our awareness, instead of allowing words and concepts to stand in the place of wisdom? Only the consciousness of surrender could bring about such a shift.

"The wise speak of One in many ways,"[43] proclaims the Rig Veda. Like white light through a prism Truth splits into many colors when run through the prism of human understanding. A fundamental characteristic of wisdom is the ability to see that behind all the conflicting truth claims lay a deep and ineffable unity. This is why Socrates wrote nothing. And this is why the Buddha, when asked to explain the meaning of life, simply held up a flower.

Whether one subscribes to a dualistic concept of reality or a nondualistic one; whether one is an atheist, theist, deist, or agnostic; whether one is a pantheist, polytheist, or monotheist; whether you believe God is a man, a woman, or an impersonal First Principle—all of these are concepts. As we have seen, whatever God is, is beyond all concepts. Now we can relax, resign from the debating society, and enjoy this glorious gallery of masks in which we find ourselves.

The good news is that we needn't abandon our current concept of the infinite. Because every concept of God is partial, provisional, and incomplete, what's the use in fighting over whose mask is the right one? As long as we understand that our *idea* of God is not God but only a reference, we can safely use any mask we like. God the Father, Mother Goddess, monotheism, polytheism, pantheism: because all words and concepts are only a "finger pointing at the moon," the debate begins to subside, and we can peacefully coexist alongside people who use different words and concepts to point to the transcendent. The ancient Rig Veda still stands as the definitive statement on the matter: The truth is One. The sages call it by many names. It's just that simple.

Are we then to rip away all masks? That will prove challenging. Another option might be to embrace all masks—the more, the merrier. Rather than trying to strip God of all associations, how about going the other way, piling them all on? Perhaps in the cacophony, the din will drown itself out, and the silence will shine through as we grow less and less interested in defending any one mask.

Another way to think about the ineffability of God is this: theologies and ideologies are maps. If I ask Google maps for driving directions from my house to Disneyland, and you do the same, we will end up with two very different and utterly incompatible routes. But I'll see you at Disneyland. It would be strange indeed to confront you in the parking lot at Disneyland, condemn your map as heresy, and praise mine as the inerrant word of God.

For the purposes of our study, let's use the word *God* in the most inclusive way possible. If the word *God* has negative associations for you, then use another word. Buried resentments against organized religion hinder our inquiry and must be released. Don't throw out the baby with the bathwater. In this book, the word *God* contains all of the masks without being bound by any of them.

If all is one as the Upanishads claim, then what becomes of all this seeking? If God is within us, then not one of our steps leads away from God. "What was never lost," said twentieth-century Vedanta teacher Nisargadatta Maharaj, "can never be found."[44] Nisargadatta counseled his students to stop seeking and instead simply ask the question, "What am I?" Get to the bottom of that, and everything else falls into place. Turning God into an external object to be discovered only after a long and arduous search, in contrast, is doomed to fail.

The biggest obstacle to this depth realization is our own illusory sense of separateness. The ego's primary task is to continually shore up its own importance. Only when we relinquish the primacy of the ego does the door to heaven open. In the words of ninth-century Persian Sufi master Abu Yazid al-Bistami, "Forgetfulness of self is remembrance of God."[45] For Muhammad, Allah is nearer than "the jugular vein," and for Meister Eckhart, "the eye with which I see God is the same eye with which God sees me."[46] The entire dynamic of surrender shifts when we realize that the power we are surrendering to is not an external overlord but an internal presence.

In the nondualism of mystics the world over, the consciousness of surrender is an essential step in the unfolding of our own awakening. When the walls between us and everything else fall down, an unforeseen power begins to move through us, a power we have long held beneath the bindings of our ego and limited sense of self. Finally, it is that limited sense of self we must surrender and renounce. Ramana Maharshi, perhaps the most influential Indian teacher of the twentieth century, put the consciousness of surrender at the center of his work. "Surrender is to give oneself up to the original cause of one's being," he wrote. "Do not delude yourself by imagining such a source to be some god outside of you. One's source is within oneself. Give yourself up to it. That means you should seek the source and merge in it."[47] Echoing this idea is Adyashanti, a contemporary teacher: "Surrender isn't something I do," he wrote, "surrender isn't an act I perform. Surrender is an expression of my own truest being."[48] In this sense, surrender is a profoundly authentic, courageous, and triumphant act. We've moved a long way from the idea that to surrender is to be diminished or defeated; quite the contrary. True surrender is to be liberated from the cage of fear and transformed into beings of unlimited potential.

No-Seeking

As we have seen, the very idea of seeking is built upon an error, namely, that we are separated from what we seek. This problem is a primary focus of Zen Buddhism. "Don't seek the truth," the Zen saying goes, "just get rid of all your opinions." The consciousness of seeking clouds our capacity to see the ever present truth.

"Your relentless pursuit of wisdom postpones your actually possessing it," said the Stoic Epictetus. "Quit chasing after tonics and new teachers. The latest fashionable sage or book or belief doesn't move you in the direction of a flourishing life. You do."[49]

Again and again the world's wisdom traditions return to this basic insight: seeking, striving, and strenuous disciplined effort are required to tear us away from our complacency, yet in the end, exertion alone, no matter how muscular and adept, can never deliver us to wisdom. Instead, we must surrender to it. This is one of the great paradoxes of the spiritual and philosophical path. The word *paradox* means two truths that, according to the rules of logic, cannot both be true at the same time, yet they are. For example, "this sauce is sour" and "this sauce is sweet." The law of noncontradiction, one of the bedrock rules of logic and rationality, says that something cannot be both *x* and *not x* at the same time. A sauce cannot be hot and cold, thick and thin, or sweet and sour at the same time. Yet anyone who's ever had sweet and sour sauce knows that the law of contradiction is apparently not taught in Asian culinary schools.

Learning to live with paradox, as we have seen, is one of the qualities of the enlightened mind. The road to wisdom is littered with paradoxes, a topic we will take up in much greater detail in the final chapter of this book, "Wisdom as Integration." Paradoxes speak not to the irrational nature of reality but to the limits of reason. Logic and reason work just fine in most scenarios. In fact, we would be lost without them. But at the higher rungs of the epistemological ladder, they begin to flounder in the rarified air of transcendent knowing. Language and reason begin to break down under the pressure of paradox. Language and truth statements offer only partial portraits of a reality forever beyond their reach. This is why to the uninitiated ear the mystics of all traditions begin to sound like babbling idiots. In the end, out of frustration at being continually misconstrued, they usually fall silent.

Recovery

In the worldwide recovery movement surrender is a core principle. The first of the twelve steps of Alcoholics Anonymous reads in part, "We admitted that we were powerless over alcohol."[50] For many people caught up in the destructive cycle of compulsive drinking or any other addiction, it seems absolutely counterintuitive to begin by admitting defeat. Wouldn't we much more effectively gain control over our lives by knuckling down and asserting our willpower?

Founded on widely held spiritual principles, the discoveries of modern psychology, and secular philosophies like Stoicism, AA emerged in the 1930s as an effective treatment method for chronic alcoholics. The principles and methods of AA have since been adapted to treat drug addiction and a host of other compulsive disorders. While overtly spiritual, AA and its sister organizations remain distinctly nonreligious. Above all, they are pragmatic. They're not interested in debating the merits of conflicting theories. They're interested only in what works. Hard statistics are difficult to come by because of the anonymity of its members, but numerous studies and reams of testimonials show that AA has saved the lives of millions of people worldwide and healed countless marriages and families. It's difficult to say why it works. But for people who surrender to its principles and follow its suggestions, it often does.

How is it possible to regain power over one's life by admitting powerlessness? How can victory begin in an act of surrender? Again, what are we surrendering to?

The second step says that we "came to believe that a power greater than ourselves could restore us to sanity." Here begins the idea of a higher power. Embedded in the fabric of AA is the idea, familiar to us now, that any specific idea of God is merely a mask. In AA, one is encouraged to find and utilize a concept of a higher power that seems most authentic and genuine for them. Even atheists are able to conceive of a power greater than themselves, even if it is only the community of fellow alcoholics. AA does not require belief in God, nor does it demand compliance with any specific religious ideology. This open-endedness is deeply welcoming to legions of sufferers for whom the doors of many churches, synagogues, mosques, and temples have long since closed. The architects of AA knew from their own experience that initiates would eventually come into an experiential knowing of an authentic higher power through the stages of their own evolution. No elaborate theological defense need be mounted. In the beginning, new members of AA are simply invited to surrender to the possibility. Experience will take care of the rest.

Then comes the third step: "Made a decision to turn our will and our lives over to the care of God *as we understood Him*." Notice that this does not say that we should abdicate or eradicate our will—it simply says that we should shift from solely relying on self-will to a deeper sense of cooperation with our higher power, whatever we understand that higher power to be. Making a decision is, after all, an act of will. Choosing to get well and setting the intention of healing, even though one does not know how it's all going to work, is yet another example of the curious way surrender and active engagement go hand in hand in the journey toward a full and rewarding life.

Whether or not one is struggling with an addiction, the principles and practices of the recovery movement offer a window into a world where the consciousness of surrender is fully embraced and practiced with great effect. The paradox of gaining power through the admission of powerlessness is a perfect example of the limitations of language and reason. What on the surface seems nonsensically contradictory becomes eminently sensible and therapeutic in the depths of our own lived experience. Countless alcoholics and others have found serenity through the practice of these principles. With the serenity prayer and mantras like "Let go and let God," people all over the world have found refuge from the circular machinations of their own compulsive and dysfunctional thinking. For those of us lucky enough to be free of addictions, there is still much to learn from the recovery movement about the power of surrender.

What if the dilemma of power versus powerlessness is a false dilemma? In the *Dao De Jing*, Laozi wrote, "The Master doesn't try to be powerful; thus he is truly powerful. The ordinary man keeps reaching for power; thus he never has enough."[51] Here again we see the irony of the futility in seeking. Like playground bullies, those who clownishly ape what they mistakenly perceive to be power are, in the end, impotent. Only through peaceful cooperation, said Laozi, do we "win." In surrender, we gain mastery. Seeking to control, we slip into failure. "The soft overcomes the hard," wrote Laozi, "the gentle overcomes the rigid. Everyone knows this is true, but few can put it into practice."[52]

Easy does it. Hard does not.

Self-Will vs. God's Will

One of the most psychologically astute and insightful teachings in the Bhagavad Gita is on the relationship between self-will and the will of God. In chapter six of the Gita, Krishna tells Arjuna:

> Reshape yourself through the power of your will; never let yourself be degraded by self-will. The will is the only friend of the Self, and the will is the only enemy of the Self. To those who have conquered themselves, the will is a friend. But it is the enemy of those who have not found the Self within.[53]

Clearly, the word *will* is moving around on us a little, and at first glance this passage is confusing. But as we look closer, it is plain that Krishna is suggesting something very similar to the third step of Alcoholics Anonymous. In other words, we must decide (with our will) to surrender to and cooperate with the will of God or our higher power (in Krishna's vernacular, the Self) in order to awaken to our own deeper purpose. If we use our will constructively this way, the will is our friend. If, however, we choose to ally the will with the lower "self," that is, the ego and its fearful attachment to destructive cravings, then the will becomes our enemy. A drug addict destructively utilizes their will to commit crime; deceive their spouse, friends, and employer; strive diligently to procure their narcotic of choice; and continually poison themselves. The will is neither good nor bad, just as a knife is neither good nor bad. It simply depends on what you do with it. This is what the third step of AA means when it suggests that we make "a decision to turn our will … over to the care of God." Far beyond mere obedience to some external deity, this alliance with the divine mind frees us and empowers us beyond the wildest imaginings of the limited ego. Once again, surrender surprises us.

Confucius and the Communal Will

Kungfuzi, or Confucius as he came to be known in the west, is arguably the most influential philosopher of all time. Born in the fifth century BCE, he distilled the wisdom of ancient China into a humanistic vision so compelling that within a hundred years of his death, he was known throughout China simply as "the teacher." To this day, his vision of the ideal society predominates throughout Asia. Confucian values lay at the core of Asian life from the arts to corporate culture.

Confucius lamented the decline of morality evident in his own time. He actively sought ways to harmonize society around a set of values that honored individuals while nurturing social relationships at every level of society, from the family to the empire. Like the Daoists and the Stoics, Confucius believed that the universe was an orderly place governed by a benign goodness. As individuals and as societies we flourish to the extent that we lived in accord with the existing order. Bringing the mandate of heaven down to earth through our choices and actions was the moral obligation of every member of the human community.

According to Confucius, the primary task of any teacher is to distill the best values and ideas from the past and apply them to the changing context of the modern world—a world our ancestors could never have imagined, let alone guide us through. In our own time, for example, technology has outpaced social etiquette. No one yet quite knows what's "right" or "wrong" when it comes to our cell phones. Is it all right to take a call while eating in a restaurant or while in a movie theater? Is it polite to set your phone on speaker and talk loudly as you walk up and down a crowded grocery story aisle, confusing or bothering all the other shoppers? Some people have strong feelings about this issue. They claim that such behaviors are the height of boorishness and inconsideration. Others seem entirely oblivious to the allegedly offending nature of these behaviors and make and take calls regardless of the impact it has on those around them. There is no consensus. The result is a lot of misunderstanding, frustration, and friction leading to recriminations, judgments, and disharmony. This is precisely the sort of mayhem Confucius believed could and should be prevented by developing a shared, communal consciousness surrounding the conundrums presented by our ever-changing world. We don't need new values. We simply need to creatively and thoughtfully apply the best of our old values to each new situation.

One of the core values Confucius held dear was *shu*, or reciprocity. We must come to realize, he argued, that we are all interconnected and that everything we do impacts those around us. We must develop our awareness to the point where we are continually conscious of the impact we have on others. This universal idea, often called the Golden Rule (do unto others as you would have them do unto you), is the beginning of harmony. Without self-awareness and sensitivity regarding the needs and feelings of others, we cannot begin to heal our strained relationships with the family members, friends, and strangers who fill the days and hours of our lives. Another word for this shift in consciousness is empathy, an act of imagination where one steps into the skin of another and sees the world through their eyes. Without empathy, the project of moral transformation never even gets off the ground.

In order for us to manifest shu and reap its benefits, we must first surrender our own immediate interests. If I want to talk in a crowded movie theater, whether on my phone or to the person next to me, I should first realize that the sound of my voice will disrupt the aesthetic experience of scores of people sitting around me, greatly interfering with their immersion in the film, an experience they paid their hard-earned money to have and certainly deserve. In order to create the greatest amount of good, I have to relinquish my self-interest for the good of the many. On the surface, this utilitarian decision seems like a sacrifice. Upon deeper examination, however, it becomes clear that by helping to maintain a quiet movie-going experience for others, I share in the cocreation of an environment that benefits me. In other words, the false dilemma between self-interest and group-interest dissolves. What's good is good and what's right is right. We all benefit. That thing I was going to say to my friend? Not that important.

If everyone awakens to the consciousness of shu, the world becomes a much more pleasant place where each of us is honored, feels respected, and in turn enjoys the even deeper pleasure of having a positive impact on the lives of others. Surrendering private good for public good feeds a deep, communal need within each of us. Especially when we mature enough to realize that our best self-interest and the interests of others are one and the same. By contributing to and maintaining healthy, constructive, and mutually beneficial relationships with everyone we meet, we open ourselves up to a world of endless abundance and opportunity. This is not a crude quid pro quo—I'll scratch your back if you scratch mine. This is a genuine realization of interwoven fates and the willingness to surrender our arbitrary and limited private desires in the interest of mutual well-being. In this way, surrender is once again shown to be a strong, courageous, and empowering act.

What Surrender Does Not Mean

By now we've seen that surrender, if understood correctly, is not weakness. Nor is it ineffective. Surrender, understood in its positive sense, is a way of being in the world that opens us up to a realm of opportunity and abundance unavailable to anyone still struggling at the level of self-will.

As compelling as this portrait of surrender might be, many questions remain. What about evil? What are we to do when confronted with injustice, cruelty, and violence? Are we simply to lay down our arms and let powerful, vicious people impose their will on us? In a word, no.

Surrender does not mean walking blindly toward our own destruction or allowing evil to go unchallenged. The consciousness of surrender has nothing to do with apathy, avoidance, or denial. In fact, it is quite the contrary. It is only from the consciousness of acceptance and surrender that truly effective action can emerge. Action rooted in the consciousness of fear, revenge, hatred, and the need to control isn't action at all—it is reaction, hopelessly bound by the laws of karma to remain in a futile downward spiral of endless, mutually destructive warfare, whether in the bedroom, in the boardroom, or in world affairs. When we arrogantly dehumanize the other and seek to impose our limited sense of right and wrong onto them without first affirming our underlying unity, our actions are not only ineffective, they are counterproductive to our larger aims. Force is never as effective as influence. "Try to make people moral," writes Laozi, "and you lay the groundwork for vice."[54]

So what is right action? And how is it rooted in the consciousness of surrender? In the next chapter, "Wisdom as Engagement," we will take up the challenging task of describing what Buddha called "right action" and what Krishna called "action without attachment to the fruits of action." From these and other sources, we will draw a portrait of action that not only achieves its aims but does so without carrying the seeds of destruction into new ground. For now, suffice it to say that surrender does not mean lying down. Surrender is an internal condition of consciousness, not an outer plan of action.

Make Me an Instrument

Saint Francis was a twelfth-century monk who transformed medieval Christianity by bringing simplicity, compassion, and heart to what many saw as a Church overly reliant on authority, dogma, and material acquisition. Today he is best known for two things: being the monk who loved nature (hence his ubiquitous statue in so many gardens), and the St. Francis prayer. Although not found in his writings, and not traceable any source earlier than an obscure 1912 French Catholic publication long out of print, the so-called St. Francis prayer is nevertheless a powerful expression of the consciousness of surrender. Naturally, it expresses a theistic, specifically Christian, point of view, but the transformation in consciousness it portrays is available to anyone regardless of their religious ideology.

> Lord, make me an instrument of your peace,
> That where there is hatred, I may bring love,
> That where there is wrong, I may bring the spirit of forgiveness,
> That where there is discord, I may bring harmony,
> That where there is error, I may bring truth,
> That where there is doubt, I may bring faith,
> That where there is despair, I may bring hope,
> That where there are shadows, I may bring light,
> That where there is sorrow, I may bring joy.

Lord, grant that I may seek rather to comfort, than to be comforted,
To understand, than to be understood,
To love, than to be loved.
For it is by self-forgetting that one finds,
It is by forgiving that one is forgiven,
It is by dying that one awakens to Eternal Life.[55]

The St. Francis prayer lifts from our shoulders the burden of having to single-handedly create from whole cloth the goodness and healing the world so clearly needs. We do not have to arduously manufacture peace, love, forgiveness, harmony, truth, faith, hope, light, and joy through the exertion of our own cleverness, tenacity, and self-will. Instead, we are invited to open our hearts and minds and let the real source of those qualities pour through us the way rain pours through downspouts. In a word, the St. Francis prayer suggests that we surrender.

There are at least two ways of understanding this. In the dualistic theism of traditional Christianity, it is God the Father who works through us to bring His love and mercy to the world—that is, if we humble ourselves enough to let it happen. If, however, you subscribe to a nondualistic worldview where God is simply the name of the one presence and power within all things, then the dynamics of the process shift. In nondualism, becoming an instrument means surrendering your false sense of separateness and entering into an open-hearted awareness of your unqualified oneness with the ground of Being and all its manifestations. When you live and think and feel and act from this awakened consciousness, you are no longer acting alone; you are indeed the presence of God. In either case, the St. Francis prayer encourages us to surrender our small and limited ego in exchange for something greater. By letting go of something insignificant, we gain the opportunity to experience the presence of God-consciousness in every moment of our lives.

An entire book could be written about the last three lines of the prayer alone, but for our purposes, it is worth noting that the transformation those lines describe occurs on the inside as well as on the outside of our lives. When we practice "self-forgetting," replacing egocentricity with humility and compassion, we arrive at the end of all seeking. The world stops being such an impossibly difficult and complicated place. When we forgive others their trespasses, our own self-loathing and suffering ends. And when we die to the ego, we awaken to God-consciousness.

Enlightenment, then, is not something to be achieved. It is our natural state and emerges when the impediments fall away, one by one. The St. Francis prayer helps us "put first the Kingdom of Heaven" so all else may be given to us. All that is required is that we stop struggling and surrender to the depth reality of what we are and have always been.

On September 11, 2001, the first reported casualty was Father Mychal Judge. A Roman Catholic priest of the Franciscan Order, Father Mychal was, among other things, chaplain to the Fire Department of New York. He arrived at the World Trade

Center along with hundreds of police officers, firefighters, and paramedics minutes after the first plane struck the south tower. Working near the command center in the ground floor lobby of the north tower, Father Mychal was killed by falling debris when the south tower collapsed at 9:59 a.m. Reuters photographer Shannon Stapleton's photograph of Father Mychal's lifeless body, slumped over in a chair and carried by five dust-covered fire fighters, is one of the most iconic images of that unforgettable day.

In Father Mychal Judge's pocket, they found a prayer. It was a prayer he always carried with him, a prayer he had shared many times with others as he ministered to grieving families, wounded firefighters, dying AIDS patients, and all of the other sufferers who crossed his path. But on September 11, Father Mychal's prayer took on a new significance.

"Lord, take me where you want me to go, let me meet who you want me to meet, tell me what you want me to say, and keep me out of your way."

A perfect embodiment of the consciousness of surrender, Father Mychal died the same way he lived—in deep submission to holiness. By inhabiting the presence of God everywhere he went, he was able to bring that presence to those who needed it most. Father Mychal often visited the sick and dying in the hospitals of New York City, particularly in AIDS wards. With fear and shame in his eyes, one young man dying of AIDS pulled Father Mychal close and asked, "Father, does God hate me?" Father Mychal leaned down and held the man in his arms, rocking him and whispering in his ear until the tears stopped falling.

After his death, many of Father Mychal's closest friends and associates shared the fact that he was gay. As a celibate priest, his homosexuality was more orientation than behavior, yet the revelation caused a firestorm of controversy in and out of the church. For Father Mychal, accepting and surrendering to his own true nature was just another act of obedience to God. To live in the truth of who you are is to honor our creator and sanctify our lives. "Within the divine order," Epictetus wrote, "we each have our own special calling. Listen to yours and follow it faithfully."[56] When we surrender to and honor the truth, how can God hate us?

Besides humility, honesty, and unwavering faith in the power of God, another pillar of Father Mychal's strength were his beloved AA meetings in the basement of an Episcopalian Church. As a recovering alcoholic Father Mychal was living out the promise of surrender every day. He had enormous respect for the principles and practices of AA, seeing firsthand their pragmatic value in his own life and the lives of countless others. At a White House reception, he once told President Clinton that he thought the founders of AA had done more for humanity than Mother Theresa.

Following Buddha's suggestion that we test philosophical ideas in the light of our own experience, I've been experimenting with Father Mychal's prayer. Roman Catholicism is not my tradition, but as I step out of my car in the parking lot at Southwestern College and walk toward my office to prepare for another day of teaching, knowing that I am going to face hundreds of students, scores of challenging tasks, and maybe even a few cantankerous colleagues at a department meeting, I silently repeat Father Mychal's prayer: "Lord, take me where you want me to go, let me meet who you want me to meet, tell me what you want me to say, and keep me out of your way." All my rational protestations aside, I feel my anxiety and worry subside. I remember that I am not in charge. I just work here. Throughout the day, I find myself smiling rather than fretting when events fail to conform to my expectations. Father Mychal's prayer grants me the serenity to accept the things I cannot change. In fact, it offers something far richer than mere acceptance: it leads me into the awareness that this moment, this person, this question, this problem, this challenge is exactly what is supposed to be happening right now, and there is great depth, beauty, and value in remaining present to it and not running into the ever-waiting arms of avoidance, denial, or self-importance.

The next time you have to walk into a difficult meeting, the next time someone interrupts your "important work" with an annoying request, or the next time you're faced with the grief of a friend and don't know what to say, try surrendering and getting out of the way. No more fighting to control everything, fix everything, or stamp everything with the mark of your egoic expectations. Assume, for once, that this is what is supposed to be happening. Trust that by shifting from the consciousness of struggle to the consciousness of surrender, the right people, the right situations, and the right words will flow from the channel your loving-kindness has made.

The mystical Sufi poet Jeladuddin Balkhi was born in 1207 in Persian-controlled Afghanistan. For Rumi, as he later came to be known, not only are we instruments of grace, but the whole world is. Every bird flight; every ripple in the lake; every thought, word, and gesture; every pebble on the shore; and every breath of wind is a manifestation of God-consciousness, laden with the power to tear away the fabric of our complacency and lay bare the beating heart of our endless longing. In a poem called "Each Note," he wrote:

> God picks up the reed-flute world and blows.
> Each note is a need coming through one of us,
> a passion, a longing-pain.
>   Remember the lips
> where the wind-breath originated,
> and let your note be clear.
> Don't try to end it.
> *Be your note.*
> I'll show you how it's enough.
>
> Let *everyone* climb on their roofs
> and sing their notes!
>
> Sing loud![57]

In Rumi's vision, everything is an instrument or a channel of Spirit. In the boundless awareness of the mystic, there is nowhere where God is not. Divine mind pours down like shafts of light through a forest. It is for us to awaken and walk through the trees of our ignorance, first on paths others have made, then at last where there are no paths, just the shapeless arcs of our own meandering. The light does not shine more sweetly on that meadow than this one. Without the consciousness of surrender, we would never rise above our own cleverness, our own cynicism, our own weariness, to move like geese flying north to their birthing grounds for the summer, to our rightful place in the home and hearth of our unalienable unity with the divine.

For Rumi, the longing we feel is God's longing. Our yearning to know more, have more, and be more is the natural expansion of our sacred nature. When we surrender to our song, we become who we really are and honor the source.

Would we speak differently if we knew that our words sprang from a well of sacred wisdom not of our own making? Would we gently shape our thoughts differently if we knew that our best thoughts were the dreams of sacred consciousness moving through us, yearning to be born in our words and actions? Would we act differently if we knew that into every room we entered, we entered as the presence of God? Let us think and speak and act as if we were the magnificent beings we are. Let us surrender to our essential nature. Let us finally live as if we were instruments and God was music.

Giant Sequoia

A few years ago, my wife, Lori, and I celebrated our twenty-fifth anniversary at the Wawona Hotel in Yosemite National

Park, the site of our honeymoon. Seven miles to the south of Wawona, there is an ancient grove of sequoias called the Mariposa Grove. Walking among the giant redwoods on a cold, late spring morning—the ground spongy and damp, the low-hanging clouds torn by shards of icy wind revealing ribbons of blue sky above—you feel in your bones the deep silence of the forest and the immeasurable patience of the sequoias, the largest, oldest living things on earth. Some of these trees are three thousand years old. They have withstood three thousand winters, three thousand fire seasons, and just recently the coming of industrial man, a myopic creature with an overblown ego and a penchant for clear-cutting. Fortunately, Galen Clark, John Muir, and others worked tirelessly to preserve tiny islands of wilderness called national parks, where nature is allowed to exist unmolested by the hands of rapacious commerce.

As we walked through an ever-changing array of rain, hail, and sun showers, the trail climbed over a ridge and dropped into a meadow ringed round with snow. Through the center of the meadow ran a winding creek of snowmelt. One lone sequoia, its bark glowing red in the diffuse light, rose up out of the earth like a colossus. It stopped us in our tracks. Out of the silence, a stellar jay squawked high in the canopy. Far from breaking the spell, his cry only deepened it, like the penetrating peal of a gong in a temple. Here this tree has stood, in this meadow, since the time of the pharaohs, a thousand years before Christ. Throughout all of the agonizing and glorious centuries of human history this beautiful tree has stood in perfect, absolute surrender. You'd be hard pressed to find a grander, bolder, or more obvious display of power than this. And yet on this cold, gray morning, I was struck not by its might or mass but by its humility. Its entire existence was characterized by a complete and utter surrender. Three thousand years ago when it was merely a seedling, as it felt its roots sink deep into the forest floor and its tiny limbs unfurl toward the sky, it knew that this was where it was going to live, in this meadow, in these mountains, with these sister trees. It did not long for some other life. It did not yearn to be anything other than what it was. It knew instinctively that its highest honor was to be itself. It knew that its very existence was a prayer, and that every day for thousands of years it would stand as a testament to life and the sacred source of life beyond the veil of all dualities.

All of these thoughts swept through me in an instant, and as a gust of wind knocks snow off high branches, this awareness tore away from me my smallness, my weariness, my restlessness to be someone other than who I am. Deeply rooted in the earth, reaching high into the sky, silent and still, feeling every breath of wind, washed clean by the rain, shining in the sun, this tree stood before me like a vast and silent force. Its selfless humility and unabashed authenticity gave me to myself. I surrendered.

In the words of Epictetus,

> We are like actors in a play. The divine will has assigned us our roles in life without consulting us. Some of us will act in a short drama, others in a long one. We might be assigned the part of a poor person, a cripple, a distinguished celebrity or public leader, or an ordinary private citizen. Although we can't control which roles

> are assigned to us, it must be our business to act our given role as best we possibly can and to refrain from complaining about it. Wherever you find yourself and in whatever circumstances, give an impeccable performance.[58]

I think of that sequoia often now that I am back in the lowlands, working for my daily bread alongside my fellow travelers, weary and hungry from the road and wondering if it's all worth it. I remember that, like that sequoia, we each have our place in the sun and our role to play—no role worse or better than any other—and that our lives are prayers if we live them with humility and courage and joy, in harmony with our true inner nature. To grow where we are planted, to accept and surrender to our sacred place in the world, is one of the greatest gifts we can give ourselves.

Going Under

I grew up in Ventura, California, a small town on the Pacific coast between Los Angeles and Santa Barbara. All summer long someone's mom would drop us off at the beach. We spent the long days of our childhoods playing in the waves. Later in adolescence, some of us took up baseball, basketball, or football and drifted away from the shore. But a few of us never got out of the water, unable to tear ourselves away from the ever-changing sky, the solitude, and the restless surface of the sea. Surfing became a way of life.

Every day, conditions change. Sometimes there are no

waves; the sea becomes a flat pond, and it seems like you could reach right out to the horizon and touch the Channel Islands. Other days huge swells rise up out of the south, break along the outer reefs, and crash over the top of the pier. I don't know if it was just the inherent hubris of youth, but somehow we found the courage to paddle out into surf that to any sensible person appeared lethal. Our willingness to go out into huge surf was not an act of extraordinary courage. It came simply from years of experience with waves.

When a giant wave crashes over you, it pulls you under and spins you around like a sock in a washing machine. There's no point in struggling. It's best to simply hold your breath, relax your body, and wait. The wave will pass. It always does. If you're struggling and panicking, it seems to take forever. If you're relaxed and calm, it passes quickly. As the water grows still, you rise to the surface, climb back on your board, and paddle hard for the horizon, hoping to make it over the next wave before it breaks. If not, you repeat the process.

Learning to cooperate and indeed play with such power liberated us from anxieties that no longer served us. It was a revelation to realize that waves can't really hurt you. It's just a bunch of water. The fear of waves is much more lethal than the waves themselves. Panicking causes drowning, not water. Surfers carry this lesson into their lives, knowing that no matter how big the challenge, it looks worse than it is, it is always temporary, it will pass, and perhaps most important, there are some forces in life that we cannot overpower with sheer strength and grit. Sometimes we are better off surrendering and waiting for conditions to change. There are many kinds of waves. Through the rise and fall of fortune, we learn when to actively engage and when to wait. If "power" means "effectiveness," then waiting is just as powerful as assertion. When we encounter something that's difficult to get through, sometimes it's best just to go under.

A Wise Person

A wise person surrenders to the conditions of this moment, knowing that everything will soon change.

A wise person surrenders to their own nature and doesn't long to be anyone other than who they authentically are.

A wise person surrenders to the laws of nature, trusting that their highest good is manifesting in unforeseen ways.

A wise person surrenders to the conditions and circumstances they finds themselves in, knowing that it is only from the consciousness of surrender that the will to change and right action can truly emerge.

A wise person surrenders to their own transformation and growth, letting go of what needs letting go and actively participating in their own evolution in a stance of deep cooperation with the larger forces around and within them.

A wise person surrenders their attachment to limited and limiting conceptions of self that no longer serve them.

A wise person surrenders to a concept of a higher power that works for them, whether it is a personal God or an impersonal energy, and takes a leap of faith into a formless awareness of their ultimate identity with this sacred source.

A wise person surrenders slavish attachment to ideologies, knowing that ultimate reality lies beyond the grasp of language and thought.

A wise person surrenders their attachment to destructive emotional patterns like misplaced anger, resentment, despair, self-loathing, condescension, cynicism, and pessimism, realizing that these are symptoms of the ego's relentless effort to shore up its own importance.

A wise person surrenders and moves willingly into this next moment, no matter what it brings.

Closing Meditation

As we did at the end of the previous chapter, let's close with a meditation. Sit back comfortably, close your eyes if possible, and take several slow, deep, and mindful breaths. Begin to relax any tensions you feel in your body. Drop your shoulders and let a certain softness come into your muscles. Allow your breathing to settle into its natural rhythm.

Imagine that you are sitting alongside a gently flowing river. Now imagine that you are in the river and sinking slowly down beneath the surface like a stone. Soon you are resting on the soft sand of the river bottom. Above you, the surface of the river is flowing along, carrying with it bits of leaves and twigs, but you are safe and still on the river bottom where the water is hardly moving at all. If any thoughts cross your mind, let them go like those bits of leaves and twigs. Watch them come and watch them go, neither resisting them nor clinging to them. They are simply floating by like clouds in the sky high above you.

Now we see that there are two stones on the soft sand of the river bottom—the stone of acceptance and the stone of surrender. We have these deep within us now. We carry them with us wherever we go. We know that no matter what we face and no matter what we have to do in the coming hours, days, weeks, months, and years, we will always have within us the capacity to accept the conditions of our lives and surrender to the sacred flow of the universe, knowing that our energies and the energies around us exist in a unified plane of being, and that we are safe, and that we are loved, and that we are valuable in the grand array of things, despite our passing glimmers of fear and insignificance. We surrender to the ineffable, formless knowing that all is well, even if we don't understand all of it. We surrender to the wonderful, surprising, nurturing, challenging, and beautiful stream of lights we call our life, and we surrender to the loving souls who share this journey with us, whose pain and fear sometimes make it difficult for them to see us, and know us, and understand us, let alone love us or themselves, but who nonetheless walk alongside us, even in their unconsciousness. And in our heart we see who they really are, and in our forgiveness we surrender our resentment, our defensiveness, our lazy willingness to hate and hold grudges. We surrender all of that to the river. We release it all to the pull of the water, and we know that by letting go we gain the whole world.

Now we rise up through the water and sit again on the river bank. We watch the river, the clouds, the trees, the colors of the sky, and the light of the sun broken into a thousand jewels on the water. We listen as the voice of the river sings a wordless song without beginning or end, a song that contains all of the songs ever written, and all of the songs yet to be written, and all of the songs that will never be written. We smell the earth and the grass and the reeds and the moss and the wind from the distant mountains, a wind that tastes like rain and stone and cedar.

With this surrender, we feel a deep peace welling up within us, filling us, holding us, moving through us like blood, showing us that all the years of struggle and resistance and denial and avoidance and conflict are behind us now, moving away from us, flowing downstream with the river, leaving us in a place of quiet and stillness, a place of safety and serenity, a place of empowerment and willingness, a place of hopeful optimism, a free-form conviction that what is ours to do will be shown to us, and we will feel in our hearts a blissful, loving knowing when our path and our purpose appear before us, and we move earnestly into the field of action, and our actions will always be in service of the good, and our actions will always be deeply rooted in the consciousness of acceptance and surrender.

When you are ready, bring your attention back to this moment and these surroundings and open your eyes. Take a deep cleansing breath and stretch and move your body. Allow the awareness of acceptance and surrender to take their rightful place deep within you. Let them slip from your immediate awareness knowing that they are ever-present and immediately accessible whenever you need them. With these first two stones in place, we can now begin to move toward the third stone, the wisdom of engagement, and explore how right action carries us forward as we create a life of deepening wisdom, compassionate service, and joy.

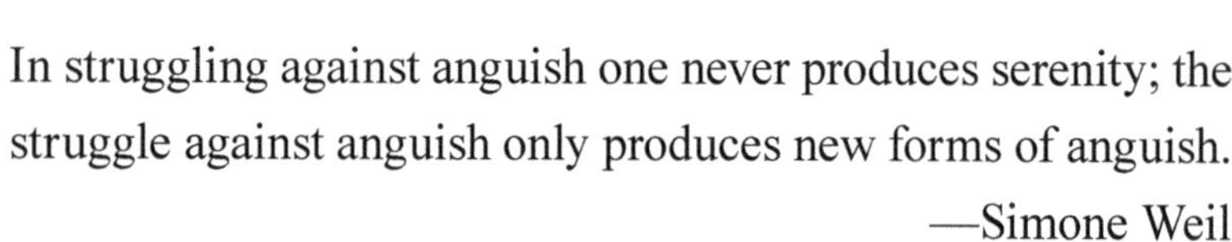

In struggling against anguish one never produces serenity; the struggle against anguish only produces new forms of anguish.

—Simone Weil

The creative process is a process of surrender, not control.

—Julia Cameron

The Master acts without doing anything and teaches without saying anything. Things arise and she lets them come; things disappear and she lets them go. She has but doesn't possess, acts but doesn't expect. When her work is done, she forgets it. That is why it lasts forever.

—Laozi, *Dao De Jing* 2

The Third Stone

Chapter 3

Wisdom as Engagement

> The master allows things to happen. She shapes events as they come. She steps out of the way and lets the Dao speak for itself.
>
> —Laozi, *Dao De Jing,* 45

The Field of Action

With both feet planted in the consciousness of acceptance and surrender, we are ready to stand tall and engage in the field of action. But what kind of action should we take? Upon searching the world's wisdom traditions, we find a wealth of experience and advice left behind by those who went before us. We needn't drown in indecision nor rashly push ahead without clarity or purpose. The good news is that it is possible to craft a plan of action that honors ourselves and others, champions the good, and brings conscious compassion to a world in dire need of it, all the while leaving us edified, ennobled, and richly satisfied. We've accepted current conditions, we've surrendered to what is, and now it is time to act.

No matter how much inner work we do, and no matter how intelligent, knowledgeable, perceptive, and wise we become, it amounts to nothing if we do not show up in the field of action willing to take a stand and engage with the world, no matter what we think we might lose. Our own well-being, indeed our very happiness, depends not so much on all those pretty ideas locked away in our heads but on how we bring those ideas to bear on the concrete facts of our existence. Wisdom will forever elude us if we continue to equivocate, debate, waffle, stall, avoid, intellectualize, or in any other way fail to fully engage in the field of action.

Shaping Our Lives

In the *Dhamapada*, Buddha left us a beautiful trio of analogies on the power and necessity of action: "As irrigators guide water to their fields, as archers aim arrows, as carpenters carve wood, the wise shape their lives."[59] Let's take these three metaphors one at a time and see what we can learn about the role of action in the acquisition of wisdom.

Buddha begins with an agricultural reference, "as irrigators guide water to their fields." Water is necessary for the successful cultivation of crops, just as crops are necessary for the sustenance of human life. And yet a farmer cannot make water, no matter how clever or ambitious they are. Instead, channels must be dug into the ground—low, empty pathways that allow the water to fall toward your seeds. Drawing water toward your seeded soil requires a cooperative collaboration between intention and acceptance. The two major elements, water and gravity, are beyond our control. They are created and governed not by human desire but by natural law. The success of our harvest is determined by the extent to which we act in accord with the laws of nature.

How good are we at carving channels, leaving openings, and allowing the life force of the universe to enter into and nourish the things we are trying to grow? Are we opening doors and asking for what we want? Are we clearing the clutter, removing what no longer serves us, and leaving space for sustenance to enter our lives?

Next, Buddha employs an archery metaphor, "as archers aim arrows." In archery, it is we who choose the target, it is we who pull back the bow string, it is we who aim the arrow, and it is we who choose when to release. But when we open our fingers and the bowstring leaps from our grasp flinging the arrow into space, we relinquish control. We can never be certain whether or not we will hit the target. A sudden wind might blow our arrow off course. An unfortunate bird might fly between the arrow and the target. The target might be knocked over in an earthquake. In life we train, set goals, and aim as best we can. We may intend outcomes, but we do not control events and we certainly cannot claim that any victory is ever ours alone—there are simply too many other contributing factors.

How good are we at preparing, intending, and aiming, while also letting go of the outcome? Can we act assertively and in the same moment accept whatever happens?

Buddha's third metaphor involves woodworking, "as carpenters carve wood." When a wood-carver carves wood they remove everything that isn't needed. Stroke by strenuous stroke, the carver wields their chisel with patience and vision, letting the sharp steel blade do the cutting, one cut at a time. There's no sense in hurrying, and even less sense in putting the chisel down and giving up. Wood doesn't carve itself. Guided by inner sight and a vision of the intended object, the woodcarver acts with discipline, consistency, sensitivity, awareness, and strength. They feel their way, working with the grain, and moving forward stroke by stroke until the work is done. Steadfast and strong, the woodcarver marries together into a seamless whole the disparate energies of acceptance, surrender, willingness, intention, and vigorous action. The resulting beauty is the daughter of all of these mothers.

Then another aspect of the wood-carving metaphor looms into view: that wood carving is not a process of addition, it is a process of subtraction. Whether they are carving a bowl or a Buddha, wood-carvers don't build a bowl or a Buddha from scratch. They remove everything that is not the bowl or Buddha. So too we sometimes misconstrue self-improvement as a process of addition—*I need to acquire this new information, this new resource, or this new skill*—when instead, all that might be needed for wisdom to flourish would be the clearing away of everything about ourselves that is not authentically essential.

Of course Buddha isn't talking about irrigation, archery, or wood carving. These are metaphors for the cocreation and manifestation of wisdom, the sacred process by which we gradually arise out of our dream of separation and awaken into the deeper reality of our unity with all things.

The Nature of Action

When we last discussed the Bhagavad Gita in chapter one, we saw our hero Arjuna at the precipice of battle, paralyzed by despair. Arjuna had dropped his bow and refused to take his rightful place on the battlefield. While honoring his compassionate, pacifist leanings, his chariot driver and soon-to-be-revealed spiritual teacher Krishna nevertheless counseled his archer to get up and fight. Krishna correctly discerned that it was neither compassion nor pacifism that Arjuna was experiencing; it was the intellectual paralysis of ambivalence. Arjuna knew very well that the soldiers facing him across the battlefield were hell bent on killing him, his family, and everyone he knew. It was up to Krishna to convince Arjuna that he must do his duty and take action.

We have already seen that Krishna taught Arjuna the true nature of reality and the Self. The Ground of Being or Brahman-atman was never born and can therefore never die. On the temporal plane, forms arise and fade, but behind the veil of maya, the Changeless stands witness to it all. "Realize that which pervades the universe and is indestructible; no power can effect this unchanging, imperishable reality," said Krishna. "The body is mortal, but he who dwells in the body is immortal and immeasurable. Therefore, Arjuna, fight in this battle."[60]

In one of the boldest statements of immortality ever made, Krishna reminds Arjuna, "There has never been a time when you and I … have not existed, nor will there be a time when we will cease to exist."[61]

As we contemplate the nature of right action, our first priority is the realization of our true nature. Without clarity about the nature of reality, our actions are rooted in ignorance and ego. But in the light of self-realization, our actions begin to move in accord with a higher purpose, a purpose implanted deep within us. This purpose is our dharma.

If everything is one, and if we are all manifestations of the one divine reality, then it is our moral and metaphysical duty to set aside whatever personal, private, and egoic desires we have that do not in some way serve the good. Our dharma is our deepest, most sacred purpose. We needn't think of this as a specific career or task, but rather as a generalized consciousness of service that we bring into whatever work we are doing.

Action without Attachment

According to Krishna, the best kind of action is action without attachment to specific outcomes. Naturally, when we undertake an action, we intend a result. It is crucial, however, to carefully distinguish between intention and attachment. Intending to shoot a basketball through the hoop from the free throw line is an entirely different state of consciousness than being egoically attached to making a free throw. Intention is a necessary preliminary stage that creates alignment between all of the requisite energies—training, perception, attention, and skill. Attachment, in contrast, erroneously conflates the achievement of the goal with one's self worth. If you miss the basket while rooted in the consciousness of egoic attachment, you suffer. If you miss the basket rooted in the consciousness of intention, you simply try again.

Action with attachment to a specific outcome is inherently different from action in accord with one's dharma. When you perform action in the consciousness of service, it is no longer your ego carrying out the action for some extrinsic reward; instead, you become an instrument of the good. "Every selfless act is born from Brahman, the eternal, infinite Godhead," Krishna told Arjuna.[62] Selfish acts performed for personal aggrandizement create only more attachments and craving; an endless spiral of deepening ignorance and misery. "The ignorant work for their own profit," said Krishna, "the wise work for the welfare of the world..."[63] Our edifice of right action must be built on this foundation.

The Owl and the Fisherman

Lori and I live near a lake—an unusual occurrence in southern California—and we often walk along the shore with our dog. One day we saw a beautiful barn owl hanging upside down from a tree limb, its ghostly white wings extended, its feet hopelessly tangled in fishing line. Who knows how long it had hung there struggling before it died. It was a wrenching sight, knowing that this magnificent bird of prey had died a slow, meaningless death from dehydration, exhaustion, and shock. You only have to see this once. From that moment on, you pick up every single wad of abandoned fishing line you find along the shore.

One day as I gathered tangled strands of discarded fishing line and other assorted trash from the lake shore, I grew increasingly angry. *How can people be so thoughtless, so cruel, so stupid? Leaving behind fast food trash and beer cans is one thing, but fishing line? These people are unconscionable murderers,* I thought. Before I knew it, my anger had turned into self-righteousness. An unmistakable sense of superiority surged through me. Because I was picking up their trash and saving the lives of innocent wild animals, I was better than these low-consciousness litterers, or so I told myself. In the time it took for me to draw one breath, all these thoughts coursed through me like a flood, washing away my good intentions and what little compassion I had left.

I had to laugh.

In an instant, my simple act of service had morphed into a self-serving ego trip. The ego rarely misses an opportunity to bend reality toward its needs. With the cunning swiftness of a barn owl in the dark, my ego had silently and without warning swooped in and turned a simple act of selfless service into a celebration of self-importance. For me to be right, someone else had to be wrong. The consciousness of anger and resentment, no matter how regally dressed, drives a dagger into the heart of compassion and kindness. The only cure is humility. I quickly found my equilibrium as the Gospel line came to mind: "Forgive them for they know not what they are doing."[64] What we call "evil" is always rooted in ignorance and self-absorption. The people who littered the lake shore were guilty of one simple failing, unconsciousness, a crime I had committed innumerable times. They were so caught up in their own small sense of self that they were unconscious of the impact their actions would have on others. Resenting them only destroyed my own equilibrium.

As I gathered discarded fishing line along the shore that day, I was working for my own profit, fueling my sense of self-importance, and healing my deep-seated feelings of inadequacy and imperfection. By feeling superior to others, I could momentarily drown out my disappointment in my own numerous shortcomings. In other words, I too was caught up in a woefully limited and limiting sense of self. Once I recognized this pathological shift, I was able to let go of it and move back into the far happier state of mind that simply and humbly performs works of service for the welfare of the world without any egoic attachments. I didn't have to make them wrong because I no longer needed to be right. In the end, I'm just like those littering fishermen. I bring all my imperfections and unconsciousness with me wherever I go, and I leave a trail of debris of one kind or another in my wake. We are all tangled in the invisible binds of ego. But in the simplicity of selfless service, clarity replaces the murky clutter of unconsciousness, leaving us edified and grounded in the awareness that we are neither less than nor more than anyone else—a truth both humbling and exalting.

The Sniper and the Doctor

At four o'clock in the afternoon on July 18, 1984, an unemployed security guard named James Huberty entered a McDonald's restaurant in San Ysidro, California, a small town south of San Diego near the Mexican border. He was carrying an Uzi semiautomatic carbine assault rifle, a Browning semiautomatic pistol, a Winchester pump action twelve gauge shotgun, and hundreds of rounds of ammunition. In the hour and seventeen minutes that followed, he shot forty people, killing twenty-one. The dead ranged in age from eight months to seventy-four years. He murdered entire families.

At the time, it was the largest mass murder in US history.

This was years before the mass shootings at Columbine, Virginia Tech, Aurora, Newtown, Orlando, Las Vegas, and all of the others. Police struggled to strategize. In 1984, this was still a new phenomenon. As the gunfire continued to ring out from inside the building, 175 police officers were pinned down outside, unable to safely approach and disable the shooter. Finally, a lone police sniper perched on the roof of the post office next door got a clean shot. He fired a single round through the window of the McDonald's, hitting Huberty in the chest, who collapsed in a heap.

In the process of medical triage, no distinctions are made between victims and alleged perpetrators—emergency medical personnel tend to the wounded based on the severity of their injuries. It is not their role to adjudicate guilt and withhold care. It turns out Huberty died on the scene, but had he been alive, he would have been transported to the emergency room where a team of highly trained doctors, nurses, and technicians would have struggled valiantly to keep him alive alongside his victims.

In this scenario, the police sniper and the emergency room doctor would have both been performing their dharma. The sniper and doctor, utilizing very different tools, training, and methods, were using their considerable skills to serve the good. Without personal attachment to outcomes, they brought years of training and mastery to bear on this tragic and violent situation. Dharma or duty does not mean rote repetition of traditionally prescribed actions; it means responding to the moment as channels for the good, a divine energy that is always trying to emerge through us. It is easy to see that the doctors, nurses, and paramedics work for the good. Yet in the moment before the police sniper took his shot, as Huberty moved through the restaurant checking the pulses of his victims and finishing off the wounded, it is also easy to see that the sniper was serving the good as well. If it is your dharma to be a warrior, then in your service it is sometimes necessary to put a bullet through someone's heart. And if it is your dharma to be a healer, it is your duty to stop arterial bleeding and stich torn hearts back together.

None of us controls or comprehends all of the factors that lead to an event as horrific as the McDonald's massacre, let alone the ordinary unfolding of our everyday lives. Every action is accompanied by murky motives and unintended outcomes. The message of the Bhagavad Gita, however, is clear. We must act. We cannot bog down in endless rumination. Sometimes "thinking it over" is a way of avoiding duty. It is good that we ponder deeply. But in the end we must set aside trepidation, pick up our tools, and burst forth.

Where There's Fire, There's Smoke

Arjuna's battlefield is a metaphor for the human condition. We are all caught in trepidation between action and inaction, ringed round by fear and the knowledge that whether or not we act, much will be lost. Part of the problem stems from the fact that every action sets into motion effects we neither desire nor foresee. Every action is necessarily imperfect. The unavoidable messiness of real life does not, however, release us from our moral obligations. "No one should abandon duties because he sees defects in them," Krishna tells Arjuna in the last chapter of the Bhagavad Gita. "Every action, every activity, is surrounded by defects as a fire is surrounded by smoke."[65] Even as perfect clarity eludes us, we must move forward in the work of manifesting the good. Trying to see through smoke isn't easy, but we have to keep walking.

No matter what you try to do, unintended results arise. Feeding the homeless has the potential to create a dehumanizing cycle of dependency. Legislating reasonable laws to protect people from deadly recreational poisons fills the jails with harmless drug addicts, draining public resources that could be better used in drug treatment. Sending humanitarian aid into war-torn regions often enriches local warlords who in turn perpetuate the very suffering our good intentions sought to alleviate. You were just trying to do something good, and people ended up getting hurt.

When we contemplate these and countless other examples of the multifaceted complexity of action, we feel Arjuna's frustration. He knows that no matter which course of action he chooses, people will die. It sometimes seems better to do nothing at all. But doing nothing sets into motion a series of consequences just as surely as our action would have. Not choosing is a choice. Not acting is a form of action. We are already on the battlefield. Despite the imperfection of any action, we must act. The Gita teaches that our longing for inactivity is just another self-indulgent manifestation of fear—a deep-seated unwillingness to fully participate in the throng of life unfolding around us. "Fear not," said Jesus again and again to his disciples, knowing that he was sending them forth into hostile territory. When you are grounded in the consciousness of acceptance and surrender fear begins to lose its grip. The ego shrinks away, and you become an open channel for the sacred emergence and expansion of Brahman or God-consciousness moving in you, through you, as you. Your actions are no longer purely your own. You've become an instrument.

Action vs. Inaction

Is it possible to refrain from action? What if I stay in my room, hold still, and do absolutely nothing?

Although on the surface, it may appear as though I am inactive, is not my heart beating? Are not my thoughts racing? Is not my body in fact a furnace burning the fuel I ate for breakfast to maintain a body temperature of 98.6 degrees Fahrenheit in this 70-degree room? And the bowl of cereal I ate, made of grains harvested by machines consuming fossil fuels and emitting fluorocarbons, and the milk from a cow living in a factory farm four hundred miles away, transported by trucks that killed thousands of bugs on its grill as it barreled down the interstate on its way to the supermarket with its rows of open-air refrigeration units, consuming electricity generated largely from coal—am I not in fact responsible for all of this? As the molecules of the milk and the grains are transformed by my digestive system into the energies of my body, even though I am sitting perfectly still, am I not in fact acting? And do not these actions have consequences? Of course I am, and of course they do.

If you are alive, it is impossible to refrain from action. We can, however, bring our free will to bear on our actions in two key ways. We can choose to become as conscious and aware as possible about the impact our actions have on others, and we can choose to act in ways that minimize suffering. It is impossible to be alive and have no impact, but we can practice conscious compassion with our eyes wide open and roll back the amount of suffering our existence causes.

Ahimsa

Ahimsa means nonharm or nonviolence. Jains, Hindus, and Buddhists share this ethical principle made famous by Gandhi in the twentieth century. The principle of nonharm is in no way a sentimental, naïve pacifism. It is grounded in an awareness of the sacred nature of all things, yet pragmatic in its recognition that some violence is unavoidable in the very processes of life itself. Ahimsa does not counsel avoidance, nor is it the naïve fantasy of eliminating all violence from the world. In fact, the principle of ahimsa calls us to carefully discern a path of least harm through a thicket of necessarily painful realities.

If a tiger comes into your village and is eating your children, you must kill the tiger. Though regrettable, killing the tiger is taking the path of least harm. It is the compassionate thing to do. A dogmatic pacifist might attempt to appease the tiger by saying, "Look, the tiger is still hungry. Bring out the rest of the children. We can always have more." Preventing harm and nurturing ahimsa requires swift, decisive action. The tiger is not evil. It is the tiger's dharma to kill and eat small animals, including human children. But it is our dharma to protect our children from harm. When dharmas collide we move beyond the realm of good and evil.

When we cut down an acre of forest to plant wheat to bake bread for our family, we necessarily kill snakes and trees and birds and mice. And when we store the harvest in a granary, we must kill the rats that try to steal our food—not with rancor and resentment, but with decisive action free of personal attachments or misguided sentimentality. This is what it means to stay engaged in the field of action and fulfill our duty.

Life is predicated on the taking of other life. It's not our fault. We didn't make the rules. Every day we have to put thousands of calories of food into these holes on the front of our faces, and the food is comprised of formerly living things. Even if you are a vegetarian or a vegan, your existence results in the death of innumerable life forms. Despite our best intentions, all agricultural processes result in unintended harm to wildlife and wilderness habitats. We are all killers. The difference between omnivores, vegetarians, and vegans is merely one of degree. Life is death-defined. Our simple existence results in the suffering of other sentient beings. Life is in many ways defined by suffering, as the Buddha taught in the First Noble Truth. Some suffering is unavoidable. The goal of ahimsa is to avoid needless suffering.

When we refrain from needless harm, we embody compassion. And when our necessary actions cause harm to other beings, we do so consciously, mindfully, respectfully, and in deep gratitude, knowing that our life too is a temporary form that will one day dissolve and return to its elemental particles.

In college I read an unforgettable account of a Navajo deer hunt in an essay called "Seeing with a Native Eye: How Many Sheep Will It Hold" by Barre Toelken. It was in a book called *Seeing with a Native Eye: Essays on Native American Religion*, edited by Walter Capps, one of my favorite professors at the University of California at Santa Barbara. According to Toelken's account, knowing that a mule deer is a good sprinter but a poor long-distance runner, a Navajo hunter simply runs the deer down. After a long and difficult chase, the deer becomes exhausted as the hunter catches up to her. Then he gently puts his arm around her neck. As he slowly suffocates the deer, he sings a song of gratitude into her ear, thanking her for being a willing sacrifice and promising to use every fiber of her body for food, her bones for tools, her skin for drums, clothes, and shoes, and her sinew to bind the papoose for his newborn granddaughter. Nothing will go to waste. When the doe is near her final breath, the hunter takes a pouch of corn pollen from his belt and holds it over the deer's nostrils so that with her last inhalation, her entire being will be infused with the most sacred substance in the Navajo universe. In this deeply conscious and compassionate act of killing, hunter and hunted are united in a reverent embrace. The people must eat, be clothed, and gain new materials for tools. Killing the deer is not a personal act. The hunter is performing the work of nature. Despite our normal way of thinking, the hunter's actions are a channel for the incessant flow of life.[66]

Bedagi (Big Thunder), a nineteenth-century hunter of the Wabanaki Algonquin tribe, put it this way: "When we go hunting, it is not our arrow that kills the moose, however powerful the bow; it is nature that kills him."[67] Deeply imbedded in primal consciousness is the realization that birth and death are two points on one circle, and that when we engage in necessary killing we are in fact honoring life's innermost principle; forms arise and fade, but life is eternal.

Despite the apparent violence of the act, the police sniper that shot James Huberty on that terrible day in 1984 was acting in accord with the principle of ahimsa. His actions prevented harm. Who knows how many lives the sniper's bullet saved? This is the stark lesson of the Bhagavad Gita: our lives are a battlefield, and we are duty-bound to act. We can act in cruel and ignorant ways like James Huberty, lost in a maze of our own darkness, confusion, and despair, utterly blind to the infinite value of our own life and the lives of others, or we can act nobly in accord with our higher purpose, becoming a channel through whose actions Brahman is realized. Most of us aren't police snipers or emergency room doctors—we are students, teachers, laborers, parents, service workers, clerks, salesmen, managers, truck drivers, entrepreneurs, and artists. In our work, every day we have the opportunity to bring to bear these same principles. Working not for our own gain but in the consciousness of service, we feel a deep and abiding joy as we play our small part in the symphony of emergence unfolding around, in, and through us. And when it comes time for us to commit a difficult and unpleasant action—firing a subordinate, flunking a student, disciplining a child—we do it not out of anger or resentment as if our pain and disappointment were all that mattered, but as an act of compassion for the greater good, knowing that through this action, we build the world and honor what is best in all of us.

Means and Ends

Means are the specific actions or methods we employ to reach a goal, and ends are the goals we intend to reach. In *Satyagraha*, his campaign of nonviolence, Gandhi made a careful distinction between means and ends. What Gandhi wanted to challenge was the conventional notion that ends matter more than means—the common but destructive notion that so long as our goals are reached, it doesn't matter how we got there.

Beginning with the principle of ahimsa, causing as little harm as possible, Gandhi conceived of all action, both personal and political, as an opportunity to cooperate with a divine unfolding already underway. Remembering that Brahman comes from a Sanskrit root meaning "emerging" or "expanding," Gandhi realized that our actions, if grounded in the right consciousness, carry with them the weight of divine inevitability. For Gandhi, as long as the means are pure, the ends will take care of themselves.

This view is in stark contrast with the normal way of thinking. For many people, the ends justify the means. As long as we get the intended outcome, it doesn't really matter how we got there. For Gandhi, it's the other way around. The methods by which we achieve our goals leave their indelible shape on the end-product, so if we work for justice by unjust means, we are doomed to fail because whatever version of justice we reach via unjust means is counterfeit and short-lived. It's rotten from the inside. We will indeed reap what we sow.

For example, terrorism seeks to right perceived wrongs by murdering innocent bystanders. Justice is the end, but injustice is the means—a recipe for failure. In contrast, working with just methods that honor and respect all parties while sacrificing only our own comfort ensures that justice will eventually prevail. This view, as Gandhi, Martin Luther King Jr., and others so valiantly exemplified, requires enormous courage, faith, and willingness—courage to face great danger, faith in the unwavering power of truth, and willingness to sacrifice not only personal safety but all of one's precious opinions and ideological rigidity. We must acknowledge that the path to truth winds around in ways we may not recognize and find difficult to follow. We may have to abandon timetables and specific means that no longer serve the greater good. And above all, we must abandon the notion that there are enemies. "Love your enemies," said Jesus, and if we follow this teaching to its logical conclusion, there are no such things as enemies, just other people with whom we find ourselves in temporary conflict.[68] For Gandhi, Satyagraha was not only a campaign predicated on nonviolence. It was above all a state of mind that saw political "enemies" through a lens of compassion and respect. Only when we refrain from vilifying our opponents, and only when we see them as beings of infinite value, can we begin to effectively move society in the direction of justice. Making sure that the goal—peace, justice, compassion, and wisdom—is deeply embedded in our means and methods ensures our success.

Deeply inspired by Gandhi, and paraphrasing nineteenth-century American Transcendentalist Theodore Parker, Martin Luther King Jr. said that "the arc of the moral universe is long, but it bends toward justice." President Obama often quoted King's famous line and even had it woven into the rug on the floor of the Oval Office. If we stay true to our ideals, King believed, we will one day get to the Promised Land, even if in our darkest moments it seems impossible. "Faith," he wrote, "is taking the first steps even when you don't see the whole staircase." The power of intention, born in the love of wisdom and the spirit of compassion, allies itself with the divine will and manifests a power far greater than any mere human desire. As Krishna told Arjuna in the Gita, when we perform our work in the consciousness of selfless service, we are performing the work of Brahman. We become a channel through whose efforts the Good is manifested. But only if our methods are pure. Echoing the wisdom of Gandhi and King before him, contemporary Buddhist monk and teacher Thich Nhat Hanh often said that "there is no way to peace—peace is the way."

King and Gandhi both believed that society was slowly moving in the right direction and that God or Truth would one day prevail. Still, it would be wrong to suggest that moral progress happens automatically. Moral progress is only possible when courageous individuals step forward and take great risks. Without the wisdom of engagement, all the good intentions in the world come to naught. No matter how eloquent our words, actions always speak louder.

The Law of Karma

The Sanskrit word *karma* means "action" or "activity." The law of karma is on the surface a simple and easily verifiable claim; every event is caused by something that came before it, and every event in turn sets into motion subsequent events. Nothing happens without cause, and everything has an effect. Karma is not divine intervention, nor is it managed by the gods. In fact, in Hinduism it is said that even the gods are subject to its ironclad rule. Karma, like a law of physics, is an elemental principle imbedded in the very fabric of reality itself.

In Indian philosophy, the concept of karma reflects a deep awareness of the way all actions in the universe are interconnected in an infinitely complex web. Given this understanding, it is never possible to definitively declare that one event is singularly caused by another—there are too many threads in the karmic weave to trace down to a single source. As the Hindu guru Nisargadatta Maharaj put it, "Causes and effects are infinite in number and variety. Everything affects everything. In this universe, when one thing changes everything changes."[69] This subtlety is usually lost in the West, where karma is often misunderstood as a simple, mechanical tit for tat. The familiar trope "what goes around comes around" is at best misleading, at worst a gross distortion. The emotional appeal of such clichés is based, I suppose, on our deep longing for fairness. We want to see good people rewarded and bad people punished. But as we know from our own experience, this is not necessarily so. Bad people often thrive in the world, accruing wealth, fame, and prestige, while good people fall through the cracks. Despite the appearance of this unfortunate pattern the universe is still ultimately just. It's just not easy to see all of its intricate workings. No event has a single cause, just as no event has a single effect.

What's most disturbing about the common and overly simplistic mechanical model of karma is that it leaves us with untenable and obscene equations. Do we really want to say to a rape victim, "Well, you must have been a rapist in a former life"? Do we want to say to the victim of any violent crime that they somehow earned it, that what goes around comes around? Of course not. It is far more reasonable, not to mention more humane, to say that there are billions of human beings on earth living out their own karmic paths, and sometimes paths cross with dire results.

Another common misconception about karma is that there is "good karma" and "bad karma." Saying there is good karma and bad karma is like saying there is good gravity and bad gravity. Gravity is good when it keeps you in your seat at the top of the Ferris wheel, and it is bad when you fall off a ladder picking apples. Gravity, like karma, is neither good nor bad. Words like "good" and "bad" only apply to specific human judgments, not cosmic laws. Water is good when you're dying of thirst, and it is bad when you're drowning.

Still, every thought, word, and deed plants a seed that will bear fruit. Every event (and a thought is an event) stems from some cause and every event in turn sets into motion future events. Put another way, nothing happens without a preceding cause or set of causes. "A man reaps what he sows," wrote Paul in his letter to the Galatians.[70] We are responsible for our thoughts, words, and actions. Everything we think, do, and say is a pebble tossed into the cosmic pond. The ripples move inexorably outward. You cannot stop them, and you cannot pull them back. You can only throw in more pebbles.

Free Will vs. Determinism

In the rich diversity of Indian philosophy and religion, there are a variety of ways of thinking about karma. In simplistic, mechanical terms, everything happening in your life is the result of actions that came before. In this portrait, we are a feather riding a powerful wave of fate set into motion by our own past actions and the actions and influences of countless others. Every event is simply the playing out of past effects. This portrait contains a fatal paradox. It requires that at some point in the past, we were free to act as we chose, unbound by karma, thus setting into motion all of these unfortunate events. But you can't have it both ways. Either we are free, or our actions are determined by forces larger than our will. Perhaps it is more reasonable to take a middle position: that our past thoughts, words, and deeds (as well as a thousand other conditions we did not choose like our genetics, our culture, and the behavior of those around us) carried us to this present moment, but in this present moment we are utterly free to choose what's next. In other words, we are shaped by the past but not bound by it. As Wayne Dyer put it, "The wake does not drive the boat."

Ultimately then, the law of karma, correctly understood, frees us from the past. It says that no matter what came before, we are free in this now moment to set into motion a new karmic chain of events. The world of time, space, and matter may be shaped by the law of karma, but as spiritual beings we re-present the eternal presence in the field of time and as such have the power to envision and fashion the world and ourselves ever anew. It is with our engagement that we reshape the entire world.

The Parable of the Arrow

The Buddha told a parable of a man walking through a forest with his friends. Suddenly he was shot in the chest with a poisoned arrow. As he lay on the forest floor with poison beginning to rush through his veins, his friends hurried to pull out the arrow to save his life.

"Wait," said the wounded man. "Before you pull it out, I have to know, what kind of wood is this?" he asked, running his fingers along the arrow shaft.

"And these feathers, are they from a dove, a hawk, a raven, a rooster, or a crow?

"And the tip of the arrow that's imbedded in my chest," he said. "Do you suppose it's made out of bone, iron, obsidian, wood, or bone?"

His friends brushed aside his questions and began to pull out the arrow.

"No, wait," he insisted. "Before you pull it out, who do you think shot it? Was it a Brahmin, a Kshatriya, a Vaishya, or a Shudra? A man, or a woman? Was it someone I know, or a stranger? Did they mean to shoot me, or was it an accident?"

By the time all of these questions were discussed, the man died.

With this parable, Buddha issued a dire warning. Speculative, philosophical questions are interesting, but there is a more pressing task at hand. There is poison coursing through us. Whether you call it suffering or ignorance or any other name, there is a fundamental dis-ease infecting our unenlightened consciousness. Speculating about its origin, cause, nature, or composition detracts us from the simple, concrete task of taking action and extracting the poison. We need to pull out the arrow. We don't need to know how it got there or who's to blame. We can talk about that later.

Postponing action until after we have all the answers to our interesting metaphysical questions is fatal. If the man with the poisoned arrow in his chest had been handed a fact sheet with all the data he required, none of that information would have helped him remove the poison from his body. His well-being, in other words, is better served by action, not speculation or data collection. With this parable, the Buddha is urging us to free ourselves from the tyranny of the mind and move instead into the consciousness of acceptance, surrender, and action. Without answers, we move instinctually into right action and ultimately, healing. Once the arrow's out, we can make some tea and sit up all night discussing metaphysics. *Who made the universe? Why? Why is there suffering? Is human nature good or evil or indifferent? Is there a God? If so, what is he/she/it? If not, does any of this mean anything? What happens when we die? Do we get one life, or is reincarnation real?* Even if we could answer all of these questions right now, we would still have before us the heroic task of living our lives and wresting meaning and value from the dance we dance with these fleeting forms around us. Whether the answers come or not, we must still live our lives. And therein lies our meaning and significance.

The Myth of Sisyphus

In Greek mythology, Sisyphus was no hero. He led a treacherous, murderous life, and he was rightly punished for it. Zeus sentenced Sisyphus to an eternity of pushing a rock up a hill—only it was an enchanted rock, and every time Sisyphus reached the summit and collapsed in exhaustion, the rock rolled back down to the bottom of the hill.

Every morning Sisyphus had to begin again. But he never complained. He accepted his fate. In fact, he more than accepted it—he embraced it.

In his essay "The Myth of Sisyphus," French existentialist philosopher Albert Camus finds something heroic in Sisyphus's resignation. No one would blame Sisyphus for giving up and muttering, "Why bother?" But he doesn't. In spite of the apparent meaninglessness of his task, Sisyphus's resilience imposes meaning. Life is absurd, says Camus, yet we get up every day and do it again anyway. And it is from our struggle that meaning comes.[71]

We do the laundry even though our clothes will just get dirty again. We empty the trash knowing it will fill back up. We put gas in the car even though it will be soon be empty. We go to work and have the same conversations about the same things with the same people, drink the same coffee, tackle the same challenges, face the same absurdities, and watch helplessly as the inbox grows faster than the outbox no matter how hard we push.

It never stops. We're never done. There is no such thing as the end of the road.

Sisyphus reminds us of the cyclical nature of our work. Life is not linear—it spirals into the future in a series of concentric arcs. Here is it Tuesday again, here it is lunch again, here I am washing my bowl again. Déjà vu is simply the recognition of this fact: we *have* been here before, many times.

In the face of this repetition, we might be forgiven for slipping into despair. "What's the point?" we might mutter in our more melancholic moments. But despair isn't inevitable. In fact, maudlin resistance to the apparent absurdity of life is, when you come right down to it, a pretty lousy read. In Camus's final analysis, the world is neither absurd nor not-absurd; it is indeterminate. It is for us to decide. Only we can carve the shape of our own meaning. That is why Sisyphus is such a hero to Camus. It doesn't get any more meaningless than pushing a rock up a hill. The rock doesn't do anything, it isn't for anything, and it's just as useless at the top of the hill as it was at the bottom. Yet, as Camus writes, "Happiness and the absurd are two sons of the same earth. They are inseparable…The struggle itself toward the heights is enough to fill a man's heart. One must imagine Sisyphus happy."[72]

Like Sisyphus, we have the power to turn our fate into a blessing. We cannot change the past or most of the conditions around us, but we can always choose new thoughts about those events and circumstances. In the boundlessness of consciousness, we are radically free to impose meaning onto the absurdity of life. It is only from our willful commitment and decisive action that meaning emerges. Life is not a fantasy—it is an activity. When we come out of our head and into our body, life springs from every pore. When you throw your shoulder into the rock and push, the meaninglessness of the world disappears like a bad dream in the light of day. This is the wisdom of engagement. It is through our actions, not our concepts and theories, that the full measure of our significance takes form.

When we perform our duty, says Krishna in the Bhagavad Gita, we participate in the divine play through which the whole universe comes into being. Of course we never accurately assess the value and scope of our work. How could we? We cannot see all the ripples that emanate from every intention, every gesture, every word, and every action. We must simply trust that we are enough. What else can we do? We are only one person. There is quiet heroism in facing every challenge nobly and playing our part in the great unfolding. Despite how it feels in our worst moments, everything matters. There are no small parts, only small actors.

Seamless Continuity

Actions are the engines that drive the world. But actions do not cause themselves, nor do they arise from nothing. Actions begin as thoughts, or more accurately, as consciousness-events. It would be foolish if in our consideration of the wisdom of engagement, we did not explore the seamless continuity between thought, intention, and action. We may also need to broaden our definition of engagement to include thought. If actions arise from thoughts, then what we think about becomes vitally important. In a very real sense, thoughts are actions too.

The insoluble link between thought and action is a consistent theme in the world's wisdom traditions. Confucius, Jesus, Buddha, Aristotle, and Epictetus, to name a few, affirmed this essential fact. In the opening lines of the *Dhamapada*, Buddha laid the foundation for his entire philosophical project: "All that we are is the result of what we have thought: we are formed and molded by our thoughts."[73] Nisargadatta Maharaj put it even more succinctly: "You are what you think about."[74] At the root of any action lies a thought, an utterly malleable consciousness-event over which we exert significant control. Some thoughts arise seemingly without our permission, but those automatic thoughts can always be replaced with new, freely chosen thoughts. As we learned in chapter one while discussing the Noble Eightfold Path of Buddhism, right mindfulness is the practice of gently monitoring and shaping mental content. We do not control events, but we control our responses to them. By choosing our thoughts, we are in fact choosing our life. The wisdom of engagement therefore means so much more than taking bold and decisive action; it also means cultivating the habit of mindfulness. Over time we can train ourselves to become more aware of the primary role our thoughts have in the construction of our experience. As the Talmudic aphorism says, "We do not see things as they are, we see things as we are." We see everything through a lens of our own consciousness, a grid of concepts, assumptions, biases, prejudices, and preferences. It's a wonder we can see anything at all.

But thoughts do not occur in a vacuum. They are in turn triggered by events in the outer world and by the way our experiences have conditioned us. In a seamless, synergistic cycle without beginning or end, our thoughts and actions impact and are impacted by the world around us, so we don't know where one ends and the other begins. In authentic wisdom, however, an honest willingness emerges to claim authorship of our experience. The wisdom of engagement, in this sense, means cultivating the maturity to let the buck stop here. If not us, who? If not now, when?

Action as Medicine

When we step into the field of action and willingly take up our chosen tasks, not only do we change the world, but also we change ourselves. Action is not only the culmination of a process of deliberation and decision; it is also the beginning and the means of internal transformation. Thoughts lead to words, words lead to actions, actions build habits, and habits construct character. We become what we do.

In his essay "The 10,000 Hour Rule" from the book *Outliers*, Malcolm Gladwell questions our pervasive assumption that genius is an inherent trait encoded in DNA, like red hair or blue eyes. Instead, Gladwell argues, genius is most likely the result of a long-term, deliberate process of choices and actions undertaken by individuals in the context of a favorable social milieu. In other words, geniuses aren't born; they're made.

Citing the work of neurologist Daniel Levitin, Gladwell argues that mastery in anything—ice skating, chess, cello, poetry, baseball, you name it—is the result of time spent in practice, roughly ten thousand hours. Across the board in all activities and arenas of achievement, those at the top not only worked harder than their mediocre counterparts—they also worked much, much longer. Genetic predisposition played only a minimal and ultimately immeasurable role in success. The overwhelmingly central factor was practice—deliberate, willful, repeated action. Mozart may have begun writing music at the age of six, but he didn't write anything great until he was in his mid-twenties. Two decades of relentless touring and composition, under the lash of his taskmaster father, made Mozart, Mozart.

Gladwell cites the Beatles as another notable example. In the years before they came to America in 1964 and sparked the worldwide phenomenon of Beatlemania, they were just a hardworking English bar band working in Hamburg, Germany, often playing eight hours a night, seven nights a week. After years of playing under these grueling conditions, they were forged into arguably the greatest rock and roll band of all time. Had they stayed in Liverpool or London, playing one-hour shows once or twice a week like bands normally do, the worldwide phenomenon that is the Beatles would have remained a small, obscure, unremarkable moment, lost forever in the dustbin of history.[75]

In the ancient world, Aristotle constructed a similar vision of how human excellence is realized. For Aristotle, the ideal life was a life characterized by *eudaimonia*, an abiding sense of satisfaction or well-being. This deep-seated happiness is the natural by-product of a well-lived life in which one's potentials are realized. And one's potentials are only realized when one vigorously acts to manifest them. This requires a host of other important virtues (or excellences) like courage, temperance, and magnanimity. In the end, only those who practice vigorously the art of living will actualize their potential as fully-realized human beings.

For Aristotle, eudaimonia or happiness was not a goal or a static resting place at the end of a long and careful climb, but rather an energetic, dynamic state of continual risk-taking and renewal. The good life is a life of vigorous action, not a passive withdrawal from life's difficulties. It's not a chair in the sand and a drink in our hand that we really want—our soul is asking for something far more dangerous. It's not retreat from the world we long for. We want to feel fully alive right in the middle of the maelstrom. That's how our vibrant aliveness and intrinsic joy is birthed.

In ancient China, Confucius taught along similar lines. At the center of all of the other virtues Confucius placed *li*, or action. *Li* originally meant ritual, but it came to mean the outward expression of thoughtfulness (*shu*), willful compassion (*ren*), and righteousness (*yi*).

Thoughtfulness, compassion, and righteousness are just pretty ideas until they are made manifest in the field of action. Behavior is more important than ideological purity. Even religious ideals only go so far. As Nisargadatta Maharaj put it, "Recorded religions are mere heaps of verbiage. Religions show their true face in action, in silent action. To know what a man believes, watch how he acts."[76] Love is not a feeling; love is an action–an idea we'll take up more thoroughly in chapter six.

Like his contemporary Aristotle on the other side of the world, Confucius taught that outward behaviors create inner transformations. When we practice kindness, we become kinder. When we practice courage, we become more courageous. When we practice compassion, we become more compassionate. It is a grave and debilitating error to wait for inner growth before changing one's actions and practices. It's the other way around.

But it isn't easy. That's why Aristotle and the ancient Greeks placed courage at the top of the list of virtues. It takes stamina and guts to let go of old habits and take on new ones. It can feel overwhelming, especially when it seems like you have to do it all alone. That's when the example of the hero's journey comes into play.

In his essential book *The Hero with a Thousand Faces*, Joseph Campbell makes clear the universal nature of the hero's journey—an archetypal tale told all over the world in every culture and tradition. Campbell argues that the metaphorical power of the hero's journey is its symbolic representation of our inner journey from childish dependency to fully realized autonomy and individuation. "Each of us is the hero of our own lives," writes Campbell, and as we revel at the adventures of Gilgamesh, Frodo, Luke Skywalker, Harry Potter, and too many others to count, we are vicariously living through the stages of our own emergence, a thrilling adventure if there ever was one. In the hero's journey, great risk and danger dog our every step as we leave the known world and cross the threshold into the unknown darkness where impossible tasks and trials await. Courageous action and an almost pathological willingness to sacrifice the past is unfailingly rewarded with increasing power and insight. And in the end, if we succeed, we return to the known world transformed into what we really were all along: a being of infinite value and burgeoning strength, willing and able to serve the greater good of our community like never before. This, says Campbell, is the universal dream within each of us, the call that relentlessly fuels our perpetual restlessness and spurs us on toward greatness. Without courageous action (and a lot of help from others), the hero would succumb along the way to any one of many pitfalls. There are a thousand ways to get it wrong, and only one way to get it right: keep going.[77]

It is clear by now that we are formed by our actions as much as our actions are formed by us. The mystery of human transformation is made plain by this simple fact: practice replaces old habits with new ones as surely as spring follows winter.

Instead of waiting in my room for courage to overtake me like a viral infection, and only then setting out to live the life of my dreams, it is far wiser and far more effective to simply ask myself in the midst of my fear, "What would a courageous person do right now?" and then do that. And then do it again, and again. Eventually, and soon, a new habit takes shape. The same is true of compassion, or any quality I wish to cultivate and embody. Should I wait for compassion to mysteriously overtake me, or should I in this next moment simply choose compassion, despite my feelings? If I wish to cultivate compassion, the answer is clear. Embody the qualities you wish to become, and cement them with repeated action. This is the medicine of action, and the wisdom of engagement.

A Wise Person

Clarified by the consciousness of acceptance, liberated by the willingness of surrender, and committed to vigorous engagement, a wise person rises up out of the fog of fear and ambivalence that characterizes so much of what passes for human consciousness.

A wise person shapes their life through deliberate choices and actions.

A wise person takes responsibility for their thoughts, knowing that thoughts are the source of words and actions. As Epictetus wrote, "As you think, so you become."[78]

A wise person knows that no matter what happened in the past, they are infinitely free in this now moment to choose and act in accord with the good.

A wise person acts without attachment to the outcomes of their actions, good or bad. They simply do what is right, knowing that all action inevitably leads to imperfection and unintended consequences.

A wise person chooses actions that cooperate with the larger forces within and around them, letting go of the illusion of egoic control.

A wise person shows up in the consciousness of service, no matter the task.

A wise person knows that if their means are pure, the ends will take care of themselves.

A wise person learns how to act even in the face of uncertainty, knowing that they will never have all of the information they think they need.

A wise person knows that they can create inner transformation through the embodiment of new behaviors.

A wise person cultivates the courage to let go of the behaviors and habits that no longer serve their highest good.

A wise person knows that thoughts lead to words, words lead to actions, actions lead to habits, and habits construct character.

A wise person is not intimidated by this newfound responsibility but is instead invigorated and emboldened by it.

Closing Meditation

As before, let us close our time of reflection on the wisdom of engagement with a period of guided meditation. If you are listening, close your eyes; if you are reading, allow yourself to slowly move into deep, intentional breathing, taking care to breathe fully from the center of your body, not your upper chest. When your breathing has settled into its natural rhythm, let your thoughts drift unrestrained, and as you release them from your control, you begin to feel them receding in importance. Soon you will sink beneath the thought-stream into the quiet stillness of being. From this restful place of stillness, begin to feel the energy in your body. Start with your hands. Bring your attention to your hands and feel the subtle energy field within and around them. Notice that their aliveness is wholly independent of your thought-stream. Then allow your attention to shift up from your hands, through your arms and into your body. Notice how there is a subtle but powerful energy field of aliveness throughout your entire body.

Even though you are in a state of rest, you sense a great power, a great potential, ready to be applied consciously in the field of action when needed. In fact, even though you are still, there is already a vibrant web of action taking place within you. One hundred trillion cells, each a microcomputer in continual communication with all of the other cells in a complex series of systems nested within systems, all of it sentient, all of it conscious, all of it guided by a purpose greater than the concerns of the individual parts. We are in awe of our own immeasurability.

And we see that our lives are an opportunity—an opportunity to show up in the consciousness of service, bravely doing what is ours to do, letting go of the need to control, and letting go of our craving to see our small-minded expectations realized, knowing that we are forever in cooperation with larger forces and that like a wave in the ocean, our life is part of a larger unfolding beyond the ken of any single organism. We know that our efforts are not in vain if our intentions are pure, even though at times things seem hopeless. We trust that there is a force that comes through our actions, a divine will that aligns with our self-will if we let it, an invisible hand that shapes all things, whether we call it God or Brahman or Dao or the Nameless, and that the best action is action in concert with this flow.

We know that it is only through action that our potentialities are made manifest. We feel this knowing in the deep aliveness of our bodies. We know that as we act, so we become; that there is an abiding freedom in the aliveness within us; that when we allow our courage to carry us into the field of action, we are one step closer to the realization of our unique place in the web of the universe; and that the universe is one step closer to the realization of its end or purpose as well. So it is that our individual lives are interwoven with the one Life of all things. Just as a whirlpool cannot be lifted out of a river for closer scrutiny, so too our apparent separateness is a concept, an idea, an illusion that fades in the clarifying light of depth awareness, born on the field of action, and made whole in the integrated realization of awakening.

Shifting out of the depths and back toward the surface of the thought-stream, we return to this room, this moment, this simple presence. We take a deep breath, drawing fully from our lower chest, and let it out with an audible sigh. We take another deep breath and let it out with another audible sigh. We feel our attention returning to the space around us, the sounds of the room, and of the world outside. We know now that we are free, responsible, courageous, willing, and alive to the tasks at hand. Like a hero on a great adventure, we know there will be times of confusion and danger. We know there will be times of great struggle. We know that there will be times of staggering grief and loss. And we know that there will be times when an unearned abundance of love and joy will pour down around us, washing away all worry and fear, and in that moment we will be born from above into our own deeper nature, a reality that was already and always ours, but to which our fear and delusion blinded us. We stand now on the field of action, ready and willing to pick up the tools of our lives and shape the world after the vision of beauty that has been shown to us. We know we are not alone. There are many others around us. Together we build what needs building, and together we tear down what is in the way. This is the purpose of life. This is where our joy lies. This is the wisdom of engagement.

Caretake *this* moment. Immerse yourself in its particulars. Respond to *this* person, *this* challenge, *this* deed. Quit the evasions. Stop giving yourself needless trouble. It is time to really live; to fully inhabit the situation you happen to be in now. You are not some disinterested bystander. Participate. Exert yourself. Respect your partnership with providence. Ask yourself often, *How may I perform this particular deed such that it would be consistent with and acceptable to the divine will?* Heed the answer and get to work.[79]

—Epictetus

Detachment means being passionate about your work but dispassionate about its rewards.[80]

—Deepak Chopra

The Fourth Stone

Chapter 4

Wisdom as Allowance

Stay committed to your decisions, but
stay flexible in your approach.
—Tom Robbins

Use the Force, Luke

In the climactic battle scene of the first *Star Wars* movie, our hero Luke Skywalker and his fellow Rebel Alliance fighter pilots are struggling to destroy the Death Star, an impenetrable, moon-sized space station. According to intelligence reports, the Death Star's sole vulnerability is its exhaust port. Only an impossibly precise missile strike could take out the enemy battle station and save the Rebel Alliance.

In hero mythology, this is known as the impossible task. In *The Wizard of Oz*, Dorothy, the tin man, the scarecrow, and the cowardly lion were given the impossible task of retrieving the wicked witch's broom. In *The Lord of the Rings*, a three-foot-tall hobbit named Frodo is given the impossible task of making the perilous journey across Middle Earth to destroy the ring in Mordor, the home of the Dark Lord Sauron. By all rational standards, these tasks are doomed to fail.

In *Star Wars: A New Hope*, Luke and his companions fail to hit the target again and again despite their best efforts. Even with all their sophisticated technology and training, they cannot accomplish the goal. Only in the last possible moment does a solution arise. As the villain Darth Vader is closing in behind Luke Skywalker, the spirit-voice of Luke's mentor, Obi Wan Kenobi, whispers the immortal words: "Use the Force, Luke. Let go."[81] Luke turns off the computerized missile guidance system and falls back on his spiritual instinct. In the consciousness of heightened attention and in cooperation with the Force coursing through him, Luke fires two final shots. The missiles find their target, and the Death Star is destroyed.

When I saw *Star Wars* in a crowded theater in 1977 the first week of its release, the audience leapt to its feet and cheered when Luke successfully completed his impossible task. A cathartic wave swept through the theater, a collective emotional release I had never witnessed in a theater before or since. Writer-director George Lucas really did something beautiful when he led us through the hero's journey to the final realization that only when we turn off the machine of intellect and ego, let go of the outcome, and slip into the deeply cooperative consciousness of allowance do we achieve our ultimate aim.

The Consciousness of Allowance

So far in our journey toward wisdom, we have accepted current conditions, surrendered the ego to our larger purpose, and engaged with life in the field of action. Now it is time to move into deeper accord with the generative intelligence of the universe through allowance.

Acceptance is acknowledging the facts of existence and moving into non-resistance. Surrender is admitting our powerlessness. Engagement is entering willingly and decisively into the field of action. And allowance is ensuring that our actions move in accord with what is already unfolding.

The state of allowance is not the same as passivity. Allowance is a deeply perceptive state characterized by open-mindedness, willingness, awareness, and intuition. Wisdom traditions all over the world recognize this condition of consciousness as a requisite element of mastery. In the Daoist tradition of ancient China this soft and deep accord is known as *wu wei*.

Following the Way

In the *Dao De Jing*, Laozi draws wisdom from a deep and intuitive reading of nature. Behind the veil of surface appearances lay an unnamable source called Dao, or the Way. Dao is not God; it is not a conscious, personified entity. It is not separate or outside the fabric of being. It is the vibrant and fluid matrix of life itself, found within the minutiae of the manifest world. Hence it is ever present and hidden in plain sight. Because of its ineffable nature, it cannot be confined to any single name or concept. Instead, Laozi points to it with poetic metaphors that spark the imagination and cloud the intellect. In the end, the Dao is simply a name for the way things unfold; the myriad processes that comprise the flow of reality. In this portrait of wisdom, it is folly to act in opposition to the Dao and wise to act in accord with it. "Rushing into action, you fail. Trying to grasp things, you lose them. Forcing a project to completion, you ruin what was almost ripe. Therefore the Master takes action by letting things take their course."[82] Who has not felt the wisdom of these words rise up through the wreckage of their own failed attempts at coercion or manipulation?

Again and again Laozi upholds the value of wu wei, a model of action predicated on cooperation and nonattachment. Wu wei literally means "nonaction" or "not doing," but looking deeper, we see that wu wei does not mean paralysis or inactivity. You do not become a Daoist master by lying around on the couch all day. Instead, wu wei is a certain kind of action—action that is natural, spontaneous, nondeliberate, and in harmony with current conditions. In his book *The World's Wisdom*, Philip Novak translates wu wei as "creative letting-be," for it is both creative, that is, highly productive and engaged, while remaining fluid enough to move effortlessly through an ever-changing thicket of conditions and circumstances.[83] How does water get past a boulder in a stream? Does it stop, draw up a plan, consult with others, scheme against its enemies, indulge in anxiety, and feel sorry for itself? No. It effortlessly and without deliberation falls around the rock. While we're still thinking about it, it's already downstream. In a sense, it doesn't do anything, if by *do* you mean plan, intend, worry, strategize, or in any other way exert effort. It simply follows the natural line of the watercourse. Noninterference allows nature or the

Dao to proceed unhindered toward its ultimate outcome. This is the simple explanation behind Laozi's apparent paradox: "When nothing is done, nothing is left undone."[84]

Like Buddhism, Daoism counsels us to move toward emptiness, a state in which we are no longer attached to rigid, preconceived judgments and concepts that blind us to the fluid reality flowing around us. "In the pursuit of knowledge, every day something is added. In the practice of Dao, every day something is dropped. Less and less do you need to force things, until finally you arrive at wu wei."[85]

Only when we show up empty-handed and open hearted can we be truly effective. "A good traveler has no fixed plans and is not intent upon arriving," Laozi writes. "A good artist lets his intuition lead him wherever it wants. A good scientist has freed himself of concepts and keeps his mind open to what is."[86] Without the open stance of wu wei, who knows what you'll miss?

We often misread a flurry of activity as productivity. Under the influence of our ego, we mistakenly assume that the results we want will come only after strident effort. But in chapter fifteen of the Dao De Jing, Laozi asks, "Do you have the patience to wait till your mud settles and the water is clear? Can you remain unmoving till the right action arises by itself?"[87] In the consciousness of allowance, we are attuned to the wider currents flowing around us and are given the eyes to see where we might, with only the slightest midcourse corrections, align ourselves with what is already happening. When Luke Skywalker used the Force, he was practicing wu wei. Only then was he able to master the seemingly impossible. For the discursive mind (and for the analytical machinery of the missile guidance system), blowing up the Death Star was impossible. But in wu wei, the boundaries between impossible and possible dissolve.

In order to assure a bountiful harvest, a farmer must employ great knowledge, experience, and skill. She must understand as much as she can about the myriad biological, botanical, geological, meteorological, and economic forces at work. Nature is not a machine comprised of linear assembly chains but a system of interwoven cycles that feed endlessly into each other. In the final analysis, the farmer is not imposing her will on the processes of nature. Like a child leaping onto a moving merry-go-round, the most successful farmer finds a way to cooperate with the energies and processes already underway. The seed in the ground does not answer to the farmer's will. It follows the laws of nature written in the fabric of its cellular material, in concert with the waves of energy surrounding it, enveloping it in a womb of becoming.

In our own lives, we learn everything we can and prepare as much as possible, but on the cusp of greatness, we must allow our actions to unfold in rhythm with the beating heart of the larger forces around us.

Cooperation, Not Competition

In 1992, scientists built Biosphere 2, a large, enclosed ecosystem in the mountains of Arizona. Replicating as best they could all of the complexity of nature, their test-tube environment was outfitted with a wide range of life forms, including trees. The trees inside the sealed enclosure grew more rapidly than their wild cousins outside. But they were thinner and weaker, with underdeveloped root systems. When some of the trees in Biosphere 2 toppled over from their own weight, the scientists were mystified. Why would trees not thrive in this perfectly protected and controlled environment?

It finally dawned on the researchers that the trees inside the sealed and protected world were weakened by the absence of the one natural element *not* included in Biosphere 2: wind. In the real world outside the dome, trees withstand high-velocity winds and as a result develop what botanists call stress wood—strong, fibrous tissue that greatly enhances the tensile strength and viability of a tree. Not only does this bear out the validity of Nietzsche's famous line "What doesn't kill you makes you stronger," but it also casts light on another truth: that nature is more cooperative than competitive. At first glance, it seems that high winds and trees are in conflict with one another; forests hamper the wind and wind damages trees. But upon deeper reflection, without the hard push of the wind, trees would not cultivate the inner strength they need to survive. Trees need wind, just as we need struggles and challenges in order to cultivate and realize our excellence. As Epictetus put it, "The trials we endure … introduce us to our strengths."

Daoism is masterful at drawing metaphors from nature and asks, Which is stronger, the old oak tree or the young blade of grass? In a violent storm, the oak tree topples over while the blade of grass survives. It survives because it yields, bending to allow the wind to pass. This shows the strength of allowance. By resisting and struggling against the wind, the oak tree failed to meet its goal, namely staying alive. "The soft overcomes the hard; the gentle overcomes the rigid," Laozi writes in the Dao De Jing. "Everyone knows this is true, but few can put it into practice."[88] A clenched fist cannot enter a tiny crack in a wall, but water easily can. By remaining fluid and having no shape to maintain or defend, water accomplishes what a rigid fist never can. Again and again, so-called weakness overcomes strength. When we shift into the consciousness of allowance, we enter a deep and mutually beneficial state of accord with the powerful energies around us, thereby increasing our power and effectiveness.

It is standard fare to refer to nature as a war of all against all. Sad old phrases like "the law of the jungle" and "survival of the fittest" are drilled into us by old-fashioned wildlife documentaries. This unfortunate distortion and misappropriation of Darwinian theory has done a great disservice by spotlighting and glorifying only one half of a complex equation. Yes, in some respects we are in competition with one another for limited resources. But it is also true that like wind and trees, we rely on one another in a complex web of mutual interdependence. Nothing survives on its own. Our survival is only possible because of our symbiotic relationship with everything else.

As recounted in Eknath Easwaran's book *The Compassionate Universe*, noted naturalist Jean-Pierre Hallet was studying elephants in the Belgian Congo when he saw an elephant without a trunk. Wondering how the injured elephant managed to survive, Hallet followed the herd deep into the forest. His question was answered when they stopped to eat. One by one the healthy elephants brought branches and leaves to their trunkless companion. Before one of them ate a single bite of food, they made sure their friend had his fill. The distinction between self-interest and group interest disappeared. That the good of the whole and the good of individuals melded into one reality reveals a moral imperative that binds us all together in a mutually beneficial relationship. Cooperation transcends competition. We are hardwired to take care of one another. Maybe *this* is the law of the jungle.[89]

Kant's Good Will

Eighteenth-century German philosopher Immanuel Kant changed the conversation in Western philosophy by asserting that the only true and valid basis for moral action was adherence to the good will, an inherent principle found in the sound mind of any rational person. Other philosophers insisted that humans do the right thing primarily to bring about a desired consequence—the ends justify the means—whether that end is a selfish or a noble one. Kant, in contrast, argued that each of us carries within us an innate morality, and this good will is rightly a starting point, not an end point, of any moral consideration. We are good, Kant argued, when we adhere to duty and principle, not when we do whatever it takes to achieve a certain result.

Though the good will may be intrinsic, adherence to it is not. We must choose it. And as we choose it, over time our moral reasoning becomes increasingly habituated until finally we no longer struggle when faced with moral quandaries. In the mature moral thinker, the highest level of mastery requires the least effort.

For Kant, doing the right thing has nothing to do with conformity to social norms and laws, nothing to do with calculating outcomes, and nothing to do with sentiments or emotions. Duty and duty alone creates true moral action, aligning our actions with the principle of goodness built into all of us. All rational creatures have an internal moral compass that always points to true north. We have only to choose to move our feet in the right direction.

Contrast Kant's portrait of a good life with the life of an addict or adulterer who must constantly lie, deceive, conceal, and manipulate in an exhausting attempt to maintain the duplicitous lives they lead. In the eyes of those around them, they are a sober and honorable member of society, but in truth they break scores of promises in every single human interaction; their entire life becomes a lie. The chaos, agitation, and isolation this creates drives them even deeper into the destructive fantasy world they have chosen. It rarely ends well.

A life lived in accord with the good will, in contrast, is a life free of chaos and agitation. Gone is the exhausting task of trying to remember all the lies you told and to whom. Instead, human relationships are characterized by mutual respect, openness, and ease. You may not always get what you want, but no matter what happens in the outer world of circumstance, your inner life is simple, clean, and worry-free.

So in a sense, both Laozi and Kant advocate the cultivation of a deep alliance with the ground of being already present in and around us. Cooperation with the good will or the Dao leads us to our highest effectiveness and joy. Inner accord means accord in the outer world. As Polonius famously said in Shakespeare's *Hamlet*, "This above all: to thine own self be true, and it must follow, as the night the day, thou canst not be false to any man."

My Yoke Is Easy, My Burden Light

In the Gospel of Matthew Jesus paints a vivid portrait of wisdom as allowance. In stark contrast to the apostle Paul's dire portrait of our ardent struggle against sin, Jesus uses an agricultural metaphor—a favorite tactic—to convey the serenity and ease of a life lived in accord with the Dao, or in the vocabulary of Jesus's theism, God the Father. Instead of battling against an adversary we can never conquer, Jesus invites us to abandon the entire paradigm of life as a struggle and move instead into a condition of consciousness characterized by surrender and allowance. "Come to me, all you who are weary and burdened, and I will give you rest," Jesus said. "Take my yoke upon you and learn from me, for I am gentle and humble in heart, and you will find rest for your souls. For my yoke is easy and my burden light."[90]

The Sanskrit word *yoga* is etymologically linked to the English word *yoke*. By calling to mind this everyday object—a common farm implement—for his audience, Jesus points to a shift in consciousness. In the same way a yoke channels the vast and undirected energy of oxen toward a specific aim, the disciplines of yoga channel the vast and undirected energy of consciousness toward a specific aim: a fruitful harvest of awakening. When we are lashed to the yoke of our destructive instinctual desires and egoic cravings, we reap a harvest of suffering both for ourselves and others. When we choose instead to live in accord with our higher natures, our good will, our inner Christ, or the Dao, we feel struggle slipping away, replaced with serenity and divine alignment. Conflict is replaced with cooperation, and agitation with contentment. In his book *The Gospel of Jesus*, Stephen Mitchell puts it this way:

> For Jesus, there is no drama. The more we surrender, the more we are carried along in the current of God's love… Not that good and evil don't exist, but when you see into the realm beyond good and evil, where everything is pure grace, we are much less likely to be caught up in our own judgments and moral categories, and much more ready to experience every action as easy and natural.[91]

Pure Grace

Religious people often speak of faith. But what if you don't believe in God? Or what if you're not sure? What does faith mean then?

Is there a connection between the wisdom of allowance and the condition of consciousness known by theists as faith?

Like a lot of words in philosophy and religion, faith has many meanings. For some, faith means believing in things for which there is no evidence, like the claim that Jesus was born of a virgin, that he walked on water, or that he rose from the dead. When struggling with their own skepticism regarding these and countless other religious claims, unbelievers are often counseled to "just have faith." Faith, in this sense, is a willing suspension of disbelief, an epistemological stance where the foundation of knowledge is not rational discourse but the testimony of traditional authorities and texts. No empirical, sensory, or experiential evidence is supplied, and none is required.

For others, faith takes on quite a different meaning. Here, faith does not mean accepting truth-claims for which you have no evidence, but a confident optimism that there is a larger order at work, that the universe is purposeful, that we are supported, and that we have an opportunity to engage with a conscious, living universe toward mutually beneficial ends. Faith is a stance, a way of being in the world, and an opportunity for engagement. In this light, faith is a courageous shift, a humble mode of consciousness where intuition and awareness replace know-nothing acquiescence. Here, one trusts that the universe is a nurturing, abundant, generative field of mutually supportive energy. Success is redefined as a state of deep allowance and cooperation with the energy flowing forever around us. All we have to do is choose to allow our own creative energies and actions to align with the larger forces in play. In a theistic system, God is placed at the center of this intricate web. In nontheistic systems like Daoism or Buddhism, the intelligent universe remains impersonal yet just as deeply responsive and interactive as any loving deity.

In the last few pages of his masterpiece *Walden*, Henry David Thoreau challenges us with this profoundly affirmative promise: "…[I]f one advances confidently in the direction of his dreams, and endeavors to live the life which he has imagined, he will meet with a success unexpected in common hours."[92] Advancing confidently is a state of mind in which one assumes the best is yet to come and that the universe is inherently nurturing. You simply have this hunch that it's going to work out somehow. In fact, the universe's nurturing energy visits us to the precise extent that we allow it to. Our confidence in its supportive nature opens up channels where its support can be perceived and incorporated into the tasks with which we are charged. We don't control these energies, but we do control our perception and awareness. When we see with open eyes and open heart the beauties that move in and around us, we invite them into alignment with our own vision of the highest good. When we move confidently in the direction of our dreams, a floodgate is opened. Confidence is just another word for optimism. When we endeavor to work hard in the field of action, abundance and success will pour into the fertile rows we have ploughed to nourish the seeds we have planted. The right people, the right books, and the right circumstances come into your life, none of which you control, but all of which your wisdom convinces you to allow. When we follow the yellow brick road of our destiny, or as Joseph Campbell put it, when we follow our bliss, we live the life our soul is asking for, the life we were meant to live. Our dharma or true path leads us to a place of deep cooperation where the line between our self-effort and the nurturing support of the energies around us blurs until we no longer know where one ends and the other begins. Religious people call it faith. Others call it trust. Regardless of your views on God, perhaps we could think of it as pure grace. In this sense, grace is not an article of faith but a simple fact. We are already in accord with the mutually supportive energies of the universe. We have only to participate in the cocreation of the conditions in which those supportive energies are optimized.

Our success is assured. We have only to allow it.

The Power of Meditation and Prayer

Around the world in every religious and spiritual tradition, some form of prayer or meditation is taught as a way to move into deeper allowance. Meditation and prayer are both conscious shifts into a state of mutually beneficial cooperation between our energies and the larger energies around us. Between the various traditions and indeed within each tradition, there is a bewildering variety of techniques and guidelines for proper meditation and prayer. Indeed, meditation and prayer are not the same thing. But in a general sense, the goal of all meditation and prayer is the same: to leave behind this small jar of water and swim for a time in the ocean from which all water comes.

Some prayer is petitionary and deeply theistic, appealing to a personal God for assistance. Other prayer is contemplative, seeking only an experience of the divine with or without a specific, personified God-concept. Is the best prayer talking to God, or listening to God? And how does prayer actually work?

It is widely held in Christian theology, and throughout the Abrahamic faiths, that God cannot be coerced. Therefore, prayer doesn't compel God to do something that he doesn't want to do, nor can it show him something of which he was not already aware. Prayer then becomes a simpler thing, an opportunity for communion and connection with the divine, an opportunity for us to come out of the fear-based demands of ordinary consciousness and enter instead into a state of serenity, acceptance, and allowance. As Soren Kierkegaard put it, "Prayer doesn't change God, but it changes him who prays."

The efficacy of prayer is difficult to verify scientifically, but the beneficial effects of meditation are becoming more and more widely established. A growing body of research points to the efficacy of meditation. We know that it works; we just don't know how it works. There are, however, some reasonable assumptions to be made. It works because in the deeply receptive state of consciousness that meditation engenders, windows to a wider reality appear and we begin to see with new eyes the abundance of riches available to us beyond the walls of our conceptual minds. Moving out of the small mind with its worries and fantasies of control, we feel ourselves expanding into highly intuitive and inherently cooperative modes of consciousness where we possess less but know more. The boundaries between things begin to shimmer out of existence, or at least become provisional, no longer seen as ultimate and unwavering. A deep humility eclipses the arrogance of intellectualism—we become again as a child. Jaded tedium is replaced with wide-eyed wonder, and in our content-free awareness, we have the eyes to see and the ears to hear the ancient song of the universe, a song long-hidden beneath the cacophony of our thought-addled minds. Meditation doesn't do anything, but it works because it creates the conditions wherein our own mind-body system's inherent healing arises on its own. Meditation is a reset of our natural equilibrium in which our energy systems return into their natural alignment. Meditation is doing nothing and allowing everything.

When you cut your finger, you do not have to deliberately heal it. Healing happens. You are simply the witness of a process. White blood cells rush to the wound to fight infection all on their own. Coagulants in the blood are activated as they hit the air hardening and sealing off torn flesh. New cells begin replicating, repairing the affected tissues. In a few days, the cut heals over, with or without your consent or attention. If they're honest, doctors, nurses, and healthcare professionals admit that they don't heal anybody; they expertly cocreate the conditions in which a patient's own healing processes can unfold without impediment. Healing isn't something we do; it's something we allow. Meditation works the same way.

The consciousness of allowance is paradoxically active and passive at the same time. Meditation and prayer perfectly replicate this paradox. In the Bhagavad Gita, Krishna tells Arjuna that "there is action in the midst of inaction and inaction in the midst of action."[93] By entering into the stillness, we engage with the ground of being, the primal activity of the universe, a boundless energy beyond all limiting concepts. The Stoic philosopher Epictetus called this ground of being the will of nature. "Learn the will of nature," he said. "Study it, pay attention to it, and then make it your own."[94] How can we learn the will of nature and embody it if we do not become quiet and still enough to hear it, see it, and feel it coursing through the depths of our own awareness? Wisdom then is a state of deep allowance where we receive more than exert, allow more than achieve, and feel more than know. And from that deep awareness comes both a confidence in our abilities and an acceptance of the outer circumstances of our life.

"When you strive to conform your intentions and actions with the divine order," said Epictetus, "you don't feel persecuted, helpless, confused, or resentful toward the circumstances of your life. You will feel strong, purposeful and sure."[95] These are the fruits of meditation and prayer. The immense benefit of taking even five minutes a day for a silent retreat into the stillness will be immediately felt by anyone who tries this venerable, ancient, and universal practice.

It may be difficult to describe meditation in clear and precise terms. But it is easy to say what it is not. Meditation is not thinking. Running through your to-do list is not meditation. Planning, brainstorming, and problem solving are not meditation. Wallowing in memories is not meditation. Forcefully concentrating on concepts, even so-called spiritual concepts is not meditating. Even the guided meditation we do at the end of each of these chapters is not true meditation.

Guided meditation is a contemplative visualization process, an excellent way of deepening into awareness to be sure, but a little too linked to the conceptual mind to properly be called true meditation. True meditation has nothing to do with thinking or thought. It is to sink deeper into the cloud of unknowing out of which all thoughts arise. The eleventh-century Japanese Zen master Dogen advised his students to "think no-thinking."[96] The advice to empty our minds sounds at first like just another unattainable spiritual ideal, but it is a suggestion designed to move us in the right direction, nothing more. Let's not make emptying our minds yet another strident aspiration on our spiritual to-do list. Take it as a direction, not a goal. There are gaps between thoughts. Move into those gaps, that's all. But this takes practice. That's why meditation cannot be a once in a while thing. Like learning how to play the piano or ride a bike, it takes consistency of action and intention.

In the end, however, meditation is not an achievement, it is an allowance. If you are struggling to control the process, you are not meditating. You are doing something else. In true meditation, we come out of the consciousness of control and into the wisdom of allowance. No struggle, no strain. In meditation, there is no effort to control the mind or still our thoughts. The mind's natural state is activity. There's no stopping it. You might as well ask a waterfall to stop falling, or the waves on the shore to stop crashing on the sand. Instead, we shift our attention away from the busy mind and toward the boundless awareness beneath the thought-stream. As we observe our thoughts arise and fade, we suddenly realize that we are not our thoughts—we are their witness. With this simple insight, we shift toward freedom. We realize our oneness with the limitless awareness that we are and have always been, an awareness hidden from us behind the noise of the thought-stream. In meditation we finally become who we really are.

Being Who We Are

Our choices and actions largely determine the quality of our lives. But it is also true that we do not choose the raw materials out of which we construct a life with our choices and actions. We did not choose our genes, our parents, our families, the century in which we were born, our race, our ethnicity, our national origin, our language group, our socioeconomic class, and so on. There is even evidence that the qualities of our personality are deeply shaped by genetic factors beyond our control—traits such as introversion and extroversion, for example, or whether one is attracted to liberal or conservative political philosophies. In other words, we are simultaneously free and utterly bound. We have free will to choose, but always and only within a given context over which we have no control. The best lives then are those in which free will is used to develop the traits already present within us. We are much more effective when we work with what is.

Arbitrarily choosing a life path out of thin air, rooted in childish fantasies of self-aggrandizement or deep, unmet ego needs, is far less effective than discerning what one's latent talents and proclivities actually are, and cultivating those. Your life is already emerging according to the dictates of its own nature. Why not work with that? Why not align your energies with what is already unfolding?

Allowing yourself to be who you are is a powerful stance—perhaps the most powerful stance of all because when you cooperate with your own nature, you are in fact cooperating with the will of nature. The universe is expressing itself in you, through you, and as you. To cooperate with and contribute to your own natural unfolding is your highest calling.

Allowing yourself to be who you are is also a courageous and radical act of sedition. There is always a chorus of voices—some of them well-meaning, some of them not—who will try to discourage you and bring you back into the fold. In their attempts to erode your courage, they validate and assuage their own insecurities, always ready with a million reasons why "it won't work" or why "you're doing it wrong." Radical authenticity and freedom is inherently threatening to the status quo.

When we begin to philosophically mature by moving through the stages of acceptance, surrender, action, and allowance, we begin to uncover our own authentic nature, those bedrock talents, tendencies, sensitivities, and strengths uniquely our own. Never before in the history of the universe has there been anyone exactly like you, nor will there ever be again. You are a one-off. You are the universe's one-time attempt to express itself as you, and only by living your authentic life can you fully participate in the cocreation of this sacred outcome. You are a being of infinite value, and so is everyone else. This knowledge has to be our starting point.

When you accept who you are, when you surrender to the things you cannot change, when you step boldly into the field of action, and when you allow your will to align with the will of nature, your whole being takes on a stature and clarity unavailable to small-minded, fearful people. In the consciousness of allowance, you are no better than anyone else, and you are no worse than anyone else. You allow yourself to take your rightful place in the world, fully engaged but calm, no longer an isolated cluster of needs and fears but an interconnected member of the human community and the web of all life. The gifts you bring are precisely what the world needs, and you have a meaningful role to play in the healing of the world. Your work is the work of God, or of nature.

The world's wisdom traditions are rife with the accounts of heroes and masters who have manifested this sacred paradox of great effectiveness and great humility. Their power comes not from themselves but from the alchemy that occurs when they meld their will with the will of Brahman, Dao, or God. In the Bhagavad Gita, Krishna tells Arjuna, "Those who know this truth, whose consciousness is unified, think always, 'I am not the doer.'"[97] In the consciousness of allowance, our actions come not from the small "I" with its ego desires and separate sense of self, but from a much deeper place. When we get our small selves out of the way, Brahman-Atman or the Self shines through.

In the Gospel of John, Jesus repeatedly reminds his students that the miraculous things he does come not from him but from the Father in him. In the theistic language of his Judeo-Christian tradition, Jesus places all power in the Lord and none in himself—yet there he is, performing great miracles. Jesus deflects attention away from himself and toward his Source when he says, "It is the Father, living in me, who is doing his work." As portrayed in the final and most fully developed Gospel, Jesus has cultivated a great state of allowance, to the point where he identifies himself fully with the divine: "I am in the Father, and the Father is in me." But what he says next is the most startling passage in the New Testament. Jesus says that if a person has faith—that is, if a person enters into a genuine state of nonresistance and open-heartedness—he "will do what I have been doing. He will do even greater things than these."[98] Jesus unambiguously points away from himself and toward our own identity with the divine, emphasizing our capacity to move into powerful accord with the sacred source. Much of mainstream Christianity, in contrast, has committed itself to an understanding of Jesus as a unique incarnation of God, a lone exception to the rule, the one human being not bound to the darkness of original sin and therefore singularly capable of miraculous actions. Jesus extols and celebrates not his own exceptional nature but the inner light within us all. The Church points to Jesus while Jesus points to us. In the gospel teachings of Jesus, direct experience of the divine is available to anyone willing to allow it.

This same dynamic is at work in the Upanishads and the Bhagavad Gita of Hinduism, the Dao De Jing of Daoism, the Kabbalah tradition of Judaism, the Sufi tradition of Islam, and many other spiritual traditions. Throughout history, shamans, mystics, gurus, rabbis, and saints have tried to lead us into a state of deeper allowance. All they've asked is that we die to ourselves, or more specifically, die to that small part of ourselves that always wants to take back control.

Dying to Self

The phrase "dying to self" is a vivid and dramatic way of expressing a subtle and complex psychological shift. Dying to self means cutting ties with our self-obsessed lower nature, the I-me-mine mindset that sees the world through a narrow lens of self-interest. The part of ourselves that we are supposed to "die to" is incapable of surrendering or allowing our higher purpose to unfold. Both the St. Francis and Father Mychal Judge prayers discussed in chapter two are perfect illustrations of this shift in consciousness. "Make me an instrument," the St. Francis prayer begins, asking God to work through us in a beautiful expression of cooperation and co-creation, so that you don't know where God ends and we begin.

In the Gospel of Thomas, Jesus puts this theme in stark terms. Speaking of the inner light within all of us he says, "If you bring forth what is within you, what you have will save you. If you do not have that within you, what you do not have within you will kill you."[99] If we do not die to our small sense of self and allow our inner light to shine forth, we are as good as dead. Or as Socrates put it, "The unexamined life is not worth living."

Whether you conceive of it in theistic terms as do Jesus, St. Francis, and Father Mychal Judge, or in nontheistic terms like Buddhist nonattachment or Gandhi's renunciation, the results are the same. Great things happen only when you move into accord with the consciousness of allowance. Much to the surprise of the lower mind, humility turns out to be the most powerful stance of all.

Despite our confusion, humility is not the same thing as humiliation. Humility is strong; humiliation is a state of great weakness. Humility is selfless; humiliation is rooted in self-obsession. By identifying with the stories of our blunders and alleged inadequacies we grow attached to a self-serving portrait of helplessness and victim consciousness. Humiliation is believing someone else's story about us. Humiliation, oddly enough, forms a refuge, a safe place where we can curl up and quit. But self-forgetting is not the same thing as self-loathing. Modesty is not the same thing as self-deprecation. Humility is graceful and beautiful; humiliation is awkward and ugly. Humility is supreme effectiveness; humiliation is abject impotence. Humility needs no apology; humiliation never stops apologizing. Who knew that self-loathing and humiliation were diseases of the ego? That was unexpected. And this is the very self-absorption to which we must "die." By allowing our greatness to express itself in our work, we shift from self-obsession to selflessness. As I often tell my students, take the work seriously, but don't take yourselves too seriously. Or as Deepak Chopra put it, "Pursue excellence, ignore success."

Riding Waves

Growing up in Ventura, California, meant growing up in the presence of the sea. You could always smell it, feel it on your skin, and taste it on the fog. It was the biggest thing in town. Its gravitational pull was undeniable.

As kids, we played in the surf all summer long on inflatable rafts and Styrofoam belly boards. In adolescence, we traded in our toys for real surfboards and learned how to ride waves standing up. Then we got wetsuits so we could surf all year. We got up in the dark to surf at dawn and still made it to our first class at Buena High School. We lived and breathed the beach until being in the water seemed as natural as being on the land. Learning to read the weather, the waves, the tides, and the mercurial moods of the sea became second nature. Ten thousand hours came and went fairly quickly.

Two things set surfing apart from its wintertime cousins skiing or snow boarding: machinery and dynamic movement. Skiers and snowboarders ride a motorized chairlift to the top of the slope. Surfers, in contrast, must paddle out into the lineup under their own power. In addition, snow covered mountains aren't like waves. Mountains stand still. Skiers and snowboarders choose the moment their ride begins and navigate a stationary face. They can even stop and start whenever they want. Surfers, in contrast, must put themselves in accord with a wave of energy moving through a pool of liquid—hesitate, and the moment is gone. The entire field of action is fluid, unpredictable, and transitory.

Surfing requires a wide range of intuitive sensitivity. In order to ride waves, surfers must abandon their own schedule and, without any external help, place themselves in a dynamic energy wave that is moving through space. To surf well, one must cultivate a keen ocean sense and learn the rhythms of each particular break. Point breaks are different than reefs, and beach breaks vary over time as sand bars move around in the seasonal currents. Endless variables like wind, swell direction, size, and frequency make standardization impossible. Sure, there are different kinds of snow, and the wind does blow on the mountain. But the ocean is a fluid realm without fixed landmarks where nothing ever happens twice.

When surfing, you have to allow what is happening to happen. There's no use in interfering; you couldn't if you tried. You surf well to the precise extent to which you cooperate with what is already happening. As we saw earlier, Daoism called this wu wei, a form of action where deliberation gives way to cooperation. Wu wei is natural action in harmony with current conditions; maximum effect with minimal effort. It is action unhampered by egoic ambition or harried interference. Wu wei is effortless effort. Surfing is the embodiment of wu wei.

When you see a swell coming, you turn and paddle with it until your board speed matches the wave's speed and direction. Moving toward shallower water, the wave rises up and begins to break over at the top. As your board accelerates down the steepening face of the wave, you can hear it and feel it in your chest as much as see it with your eyes—the nose of your board drops away, you leap to your feet, and you're gliding down the face and turning left or right away from the breaking foam and out onto the rising shoulder of the wave. You feel the subtle vibration of the wave rising up through your feet as the board chatters over the surface of the water. You're moving fast, but in a way it feels like you're standing still, like everything is moving but you're not. You are the still point at the center of the cyclone. You feel supported, held, and safe. A wordless conviction comes over you: you're in exactly the right place. Everything else falls away—your worries, your problems, your thoughts, your memories, your fears. There is just … this.

What is a wave? The wave isn't water; the wave is an immaterial energy pulse moving through water the way music moves through air. Water is simply the medium in which the wave takes form. The wave, the pure energy itself, isn't made out of anything. It just is. In its pure state, it is disembodied energy, embodied for a time in water. You did not make the wave. No one did. And yet you found it, you went to it, and you learned how to place yourself in accord with it. This is a joy and a satisfaction like no other. It is a simple thing. Great things usually are. And in that moment, the duality of wave and rider dissolves. There is no more surfer, no more wave. There is only surfing.

What if we lived our lives this way? What if we learned how to wait, to watch, to read the energy flowing around us? What if we began to perceive the people, circumstances, and situations of our lives not as problems or possessions, but as opportunities for self-mastery, aesthetic rapture, and self-realization? What if we learned how to merge our so-called private concerns with the larger realities enveloping us? What if we finally heard the music and joined in the dance that is already underway? When you practice acceptance of current conditions, surrender to the grand flow, vigorously engage with the energy around you, and allow the resulting beauty to unfold without interference, you honor yourself and everything that is. You are lifted into the still point of creation, empowered beyond the limits of private ambition, and tapped into the source from which all things come and to which all things return. Becoming one is not an achievement. Oneness is an ever-present reality which need only be allowed.

Epictetus didn't surf, but it sure sounds like he did: "Your aim should be to view the world as an integrated whole, to faithfully incline your whole being toward the highest good, and to adopt the will of nature as your own."[100]

Good Will, Happiness, and Self-Esteem

As discussed earlier, Kant's notion of the good will suggests that each of us possesses an inherent capacity to know, do, and be good. This quality is not so much learned as it is cultivated, for it is lying dormant within us like a seed. It is brought to fruition, Kant says, through proper application and habituation. For Kant, this is the "metaphysics of morals," that is, the absolute foundation upon which all right thinking and right action is properly constructed.

The good life, then, is a life lived in accord with the good will. For the purely self-interested person, the person who is always busy calculating how a proposed course of action will further their own gain, life is stressful and complicated. They are always torn on the horns of dilemmas. In contrast, for someone slipping into deeper and deeper accord with their inherent good will, stress and worry begin to recede. They are not caught in a web of calculation. They live in accord with principles, not outcomes. They treat people as ends in themselves, never merely as means to an end. The inherent value of everyone and everything is a given. From this foundation, a life of simplicity and ease begins to arise. In other words, when we move into accord with the good will present within us, we become happier and freer.

The good life arises of its own accord when we live in a state of allowance with our higher nature. It is in our long-term self-interest to set aside our short-term self-interest and draw sustenance instead from roots that run deep into our inherent good will. The person with a fully developed good will is no longer torn between conflicting sets of needs and interests; their actions align with their values without a lot of drama and stress. In a word, we call this integrity, a word based on the Latin word *integer*, meaning "untouched" or "whole." Being a whole person is easier than being endlessly divided into warring factions. Given a chance to choose, who would not prefer the light yoke and easy burden of integrity to the heavy yoke and difficult burden of dis-integration?

And there is still more to gain from moving into accord with the good will. In her book *Ethics for Life*, Judith Boss makes an important link between the Kantian notion of the good will and genuine self-esteem. It turns out self-esteem is not quite what we think it is.

As we cultivate the habit of acting from the good will, we begin to include ourselves in the assessment that all human beings are beings of infinite value. Our self-worth is no longer tied to some extrinsic standard or the assessment of others. Instead, Boss argues, self-worth arises from the natural exercise of the good will. Self-esteem is properly rooted in good actions born out of moral conscience. True self-esteem can never be granted by another; it arises only from within as a result of right action and genuine, hard-won accomplishment. The empty praise of well-meaning others does not create authentic self-esteem; it only offers the fleeting pleasure of peer approval. In fact, empty praise divorced from virtuous behavior fosters an exaggerated sense of self-importance. The curious dissociation of character from values creates monsters, so that no matter how miserably you treat others, you are still "amazing." Constantly telling young people that they are wonderful, incredible, awesome, and perfect without a corresponding expectation of moral development creates narcissists, doomed to forever languish in the evolutionary backwater of their own distorted self-perceptions. Besides, kids see through this puffery anyway, and they begin to believe that praise-happy adults flattering them with "esteem-building" accolades are dim-witted fools whose judgment and motives cannot be trusted. Only by challenging young people to push past fear and low-order self-absorption can we draw them into the wider currents of their own evolving humanity. Through gentle guidance and by example, we awaken them to the joy of full membership in the conscious human community. Their authentic self-esteem properly increases as they cultivate and express their inherent moral character in the face of the failures and challenges of their lives, for it is only through struggle and genuine accomplishment that we uncover our character. Allowing children to fail, and to learn that there is no shame in failure, is powerful pedagogy. Protecting children from risk and failure while inflating them with hollow flattery, in contrast, is to doom them to an eternal state of dependency ringed round with fear and isolation—isolation from genuine relationship with others and from their own authentic nature.[101]

With a fully cultivated good will, habituated in right action, free of the chaos of moral relativism and naked self-interest, we are safe to move into the consciousness of allowance. Our thoughts, words, choices, and actions will more likely than not align of their own accord with the divine will. We will more likely become channels of light. The good will does not have to be strenuously wrestled for, only allowed. In this state of grace, where acceptance, surrender, engagement, and allowance join together in a harmonious chord, we will feel a joy welling through us, a joy that speaks a plain, wordless truth: allowance feels good.

Allowance Feels Good

By moving into the stream of our lives and allowing the energies within us to align with and be amplified by the energies around us, we begin to experience life as a joyful experience. Anxiety, depression, worry, and fear begin to recede. We become right-sized; the need to belittle others or ourselves simply drops away. Each day becomes another wonder-filled opportunity to see where this mysterious carnival is going to take us. Every stranger we meet is a magical being of infinite value. Every challenge we face is another opportunity to ply our skill and experience the kindness of others. The unearned grace of the universe pours down around us like rain. Beauty pops up in unexpected places. We see with new eyes and hear with new ears, and we can never for one single minute be bored ever again. We begin to engage in life with a sense of enjoyment and play. We do important things, valuable things, but we don't take ourselves too seriously. We laugh often. We know that we are safe, and that the things that are taken from us were never ours anyway. Everything is borrowed, nothing is owned, and we have to give it all back, sometimes suddenly and without warning. Everyone we've ever known and everyone we've ever loved will be taken from us. Even our own death is the will of nature, to be allowed and honored. Instead of fear and grief, we feel a sense of wonder and joy washing over us, grateful that we were even born and that we got to see, hear, taste, touch, hold, and love any of this. A sense of scarcity is replaced with a sense of abundance. Loneliness is replaced with boundless love. We finally feel at home in our own skin, in our own time, in our own set of circumstances. We know that despite appearances, all is well in the world—and that if it isn't, things will soon change. They always do. We know we have work to do. But we are free from the egoic burden of thinking we have to do it all. We simply suit up, show up, and do our part. And when we are tired and spent, we rest and let the joy of the work sink in, knowing that the part we play is a vitally important part, a sacred drop in the one ocean from which everything comes and to which everything returns. Awash in this knowledge, we can sleep and dream and awake the next morning to take another turn on the wheel. We are each a voice in the one song, the *uni-verse*, and the beauty of the music is partly our doing. Let us have the ears to hear our lone voice blending with the one song and revel in the beauty that arises in us, through us, as us.

A Wise Person

Grounded in the conscious of acceptance, surrendered to current conditions, and willfully engaged in the field of action, a wise person intuitively allows their own energies to align with the energies already in motion.

A wise person allows events, circumstances, and situations to unfold as they will while maintaining eternal vigilance to perceive and intuit where and when they might best engage.

A wise person allows people to be who they are. They don't waste time and energy resenting them for not being who they think they should be.

A wise person replaces interference with engagement, intellectualism with intuition, and agitation with serenity.

A wise person knows that the energies that animate their inner life are identical to the energies that animate the cosmos, and that the microcosm is a mirrored reflection of the macrocosm. They feel a deep and abiding kinship with all things.

A wise person trusts that the universe is conspiring for their success.

A wise person knows that their true purpose is revealed only when they allow it to be, in the course of a conscious and engaged life.

A wise person knows that too much effort is as futile as no effort at all.

A wise person knows how to wait and understands the therapeutic and generative power of silence.

A wise person cultivates an earnest practice of meditation or contemplative prayer, without any expectation or demands for self-defined results.

A wise person knows that their internal state, be it anxiety or serenity, is a barometer of how well they are allowing and cooperating with the unfolding of their own best life.

A wise person knows to let go of worry and fear and any other manifestation of resistance to what is, and to practice the consciousness of allowance instead.

A wise person knows the difference between humility and humiliation, and that humility is a state of great effectiveness where true self-esteem replaces self-centeredness and forgiveness replaces blame.

A wise person trusts their own inner voice and allows it to speak with authority.

A wise person knows that when they cultivate their own excellence, they become a channel through which the universe expresses its highest nature. This state is not achieved as much as it is allowed.

A wise person learns everything they can and practices their craft with great care and attention, while allowing themselves to be carried by the energies with which they have allied themselves.

A wise person knows that beneath all the conflicting desires and confusion, there lies an inner core of goodness in everyone, an inherent good will that informs the structure of all genuine ethical action.

A wise person knows that their joy is rooted in and inseparable from their willingness to allow their life to move in accord with the lives of those around them, in concert with the energies of the larger universe.

A wise person learns how to receive their own laughter as a sacred message telling them that they are on course.

The wise person trusts the pull and the feeling of ease that accompanies a well-lived life of acceptance, engagement, surrender, and allowance, moving through the channels of their life the way a stream flows through its watercourse.

Closing Meditation

Now it is time to leave our thinking behind and slip down into a richer, deeper, and more lasting mode of awareness. If you are listening to this, close your eyes. If you are reading, soften your eyes, relax your shoulders, and allow your breathing to deepen and settle into its natural rhythm.

This time, visualize a slowly flowing river. Drift out over the surface of the river. Then feel yourself slipping into the flowing water. You feel warm and safe. You have become the river. You are water.

Feel yourself flowing, pulled along by a subtle but insistent force. Everything before you is pulling you, everything behind you is gently pushing you, and still you are free and unbound. Your feelings of loneliness and isolation begin to recede. You are utterly at home in the heart of your own existence. Without worry and without fear, you trust completely the flowing of your life.

Up ahead you see an obstacle, a huge boulder. For a moment, familiar feelings of worry, fear, resentment, and victim consciousness arise. How are you going to get past this problem? Then without cleverness or effort, you feel yourself sliding around the boulder. The obstacle before you is suddenly and effortlessly behind you. Without plan, without guile, without strategy, without analysis, and without the machinations of your busy mind, the problem simply receded from view as you flowed further along. The problem wasn't the boulder. The problem was your poor assessment of the situation. You didn't have to struggle against the boulder. You simply had to allow yourself to be carried around it.

Farther downstream, you feel yourself picking up speed. Tributaries—muddy creeks from high-country rain forests—are pouring into you and you are becoming cloudy with silt. Your vision is limited, and you feel yourself tumbling over the edge of a cliff. You crash into a pool below and drift out into a wide lake. Soon without effort, you flow into deeper waters. The silt begins to settle to the bottom and your vision brightens. Cloudiness becomes clarity, and your surface becomes placid. By following the flow and by waiting patiently until the mud settled, you have become clean and clear. Where there was once agitation, there is now stillness. Where there was once obscurity there is now clarity. Where there was once darkness, there is now light. You see the sun in the sky, and you feel its rays reaching deep into your depths. The brightness is illuminating the many hidden places where once you kept your secrets. Now there are no secrets. All of your secrets are known. And in the light, you now see that your fears were wrong. You are known, you are loved, you are accepted, and you are embraced, just as you are. You are a part of the earth-body, you are part of the spirit-body, and you are joined with the myriad things in a deep and bottomless kinship.

You rise to the surface and drift up into the air, vaporized, turning into mist. Gathering together with other vapor, you form clouds and soar high over the mountains until you grow heavy and the draw of the earth pulls you back down in the form of rain. You fall through the air, spill over the ground, and gather together in rivulets and streams that slip into rivers that course through canyons, boulder fields, forests, and meadows on their way to the sea.

Feel the vast and rich power of the consciousness of allowance. Feel the freedom and the beauty of simply being, of learning to work with what is. Feel your authentic nature begin to blossom and flower in the atmosphere your allowance creates. Know that the power and grace you are experiencing could not have been manufactured by your busy mind with its schemes, fears, and endless cravings. Only in the consciousness of allowance can you tap into the infinite source from which we and all things come.

Now slowly begin to come back into your body. Feel your feet, your legs, your hands, your arms, your chest, your organs, your shoulders, your neck, your head, and your face. Notice that where there was once weariness and worry, there is now serenity and alert awareness. As you go forward into the rest of your day, your week, and your life, carry this serenity and alert awareness with you. Know that it is always with you and that not one of your steps leads away from it. Give yourself time to see with the eyes of allowance. Let yourself feel the sometimes subtle push and pull of the larger currents around you. Be free, be wise, and be true, but never confuse freedom, wisdom, and truthfulness with blind ambition, fearful striving, and pointless acquisition rooted in the consciousness of scarcity. Know that the universe is infinitely abundant, infinitely generative, and forever new.

We are here now, and we are the waves that rise up out of the one sea. Your hands are the hands that build the world. Your voice is the voice that speaks the truth. Your heart is the heart that loves without reservation. None of these things are to be accomplished. They are only to be allowed.

Take a deep, cleansing breath. And another. Open your eyes and see the world with new eyes. Go forward with a renewed conviction of your own infinite value, and of the infinite value of everyone you meet. Do the work that is yours to do, nothing more, nothing less. Let the joy of the work sink in. Know that your greatness is not solely your own doing but is born from a marriage of intention, engagement, and allowance. Be joyful but not proud. Know that you are a part of something glorious, but be humble enough to let it move through you without interference. Open your hands and loosen your grasp. Let the rising sun be your only monument, relish that you have another day to live and serve, and allow your life to be a testament, a call to others to rise up into the beauty and glory of their own lives. Our bliss depends on it.

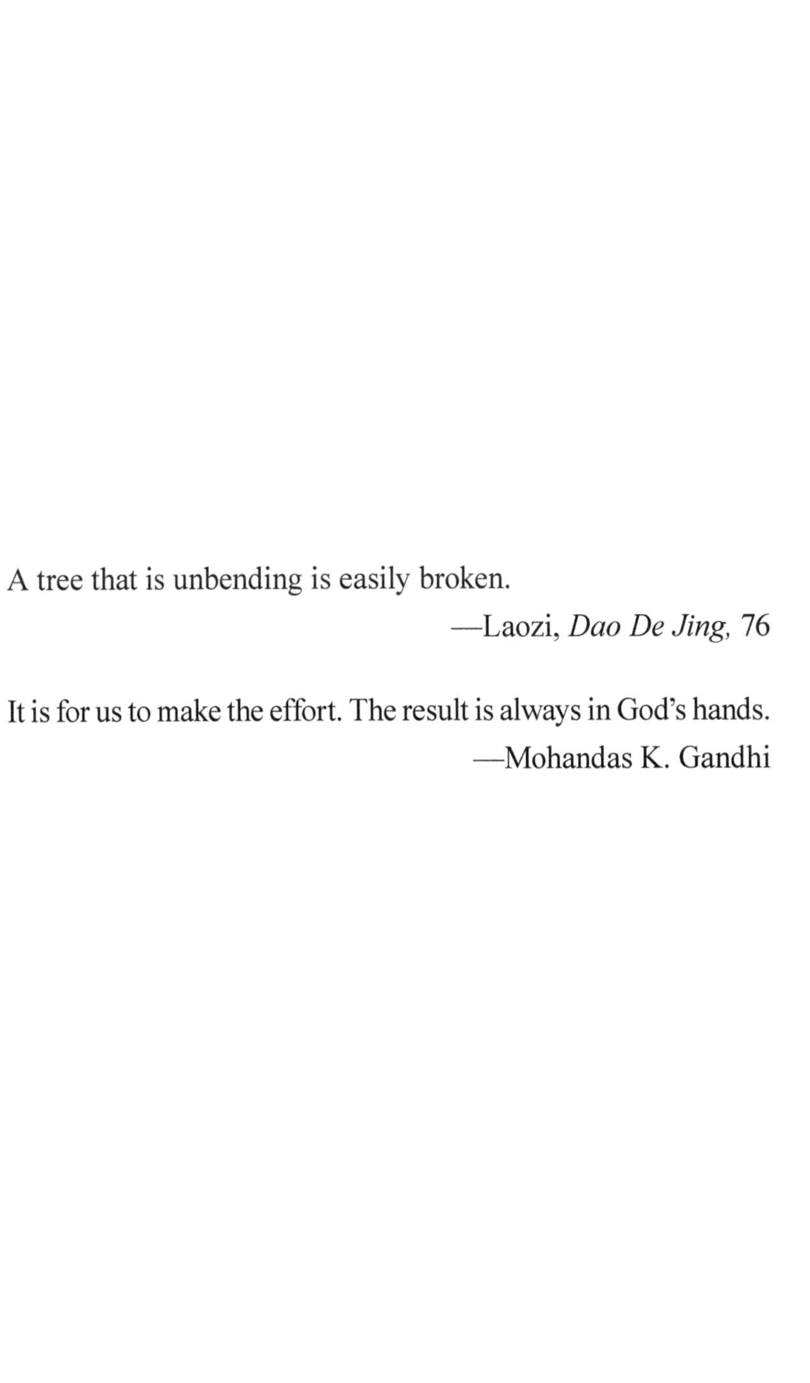

A tree that is unbending is easily broken.

—Laozi, *Dao De Jing,* 76

It is for us to make the effort. The result is always in God's hands.

—Mohandas K. Gandhi

The Fifth Stone

Chapter 5

Wisdom as Enjoyment

Live in the sunshine, swim the sea,
drink the wild air's salubrity.[102]
—Ralph Waldo Emerson

Renounce and Enjoy

Mahatma Gandhi was once asked by a reporter to describe his philosophy in three words. Without skipping a beat, he said, "Renounce and enjoy."[103] Renunciation was a word Gandhi often used to mean nonattachment, acceptance, and surrender. To renounce is to let go of the illusion that we are in control. It also means to break free from the mistaken notion that our idle desires are our authentic needs.

In our religious, spiritual, and philosophical lives, many of us practice discernment and great discipline as we learn to let go of the things we cannot control. For theists, renunciation often takes the form of "Let go and let God." For nontheists, it means acting without attachment to the fruits of action. But missing from all this arduous, well-intentioned, earnest, and often humorless work is the second half of Gandhi's formulation. Somewhere along the way, we forgot that this was supposed to be fun.

Where does enjoyment fit into all of this?

Philosophy has a bad reputation. The search for wisdom is often mischaracterized as a dour affair—wizened old men arguing about ancient texts. It's assumed that among philosophers, the worst thing you can do is break out in a fit of uncontrollable giggling. But what if pleasure and joy are an integral part of wisdom? What if pleasure and joy are an integral part of us? Is it even possible to imagine a fully satisfying and well-lived life without laughter and joy? How and why were we taken in by the assumption that wisdom and joy are two disconnected realms of experience? Let's use Gandhi's formula "renounce and enjoy" as a tool to open up an exploration of the role pleasure and enjoyment play in a life of wisdom.

As we travel the seven stone path, we see with increasing clarity that the stones or stages are deeply interconnected, and that each stage is taken up into the next. The stone of enjoyment, therefore, contains all the previous stones and is impossible without them.

In order to reach a deeper and more accurate understanding of the wisdom of enjoyment, we first need to untangle some knots surrounding the experience of pleasure and enjoyment.

Although enjoyment and pleasure are deeply interrelated, enjoyment is somewhat different from pleasure because enjoyment is internally self-sustaining and not dependent on outside stimuli. Pleasure, in contrast, is a response to a stimulus like receiving a gift, seeing a rose in bloom, or tasting delicious food. Here the pleasure only lasts as long as the stimulus. Lasting enjoyment, in contrast, is a subtler experience that reverberates long after the stimulus has passed.

Joy is not the result of a sufficient accumulation of pleasures. Nor is joy a possession. Joy has nothing to do with outer conditions. Joy is an inside job. As the word implies, enjoyment is the embodiment of joy. Joy is a complex, multifaceted state of being encompassing all of our faculties. It arises from within and leaves us with an unmistakable glow. No one has to tell you you're experiencing joy; you feel it in your body, mind, heart, and soul. And where does joy come from? What triggers it to well up within us? True enjoyment is the natural result of a life lived in the consciousness of acceptance, surrender, engagement, and allowance.

Yet pleasurable experiences can most certainly be enjoyed. We often speak of enjoying music, or a beautiful sunset. We do not, after all, live in a bubble. We are always interconnected with everything around us. Enjoyment may be a self-sustaining inside job, but it is deeply engaged with the world around it.

We can't help having mixed feelings about joy. Any feelings of joy are inevitably accompanied by a pang of longing—we know it won't last. The pain is even more acute when we're speaking of pleasures because pleasures are anchored to temporary outer conditions, and whatever enjoyment we take in them is particularly fleeting. In the experience of pleasure, we tend to slip out of the now and into the thought-stream to begin framing the experience as a memory and dressing it up in all sorts of descriptions and judgments. Instead of enjoying a beautiful sunset, we feel the need to say, whether aloud or in thought, "This is a beautiful sunset," turning a pure and unfiltered experience into a thought about a pure and unfiltered experience. Cut off from immediate experience and locked in the thought-stream, we peer out at a world just beyond the grasp of our conceptual mind. This strange and haunting quirk of consciousness is poignantly captured in a haiku by seventeenth-century Japanese poet Matsuo Basho: "Even in Kyoto / hearing the cuckoo's cry / I long for Kyoto."[104] To be both in the midst of beauty and caught up in the sadness of beauty's imminent absence—what strange and forlorn creatures we are. Our capacity to manufacture suffering from the raw materials around us is truly impressive.

In the realm of enjoyment, another problem awaits. Our pleasures are often tainted by feelings of guilt and shame: *I don't deserve this, I shouldn't be doing this, this is a waste of time, I'm busy, I have better things to do, it's wrong to enjoy myself because that means I'm being selfish.* Sometimes this comes in the form of religious prohibitions. In the dualistic religions of the West where the emphasis is often on obedience to divine commands, it sometimes seems as if every natural impulse is a sin. The portrait of the world that emerges from much of mainstream Christianity, for example, is of a fallen world that we are to resist and transcend. For the apostle Paul, even (and perhaps especially) our own bodies are dangerous minefields packed with soul destroying explosives—touch the wrong place, and *kaboom*. Pleasure, in this context, is fraught with danger.

What are we to make of all these conflicting messages regarding pleasure, happiness, and joy? Let's trace the conversation back to some ancient sources and see whether we can't clear up some of the confusion.

Hedonism

In classic Greek philosophy, hedonism is the view that pleasure is the highest good. It takes several forms, from the simple hedonism of Aristippus (c. 435–c. 356 BCE), who argued that all pleasures are good, to the subtler hedonism of Epicurus (341 BCE–270 BCE), who argued that pleasures of the mind are superior in quality to the pleasures of the body and are therefore to be preferred, even if in lesser amount or mixed with pain.

In his simple hedonism, Aristippus cared only about the quantity of pleasure: the more pleasure, the better, and tomorrow be damned. Epicurus, in contrast, was more interested in quality than quantity. The pleasure of reading a poem is of a higher order than the pleasure of scratching a mosquito bite. Epicurus favored long-term pleasure and was therefore willing to restrain his consumption of immediate pleasures if they interfered with his long-term well-being. Epicurus found simple food, exercise, and quiet friendship more pleasurable than the all-out debauchery of Aristippus. Hedonism, it turns out, is no simple thing.

In order to be effective, even the most committed hedonist must weigh their pleasures and calculate how best to achieve their goals. We have all postponed small, short-term pleasures for larger, long-term pleasures—saving money for a trip, or drinking less wine tonight to have a better, more pleasurable tomorrow.

Classical hedonism had a profound effect on the ethical philosophy known as utilitarianism. As expressed by its two most famous proponents, Jeremy Bentham (1748–1832) and John Stuart Mill (1806–1873), utilitarianism attempted to bring scientific rigor to the messy business of morality. Bentham identified what he called the principle of utility: everyone always acts so as to increase their pleasure and minimize their pain. According to Bentham, this is an unimpeachable principle, a law that has no exceptions. Even a single-celled amoeba in a Petri dish swims away from the painful electrode and toward the food. All beings are bound by this simple and irrefutable law. Freud called it the pleasure principle.

If I go to the gym to exercise, it's because I want the pleasures of losing weight, feeling stronger, being healthier, and looking better in a bathing suit. I calculate that the unpleasant aspects of exercise are outweighed by the benefits gained. Conversely, if I do not go to the gym, it's because I want the pleasure of avoiding the discomfort of vigorous cardiovascular training or weight lifting. Either way, says Bentham, I'm choosing the path that in my calculation results in the greatest pleasure. One of me is clearly wrong.

Some people smoke crack cocaine, and some people don't. Both are committed to maximizing their pleasure. Most of us agree that smoking crack is a very bad idea. This was precisely Epicurus's point. "Bad" people aren't morally deficient. They simply make unskillful calculations of self-interest. For Epicurus, immorality is purely a cognitive error, making the wrong choice and inadvertently reducing one's pleasure instead of increasing it. In the end, regular, vigorous exercise and avoiding crack results in a far more pleasurable life.

Utilitarians like Bentham and Mill argued that for centuries moral and ethical codes had been capriciously formulated to serve those in power, were based on unverifiable religious revelations institutionalized into dogma, or both. Utilitarianism sought to clear away the clutter. Because Bentham's principle of utility is rationally irrefutable, why not use it as the basis of a new and far more coherent ethical system? This is precisely the task Bentham and Mill set out to accomplish.

Applying the principle of utility to larger societal concerns turned hedonism into a radical political philosophy of great importance. For Bentham and Mill, the good is that which results in the greatest happiness for the greatest number of people—all people. With utilitarianism, we see the doors to universal human rights doctrines beginning to open because all human beings (and for Bentham all sentient beings) are part of the calculation, not just property-holding white males—an uncommon assertion in the eighteenth century. A political decision or a law is just only if it results in the greatest happiness for the greatest number of people, plain and simple. The political and societal fallout of this radical recalculation would reach far and wide.

To this day, many of our decisions—privately, in our families, in the workplace, and in our governments—are made using this utilitarian calculation.

The pleasure principle, to use Freud's term, is at work everywhere you look. Pleasure works. Evolutionary biologists point out that sex became pleasurable so that we would continue to propagate. If it didn't feel good, why would anyone bother?

If seeking pleasure is hardwired into our biology, is evolutionarily advantageous, and feels good, then why do we have so many mixed feelings about it? That's easy. Look at your own life and see how much trouble the pursuit of pleasure has gotten you into.

Maybe Epicurus was right. Maybe our moral failings have more to do with cognitive errors than with some metaphysically grounded moral weakness such as "original sin," We simply could do a much better job of manifesting our own long-term, enlightened self-interest. Pleasure itself was never the problem. The problem is our continual miscalculation of our own best self-interest and our consistent disregard of the value of others. Blaming pleasure for our problems is like an alcoholic blaming alcohol.

Setting aside the obvious damage done by poor decision-making, it is easy to see that pleasure is woven deeply into the experience of all sentient beings and at its best is a healthy and beautiful part of a deeply satisfying life. In traditional

Hinduism, we find a refreshing affirmation of the positive role pleasure plays in a well-lived life.

Kama

Why are we here? What is the purpose of life? What is the purpose of my life? What are legitimate and honorable pursuits? What should I be doing with these few short years I've been given? When these perennial philosophical questions arise, Hinduism has an answer: *kama*, *artha*, *dharma*, and *moksha*.

Kama means pleasure, artha means worldly or economic success, dharma means service, and moksha means liberation from the wheel of rebirth and returning to the source from which we and all things came. Each of these four is a legitimate pursuit if carried out with compassion for self and others and practiced within the bounds of social convention. All of these goals or aims are, at their best, authentic expressions of our divine nature. Let's focus on kama.

In chapter two, we discussed the Indian concepts of Brahman, Atman, and maya. Brahman is the name of the ground of being, the formless source from which all forms arise. Atman, or Self, is the presence of Brahman within us. And maya is the illusory nature of the perceptual field, the distracting surface perceptions and forms that arise from Brahman but obscure our direct experience of the oneness of the divine ground of Being. Where does pleasure fit into all of this?

If everything is a manifestation of Brahman, then the sensory, material world is just as sacred as the source from which it arises. In nondualistic philosophies like Vedanta, there is only one reality, and it is inherently sacred. Everything carries the stamp of God. Brahman is the vine, and all of the fleeting forms of the world are its branches. The beauty of the world and the pleasures inherent in human experience are to be enjoyed and celebrated with reverence and jubilation. In this worldview, the enjoyment of pleasure is a sacred activity. There are of course certain restrictions. The principle of ahimsa is always in place: cause no harm to ourselves or others. Also, it's important to respect legitimate group conscience by graciously aligning our behaviors with shared norms and social regulations out of respect and compassion for our neighbors, as long as those norms and regulations are just and honorable. Leaving aside for now the legitimate debate about whether or not specific rules or regulations are truly just, let's stick with general principles. The beauty and pleasure of the world is not to be suppressed, denied, avoided, shunned, or shamed. On the contrary, when we enjoy ourselves and the world, we are in fact honoring and celebrating the divine.

Every one of us was born with a healthy longing for kama. We are naturally drawn to experiences and pleasures that make us feel happy and joyful. Early on, it's pretty simple: candy, play, and laughter are enough. As we grow older, our tastes shift, and things get a little more complicated.

Experiencing the pleasures of the world isn't as easy as you'd think it would be. There are a lot of ways to get it right and even more ways to get it wrong. Wisdom teachers the world over have offered sage counsel on how best to navigate the path of kama. Buddha was no exception.

The Middle Path

As a young man, the Buddha grew up in a life of wealth and privilege. He enjoyed every indulgence. His father was trying to lead his son into a worldly life, a life of politics and achievement. But it was not to be. As he left the palace to pursue his search for wisdom in the forest, his practice grew more and more extreme. Soon he was a fervent ascetic, fasting and barely surviving in wretched conditions. Asceticism's aim is to conquer the appetites through denial and self-mortification. As in chemotherapy, the treatment is nearly as bad as the disease, and that's the point. In its efforts to clear the body of its destructive impulses, asceticism all but kills the host. Toward the end of this dangerous and arduous process of starvation and other forms of self-mortification, it was said that Buddha could grab his spine through his stomach. Despite his iron-willed self-discipline, asceticism did not deliver him to the freedom and insight he sought. Being above all a practical man, Buddha abandoned asceticism on the grounds that it simply didn't work. He began eating food and returned to his natural, healthy weight.

After a long period of meditation, he attained enlightenment and saw through the veil of illusion. He saw the interconnectedness and interdependence of all things, and he realized a deep and abiding compassion for the suffering of all sentient beings, vowing to devote his life to the alleviation of that suffering. So began the work of the Buddha.

He began to teach two core themes he would reiterate his whole life: the middle path and the Four Noble Truths. We discussed the Four Noble Truths in chapter one when we were exploring the wisdom of acceptance. But the middle path belongs here in the chapter on enjoyment.

The teaching of the middle path is simple. Sensual indulgence and slavery to pleasure is futile, vulgar, and selfish. Asceticism, it turns out, is equally futile, vulgar, and selfish. Each is the shadow of the other, and both fail to lead us to freedom. At core, both are rooted in egotism and isolation—one locks us in a pointless, never-ending cycle of craving, satiation, and dissolution, whereas the other declares war on the world and, closer to home, on our own bodies. Both extremes imprison us in a lonely, loveless narcissism. Only on the middle path, Buddha taught, do we have a shot at real happiness that is grounded in wellness and right relationship with the world, other people, and above all ourselves. Taking pleasure in food, family, friends, and the beauty of the world—this is the high art of good living and enables us to move freely through the world humbly sampling its pleasures without trying to control or grasp any of them. From this perspective, enjoyment is not a sin, nor is it a private prize to be coveted and hoarded. Enjoyment is simply a natural byproduct of a well-lived life, a life of conscious intentionality, generosity, love, community, creativity, and abundance. Our ability to take pleasure in life is a measure of our wellness.

Making Peace with the Material World

We aren't monks or ascetics, yet there is still a lot of submerged and destructive self-loathing lingering within us. Dualistic, world-denying ideologies of shame haunt us like ghosts. Many of us hold the view that the world is a fallen place, to be despised and largely avoided. Many of our religious ideologies divide the world into sacred and profane, clean and unclean, saved and damned. Selective scripture citing can be used to support this view. Jesus says he is not of this world. You can't serve two masters, God and the world, at the same time. Do not lay your treasure on the earth where moths and dust and thieves corrupt them, but lay your treasures in heaven. Where your treasure is, there will your heart be also. The apostle Paul, author of nearly half of the books in the New Testament, writes convincingly about how much he loathes his own body, how it is wretched and polluted with sin. This dualistic message is amplified in some churches but muted in others. Regardless, its echoes reverberate through us and set our feet in a battle stance—we are at war with the world, and as a result enjoyment is often viewed with guilt, suspicion, and distrust.

This world denial extends to our ambivalence about money. We want it but in the next breath mock those who have it. It's a confusing mess.

The Hindu teaching about kama and the Buddhist teaching about the middle path help us chart a course through this minefield. A closer look at the Bible reveals a similarly nuanced world-affirming perspective.

In the first two pages of Genesis, as God created each new thing—the light, the firmament, the land, the plants and animals—we are assured that "God saw that it was good." This affirmation is repeated seven times, capped with the refrain, "And it was very good." The message is clear: the world is not a malformed mistake. It is the master creator's finest work, a direct reflection of his loving wisdom. As we celebrate the world, we celebrate God.

In the nondualistic philosophies of India, the sacred perfection of the world is made even more explicit. Here we learn that all forms arise from the sacred energy of Brahman and therefore are themselves sacred. The beauty of the world is God's best work and is to be honored, not feared and despised. The medieval condemnation of the natural world has cost us plenty on a psychological and societal level. It's time to wake up from the dream of separateness.

The wise learn how to make peace with the material world.

At Play in the Field of Forms

When we view the forms of the world as expressions of Divine Mind, we move into accord with them. A beautiful garden, a canary yellow Ferrari, a Frank Lloyd Wright home, a Bach fugue, a butterfly in a Costa Rican rainforest—how can we meet these miracles with anything other than awe and rapture? In this frame of mind, we are free to pursue the cocreation of these beautiful manifestations. Build a home, buy a car, plant a garden, travel—each of these is a manifestation of the infinite abundance of the creative mind of the universe to be celebrated and honored. We don't own any of them; they simply pass through our hands for a while. The wise understand that everything we have is borrowed, not possessed, and we have to give it all back. We keep a light touch on the reins and a soft smile on our face as we note these beautiful, fleeting forms passing through our grasp. Our aesthetic appreciation is our prayer. We share easily because none of it belongs to us—it belongs to everyone. We love it all the more for its transitory nature. We open our hearts to it and to each other, knowing that only in our openness do we fully receive the bounty moving through and around us.

Correctly oriented to the forms around us, we are now ready to playfully engage with all of them. We experience great enjoyment as we meld our intention, discipline, and creativity with the raw materials we are given to build things of value. Without the fear-based restriction of egoic craving and the delusion of ownership, we are free to create in deep cooperation with the energies around us, becoming channels of manifestation. We write and perform music, design homes, cook feasts with our friends, solve scientific and medical mysteries, and bring healing where there once was disease, food where there once was hunger, and beauty where there once was banality. Like children building sandcastles at the shore, we enthusiastically create as if everything depended on it, yet we walk away at the end of the day knowing that the sand doesn't belong to us, and it never did. This is what it means to be at play in the field of forms—reaching without grasping, creating without craving, holding without clinging, caring without attachment, bonding without binding, and stewardship without ownership. We do it because we can. We do it because that's who we are. We engage with the world as fully as possible because when we do we feel our own joy bubbling inexorably to the surface.

The Importance of Play

When children play, they often pretend to be something they're not. They playfully become pirates, dragons, monsters, superheroes, cowboys, princesses, soldiers, wild animals, or space aliens. Playing roles and taking masks on and off is good practice for the more serious transformations we must undergo in adulthood if we are to actualize our potential. In our lives we will play many roles, and we must play them earnestly and well. By playing behind masks at a young age, we begin to soften our attachment to all masks, most importantly the mask we wear when all the other masks come off—our persona. Beneath all of the roles we play is this thing called *me*. Eventually, we realize that it too is a mask. Through a lifetime of inquiry and reflection, we come to understand that our persona is just another role, a creation, a transient and contingent circumstance we employ for convenience sake, despite its insubstantial nature. The fundamentally indefinable nature of consciousness defies all masks. Yet use them we must. Play becomes a deadly serious craft.

This is not to say that we're all a bunch of phonies—quite the contrary. It is through the roles we play that we interact with each other in profoundly meaningful ways as husbands, wives, fathers, mothers, brothers, sisters, citizens, artists, mechanics, musicians, poets, laborers, and professionals of all stripes, deeply rooted in our place along the gender identity and sexual orientation continuum. But we are so much more than the roles we play and the labels we bear. When we mistakenly confuse our roles and labels with our indefinable essential nature, a danger arises. We forget that we are playing a role, performing a function, and fulfilling a larger purpose, and instead we become the mask. This pathological conflation of ego and role is the root of much personal and societal dysfunction. Police officers who lose their humanity and instead become antagonists in their own community, mistakenly believing that their power lies not in their compassionate and selfless sacrifice for the greater good but in the indiscriminate use of force and the dehumanization of innocent citizens, is a painful reminder of the great damage caused by becoming the uniform. Maintaining constant awareness that each of the roles we play is an opportunity to serve and not an opportunity for self-aggrandizement keeps us out of harm's way. Who knew play would be this important?

It is unfortunate that only musicians, athletes, and actors refer to their work as play. Even if we are not playing music, playing a game, or playing a character on stage or on film, we are still very much playing an essential role in the function of our family, our workplace, and our community. We each bring to our work a rich and complex set of tools and sensibilities that no one else has; what we do matters. Calling life a game trivializes it, but the fact remains that play and work are more alike than different. If each of us entered into our work with a sense of play, wide currents of creativity would open up revitalizing our projects, inspiring our colleagues, and encouraging our loved ones. When we laugh, we open up, we soften our grip, we see things anew, and we release our fixed and rigid notions of ourselves and how the world is supposed to be. When you're serious, you're stifled. When you're laughing, you're learning.

Our Blissful Nature

Although Brahman is ineffable, that is, cannot be expressed with words or concepts, the Indian sages nevertheless attribute three qualities to it: *Sat-Chit-Ananda*. *Sat* means true being, unlimited existence, or boundless reality. *Chit* means true consciousness, unlimited awareness, or boundless knowing. *Ananda* means absolute and unlimited bliss. Sat-Chit-Ananda are the triune qualities or attributes of Brahman, the universal ground of being. And because all reality is a manifestation of Brahman, including us, we too embody these three qualities, even if we're not aware of it. We are at core unlimited, boundless, and blissful. Therefore when we experience joy, we are not simply responding favorably to external stimuli—we are drawing to the surface the submerged reality of our own essential being. So-called outer experiences simply inspire or stimulate our inherent joy. This is why when we feel joy, we feel more deeply connected to everything around us, not less. Joy draws us up out of the illusion of isolation and into our natural interconnectedness. Joy dispels loneliness the way dawn dispels darkness.

If our true nature is unlimited existence, boundless awareness, and absolute bliss, then enjoyment is nearer to us than our jugular vein. Joy is our nature, and enjoyment is our natural state, not a special or rare experience to be arduously sought and covetously grasped. It is as simple as breathing, sleeping, or being.

From this perspective, we realize that increasing our experience of joy might be as rudimentary as allowing it. Rather than having to manufacture enjoyment from scratch, the process becomes one of subtraction—removing the obstacles that hinder our naturally joyful state. Coming as far as we have with the seven stone process, we know that when we are grounded in acceptance, fully surrendered, alertly engaged, and softening into allowance, enjoyment arises on its own without effort or striving. The simple act of living begins to glow with inner beauty as enjoyment sweeps away the sadness and worry that often plague our thought-addled minds. We find joy in the most ordinary of places—a clean kitchen, an open window, the smell of bread, a birdsong, a remembered kiss, a cup of tea, a quiet acquiescence with all that is, as it is. Here, there is nothing but joy.

When Joseph Campbell's students came to him with their agonizing life decisions—Should I do what my father wants me to do? Should I do what my mother wants me to do? Should I do what society wants me to do?—Campbell famously counseled them to "follow their bliss."[105] Inspired by the Hindu concept of Ananda, bliss is that sizzling, vibrant, electrifying sense of aliveness that arises from within when you begin living in accord with your deepest and most significant purpose. It isn't going to be easy, but it is going to be amazing. In this sense bliss becomes crucial information, an inner light that guides you along your authentic path. When you are following your bliss, the universe begins to conspire in your favor. Conversely, when you ignore the call to your hero's adventure, life becomes a difficult struggle plagued by setbacks, blocked by powerful others, and in every sense miserable. Following your bliss doesn't solve all your problems—far from it. In fact, it will stir up problems you've never had before. But as your heart grows clearer about the nature of your true purpose, you will feel your wings lifted by a wind not of your own making. When you begin to follow your bliss, when you begin to live in accord with your true inner purpose, you will have all the evidence you need that you are on the right track. You will be gripped by the conviction that nothing and no one could knock you off the beam of your true life no matter how hard they tried.

Our Inner Purpose

Aristotle thought so highly of well-being and happiness that he made it the cornerstone of his entire philosophical project.

Aristotle set out to address a question his mentor Plato left unanswered: What guides the process of change in the universe? Why do things transform and evolve? Where is everything headed?

His answer was surprisingly modern. Everything is evolving, Aristotle argued, toward its highest state. An acorn's inner purpose, or *telos*, is to become a thriving oak tree. A colt's growth is guided toward the goal of becoming a magnificent horse. Everything contains within itself a blueprint of its own perfection, an ideal toward which it is moving. If the inner purpose of an acorn is to become a thriving oak tree, and the inner purpose of a colt is to become a strong, beautiful horse, what then is the inner purpose of a human being? What is our telos? To what end are we moving?

The answer, said Aristotle, is eudaimonia. From one angle, eudaimonia means happiness. From another angle, it means the deep satisfaction arising from the achievement of excellence. The inner purpose guiding all our processes of transformation is the vision, held deep within the fiber of our being, of a fully realized and magnificent life, a life in which all of our potentials are realized. The restlessness and longing that plagues our every step is the natural urge to push through our fears and take the necessary risks to bring our innate excellence to fruition. Maybe it's time we rebrand our anxiety as sacred restlessness.

Methods for self-actualization vary around the world, and what Aristotle had in mind differs from the meditative traditions of the east. For Aristotle, the principle tool for achieving eudaimonia was reason. Only our intellect, he argued, possessed the necessary skill to properly analyze and discern the path to mastery.

For Aristotle, we realize eudaimonia by realizing our excellence, and we realize our excellence by cultivating our virtues. The Greek word for virtue was *arête*, meaning excellence of function. When something perfectly performs the function for which it was designed, it has arête. When a saw is sharp, when a magnifying lens is clean and focused, when a flute's tone is clear, it has arête. It stands to reason that for a human being to achieve excellence of function, or arête, we must cultivate our virtues. Happiness and competence go hand in hand. Aristotle identified a number of specific virtues such as courage, self-esteem, and friendliness. When we manifest courage, healthy self-esteem, and friendliness, we attain excellence of function and realize our eudaimonia. But there are many ways to get it wrong.

Much like Buddha's middle path, Aristotle argued that virtue was a middle point between the two extremes of excess and deficit. If one has too much courage, for example, one is foolhardy and rash. If one has too little courage, one is a coward. Both extremes are equally ineffective vices.

Too much self-esteem is vanity. Too little is self-loathing. Both are destructive to our own well-being and the well-being of others.

Too much friendliness is obsequiousness—an annoying, overbearing, and neurotic attachment to the other. Embodying too little friendliness leaves one cold and aloof. Both rob you of your natural inclination to bond well with others. Our excellence lies between the extremes of excess and deficit.

How do we find and stay in the virtuous middle ground between these vices of excess and deficit? According to Aristotle, the only way to attain the golden mean was through the proper exercise of reason. Only our rational faculty, he argued, can discern the difference between good self-esteem and bad self-esteem, or determine how much courage is the right amount. Without reason, we are doomed to get it wrong.

The best way to cultivate the faculty of reason is to train it and use it. Proper education, according to Aristotle, strengthens the faculty of reason thereby equipping us to lead better lives. Aristotle's teacher Plato believed that the best educational curriculum consisted largely of four core subjects: geometry, gymnastics, music, and dialectics. Geometry trained the mind in quantitative and spatial reasoning, perfectly preparing us for later projects like logical, ethical, and philosophical reasoning. Gymnastics trained and strengthened the body, the vehicle that carries us through the well-lived life. Music synthesized mental and physical activity into a coherent whole, integrating our energies and harmonizing our analytical, emotional, and aesthetic lives. And finally, dialectics was that field of advanced analytical thinking so necessary to the philosophic life. (More on that in chapter seven.) The real purpose of education is not indoctrination or career training; it is nothing less than the burnishing and cultivation of the whole person, an arduous process designed to facilitate the fullest realization of our innate potential as conscious beings. Without proper cognitive strengthening, one cannot become a skilled ethical thinker. For Plato and Aristotle, it is hard to be truly good if your mind isn't functioning at its highest capacity.

After reason and education, says Aristotle, comes habituation. By exercising our reason over and over in the proper comportment of our lives, we build good habits. Repeated behaviors become habits, and habits construct character. We become what we do. Our lives are the sum total of our decisions and actions.

Finally, when we have consciously constructed our character through rational deliberation and habituation, we have in fact brought to fruition our deepest innate potentials. We have become beings of reason, sensitivity, courage, strength, friendliness, and humility—in a word, we have become excellent. We have become virtuous by embodying the virtues. And when we are virtuous, our eudaimonia is realized. We are, in a word, happy. In Aristotle's portrait, then, joy comes not from receiving outward rewards or pleasurable stimuli. Real joy wells up from within, arising from the realization of our innate potential. This is the wisdom of enjoyment.

The causal link between reason, education, habituation, character, and a deep and abiding well-being (eudaimonia) is the most inspiring contribution of the Greek philosophical project. Is there anything more heartbreaking than unrealized potential? When we are on our death bed, it won't be our failures we will regret—it will be the risks untaken. As the Afghan saying goes, "What a shame, to die like a pomegranate, with all of one's seeds still locked up inside."

This is why for the Greeks, courage was the most important virtue of all. Without courage, one cannot muster the will to face the great risks inherent in the daunting process of becoming who we really are. Old habits must be abandoned, comforts eschewed, and unknown paths traversed. Becoming fully human is not for the timid. Without courage we cannot fully love. Without courage we cannot fully live.

As discussed in chapter three, the only way to become courageous is by practicing courage. This is why the agricultural metaphor of cultivation is so powerful. When we cultivate a plant, we pay close attention to the composition of the soil, the amount of sunlight, and the frequency of watering. Cultivating our excellence is no different. What is the composition of the soil in which we are planted? What images, thoughts, and information do we allow to take up precious space in our minds? What kind of people do we spend time with? What do we do with the hours of our days? How carefully and consciously do we design the conditions of our lives? This is the soil in which we grow. In many ways large and small, we are shaped by our environment. So choose wisely. This is not a philosophy of determinism; we are not made entirely by our environment. But it matters a great deal. Still, it is our choices in the face of these conditions that shape our lives.

Perhaps nothing is as influential as the friends we keep. Our friends influence the way we talk, the way we dress, the way we think, and the way we live. Our peer group sets a thousand boundaries between cool and uncool, between sacred and taboo, and so much of our individuality is forged in the fire of our resistance and acquiescence to these restrictions. Dancing to the music of conformity—just enough in and just enough out—constructs our personality, an insidious process so mysterious it's impossible to know where acculturation ends and autonomy begins. Our friends impact us in ways we will never understand. They are the soil in which our lives take root, lending shape to our branches and breadth to our reach. Our friends become a part of us just as we become a part of them.

The Philosophy of Friendship

We enjoy our friends, and they enjoy us. Good friends open the door to enjoyment because they disarm us and draw our hearts to the surface. They put us in touch with the simple pleasures: good food, laughter, and the joy of simply being alive. In their presence, we drop our guard and experience the unusual sensation of complete and total acceptance. We are loved for who we are, not for what we are or how we benefit others.

Friends are an opportunity to experience humanity up close and personal in someone other than ourselves. Like a mirror, they reveal the patterns of our own lives. In coming to know them better, we come to know ourselves better.

A friend is an ally. They join fortunes and talents with us and stand with us against the inevitable challenges of life. They remind us that we are never alone. A friend is also a competitor, a rival in a good-natured but spirited contest to see who can run faster, jump higher, or best the other in a million other ways. They remind us that we must push ourselves to burnish the skills needed to thrive in the challenging tasks ahead.

A friend is also a place to practice the virtues of empathy and compassion, virtues that deepen our bond with the entire realm of conscious beings, awakening us to the infinite presence within us and all things.

A friend is another pair of hands, another strong back, and another pair of legs to bind, lift, and carry the load.

Because we love our friends and accept them for who they are, we are taught to love ourselves and accept ourselves as we are.

No matter what our friends have done, we are willing to look past their mistakes and see the innate goodness within them, just as they do for us. This teaches us to see ourselves not as the sum of our mistakes but as the innocence from which we came. The scorecard doesn't matter. What matters is what happens next. Our friends remind us that the most important question is not *What have you done?* but *Who are you now?*

Our friends see through our pretense and know who stands behind the mask. With a single glance, we are laid bare. With the wave of a hand, we are called back into the center of the tribe. With a laugh we are forgiven for our unskillful slight.

The art of cultivating friendships is the work of a lifetime. We begin practicing early and never finish. With plenty of errors behind us, we muddle through relying on the grace and generosity of the kind souls we meet along the way. No matter where you go, no matter what you do, there are always others around you, dancing with you in a delicate balance between distance and intimacy. There are no rules about how far to lean in or how far to lean out. Every moment is a renegotiation. It's best not to overthink it. The best friendships achieve a natural equilibrium, an effortless grace; that's what makes them so appealing. They are a welcome respite from the exhausting vigilance often required by social interaction. In the presence of our friends, we are free. We can breathe deeply, feel what we want to feel, think what we want to think, say what we want to say, and do what we want to do. Our friends give us a taste of the rarest of experiences—authenticity. When the charade is dropped, the real self emerges. This is perhaps the greatest gift our friends give us: the pleasure and enjoyment of ourselves.

Wild Strawberries

We came out of the trees and stood on the meadow that sloped down to the gravel beach where the boats were waiting, the boats that would take us across Chilkat Inlet and back to Skagway. We had spent the morning hiking through fragrant conifers and canoeing across a glacial lake to stand on the cusp of Davidson Glacier in the heart of the Tongass National Forest. Our eyes and hearts were full of the raw power of the Alaskan wilderness—we felt expanded, stronger, and more alive. Fields of bright pink fire weed as far as the eye could see, distant mountains capped in mist, old growth forests of spruce and fir, and underfoot soft moss and a chaos of grasses like walking on clouds. Then we saw them: wild strawberries, deep red and small, their floral perfume turning the air to candy, every breath dessert. Our guide heard our unspoken question.

"Go ahead," he said.

He only had to say it once.

Here in a land where glaciers grind granite into dust so fine the rivers run milky gray, where 800-pound bears and 1,200-pound moose tamped down the paths we walked, it was difficult to understand how something as fragile and delicate as a wild strawberry could exist. How could this rugged earth exude such luxury? Kneeling in the meadow, plucking one and then another, the sweetness freed me of the need to understand.

To this day, I am hushed into reverence whenever I think back on that moment. It is hard to believe how beautiful the world is sometimes, how generous, how abundant, and how miraculous. There on that patch of Alaskan wilderness, I kneeled in the middle of something sacred, at once ordinary and sublime.

When I finally looked up, I was alone. Everyone had gone ahead to board the boats that would take us north to Skagway. Hurrying down to the shore, the taste of strawberries warm on my tongue, I knew I would never set foot in this meadow again, that this moment was slipping away. I felt in my bones the sweet sadness that always comes with the wisdom of enjoyment. As Basho so beautifully captured it, "Even in Kyoto, hearing the cuckoo's cry, I long for Kyoto."

I took with me the knowing that the ability to enjoy one's life has nothing to do with exotic locales or extraordinary experiences. You can break open anywhere. Every moment holds in its core a miracle, its wild strawberry. It is not a new world we need, but new eyes with which to see the world. Enjoyment is not an endpoint that comes only after a long process of craving, cleverness, travel, or acquisition; it is a natural by-product of a well-lived life rooted in broken-open awareness. When we see the boundless beauty within every moment, we taste the sweetness of the joy that is our birthright, a joy that is the marrow of life itself—not something earned, not something achieved, but something received, like grace. Learning to take the time, to slow down and open our eyes—this is the wisdom of enjoyment.

As we have seen again and again in this process, after the practice of acceptance comes the wisdom of surrender. From that stance, we are able to engage with the processes of our lives in a way that truly serves our needs and the needs of others. Then we learn the wisdom of allowance—that our efforts go further when aligned with the larger forces around us. And when we have reoriented our lives along these lines, locks begin to fall open. The joy that was always ours but obscured by mistaken thinking begins to rise into our field of awareness. Suddenly we see that life is not a struggle—it is a beautiful field of possibility. We stop defining every situation in our life as a problem, gradually coming to enjoy the well-being washing over us, no matter how heartbreaking the arising and fading of forms. In our wise hearts, we know the strawberries will only be here for a while. The boat is waiting to take us to another shore. And winter will again come to cover everything in ice. But in this now moment, we are safe, we are warm, there are good people on the path with us, and the beauty of the world steals our words, heals our wounds, and fills our souls with a bounty that cannot be measured. Enjoyment was never about ownership. It is rightfully a nameless experience of the symmetry between our being and the being of the cosmos, a oneness that transcends the concepts and objects of the world of forms. Beauty and joy take us back to our original nature as spiritual beings at play in the field of forms. Everywhere we are, we are home. And in this knowing, there is a joy that has no beginning and no end.

A Wise Person

At peace with the world in a deep state of acceptance, committed to surrendering to our highest good, vibrantly engaged in the processes of our own lives, allowing and moving in accord with the energies surrounding us, a wise person receives and embraces the enjoyment inherent in the well-lived life.

A wise person practices ongoing renunciation, letting go of cravings, attachments, judgments, and the need to control, allowing their natural state of enjoyment to arise.

A wise person understands that joy is different than pleasure. Fleeting pleasures come from the fortuitous arrangement of outside stimuli. Joy arises from within and has little to do with outer circumstance.

A wise person practices prudence by carefully assessing their own long-term best self-interest, choosing experiences that create lasting happiness and avoiding experiences that are, in the final assessment, destructive.

A wise person understands that their enjoyment is intricately intertwined with the enjoyment of those around them, and they put themselves neither above nor beneath others in the pursuit of happiness.

A wise person understands that joy is a natural and healthy way of being in the world, a world spun from the web of being where each strand reflects the whole. Nothing is insignificant. Seen through the eyes of aesthetic rapture, the world is bereft of triteness. The beauty of the natural world; the boundless expression of artistic creation; the shimmering radiance of music and dance; the celestial marriage of reason, mathematics, physics, form, and design that is architecture; the wisdom of our animal and human friends; the yield of our gardens and the bounty of our table—every chef a shaman, every meal a sacrament, every gesture an absolution, every word a song, every thought a prayer. The very act of living is a ritual participation in the sacred energy of the cosmos. Apprehending all of this, the wise person is lifted by an ever-present undercurrent of joy, even in the midst of pain and loss.

A wise person walks the middle path between extremes, seeing the destructive egotism of both asceticism and sensual excess—the ascetic and the glutton are equally self-obsessed even if they manifest their pathology in opposite ways. A wise person understands that the practice of temperance and moderation in one's appetites increases one's joy, not diminishes it. Ironically, it is the moderate person who more ably maximizes their pleasure and happiness, demonstrating hedonism's subtler dynamics.

A wise person knows that the material, sensory world is neither good nor evil; those moral judgments pertain only to human benefit or loss. The world is a dynamic energy field filled with life forms vying for survival. It is full of beauty and terror. The very maintenance of our lives depends on the taking of other life. Yet in the depths of our awareness, we know that we are not these bodies, we are not these fleeting forms. The inner witness, the spiritual core, views the transitory nature of forms as a beautiful array without victims, without perpetrators—only participants in a never-ending cycle of arising and fading and arising. A wise person knows that they don't own any of it; everything is borrowed, and they must give it all back, sometimes suddenly and without warning. In a deep state of acceptance, surrender, engagement, allowance, and enjoyment, they play in the field of forms, celebrating and honoring each and every one of them.

A wise person understands and appreciates the value of play. They throws themselves into the activities of their life with the enthusiasm of a child, taking on the roles their responsibilities require with the abandon and commitment of a master actor. Never pretending, always authentic, the wise person nevertheless tackles the challenges of life without taking any of it personally. The wise person knows that doing what is right need not be a somber, dour affair. They take seriously their aims while playfully executing them.

A wise person cultivates their sensitivities to the subtlest of energy fields, detecting the blissful core within all things. They comes to know their own nature as Sat-Chit-Ananda—truth, awareness, and bliss, an unimpeachable realm of being deep beneath the waves of becoming that rise and fall on the surface.

A wise person comes to realize their inner purpose, planted in them from the very beginning like a seed, and cultivates their faculties of reason in order to better manifest their potential. They seek education in all its forms; they use their faculty of reason to find the golden mean, thereby realizing the excellence of courage, self-esteem, and kindness. Through repetition, their conscious choices become habit, constructing a quality of character strong enough to withstand the vagaries ahead. By manifesting their own inherent excellence, they experience a deep and abiding satisfaction—the joy of becoming their best and most authentic self.

A wise person knows the value of friendship and knows that it is only in community with others that we develop our highest potential thereby realizing our best life. A friend is a place to forgive and be forgiven, to accept and be accepted, to love and be loved. A friend is a welcoming shelter from the indifference of the world. A friend is a coconspirator in the game of life, a confidant, an ally, and a bullshit detector. A friend is an opportunity to practice the arts of conversation, imagination, negotiation, cooperation, collaboration, surrender, and assertion—in other words, all the arts necessary to create a successful and vibrant life. A wise person realizes that their fate and the fate of their friends is inextricably bound together, and when we look after each other, we are practicing the high art of self-love.

A wise person cultivates a heightened sense of aesthetic appreciation for the beauty inherent in every moment, every object, and every compound phenomenon. The flash of a yellow oriole in a cypress tree, the taste of rain, an elegantly wrought sentence, a sudden and unexpected act of kindness, the glow of twilight on a granite monolith, circling bats over a campfire, the simple comfort of a café, the smell of newspaper, the grasp of a child's hand, a wave on the shore, a cloud, a tear—all of these are miracles, ordinary and sublime, given freely by a universe incapable of anything but infinite abundance. The more we open, the more we receive. A wise person has the eyes to see, the ears to hear, the hands to touch, the heart to feel, and the mind to know the pouring forth of beauty that has no beginning and no end.

A wise person makes peace with the material world. Through laugher they continue to emerge from their egoic shell and enter the wider world, at play in the field of forms without attachment to any of them. They know that enjoyment is not a sin, nor is it a reward for enduring the necessary evils of work, accomplishment, duty, and obligation. Enjoyment is the natural state inherent in every experience, every endeavor, and every moment. Enjoyment is simply how life tastes when it is lived well.

Closing Meditation

As in previous chapters, let's end our time of inquiry into the wisdom of enjoyment with a period of guided meditation. The time for thinking is done. Now it is time to allow the insights we have discovered to sink down into our awareness, beneath the busyness of the thought-stream.

If you are listening, close your eyes. If you are reading, soften your gaze and relax the muscles in your face, neck, and shoulders. Bring your attention to your breathing. Take several long, slow, deep, cleansing breaths. Allow your breathing to settle into its natural rhythm.

As we did in previous meditations, visualize in your mind's eye that you are sitting on the bank of a slow-moving river. Now imagine that you are drifting out over the surface of the river. There is no one else around. You are alone in the wilderness. But you feel utterly safe and at home in this beautiful place.

Imagine now that you are slowly entering the water and sinking beneath the surface. The water is warm and welcoming. Soon you are completely submerged and slipping down through the soft current. Your mind doesn't understand how, but you are able to breathe. You come to rest on the soft, sandy river bottom.

Around you is a circle of five smooth, round stones. You are in the center of this circle. They are the stones of acceptance, surrender, engagement, allowance, and enjoyment.

You reflect on the path so far. You are awash in gratitude for the transformation underway; you have realized insights and released misunderstandings. You have felt the freedom of learning to accept the things you cannot change. You have known the paradoxical power that comes with the consciousness of surrender. You have found your feet and stood strong in the field of action rooted not in attachment and egotism but in service and selflessness. You have committed yourself to mindful and courageous action by embodying the truth that the best actions are rooted in the consciousness of allowance where one's energies move in accord with the larger forces around us. And finally, you have opened a door to a new and deeper understanding of enjoyment.

In the center of your abdomen, just below the navel, you begin to feel a subtle tingling sensation, a vibrant aliveness, a powerful but subtle energy field that begins to radiate throughout your entire body. It is a pleasurable wave of enjoyment. It moves through your body-mind like ink in water, moving from cell to cell and synapse to synapse, replacing weariness, lethargy, tension, and fear with the warm light of joy. It feels right. It feels normal. It feels at once rare and entirely ordinary. It feels like this is where you belong. It feels like home.

As you bask in the light of this deep and abiding joy, you notice that it welled up from within; it did not enter you from outside. It was not granted to you when you performed the right absolutions or sacrificed the proper offerings. It is of your own essence. Joy is the natural state of your own infinite and eternal being. It has always been there. You did not create it, earn it, buy it, or grasp it. You have simply, gently, lovingly, consciously, and carefully removed the obstacles that kept it hidden. The humility of acceptance and surrender increased your awareness of it. The courage of engagement helped you open the channels to it. The wisdom of allowance helped you harmonize with it. And now you have only to receive it, release it, realize it, and become it.

If regrets arise for the many years you spent in bondage to ignorance, for the many years you denied your birthright of a joyful life, release these regrets and let them drift downstream. We did the best we could. We only do what we know how to do. We did not know then what we know now. We looked for pleasure in external things—material objects, power over others, self-obsession, and fear-based acquisition. We didn't understand that joy was already and always ours, awaiting only the stillness and clarity that comes with wisdom.

Now we know with great clarity and resounding authority that joy is our essential nature, and it can never be taken from us, even if every form faded and the entire universe disappeared, for joy is the essential quality of Being itself, not the possession of one man or one woman. It was never ours to crave or achieve or hold or own. When we open our hands and open our hearts, our joy does not flee from us. Quite the contrary, it increases manyfold, for joy is allowed as much as attained, realized as much as received.

And with this deepening understanding, we now understand that there is no meaningful or lasting boundary between our joy and the joy of others; there is only one joy washing through all of us, and any man's joy is my joy, any woman's joy is my joy. All joy is our joy.

Joy is a decision. Joy is an allowance. We have only to open the valve and let it rise in us like groundwater seeping up through sand.

It is all there in our memories, the golden moments of our lives when joy overcame us. Looking back at those moments, we see now with new eyes that, yes, joy seems to be triggered by a fortuitous alignment of outer elements and circumstances, but the joy itself came from within us, not from the external world and its fleeting prizes. Joy was our response. And only now we realize we were the source of it all along.

We breathe deeply into this truth. We feel its inner authority. We know its unimpeachable reign. It is a bell that cannot be unrung, a song that cannot be unsung, a sermon that cannot be unspoken, and a vision that cannot be unseen. As we begin to rise up out of the depths of our meditation, we carry it with us into the hours, days, weeks, and months ahead. Today will feel different because of this. We will never have to look far to see beauty, to feel joy, and to know in our bones the constancy of this immutable truth: we are joy embodied and the only way to hinder it is to fall asleep to who and what we really are. But we are awakening now, and we cannot go back to sleep.

Slowly and gently, begin to move your hands, arms, and shoulders. Let your attention come back to the room, back to your body. Notice the sounds around you. Open your eyes. Stretch. Feel the peace and light coursing through you. Know that you are this peace and light. It isn't happening to you. It is happening through you. You are that.

Give thanks to the efforts—your own and the efforts of others—that have brought you here. In the consciousness of gratitude, there is great power. Know that we are on an important journey. We are learning how to live more deeply, more truthfully, more freely, and more joyfully. This is a good thing. Whatever we are giving up to move in this new direction pales in comparison to what we are receiving and what we will continue to receive. For all of these things, we are profoundly grateful.

Feel the love that you have for each other, for yourself, and for the beautiful world and all its creatures. Let that love be the echo of your awakening, like the peal of a monastery bell in a quiet, sleeping village just before dawn.

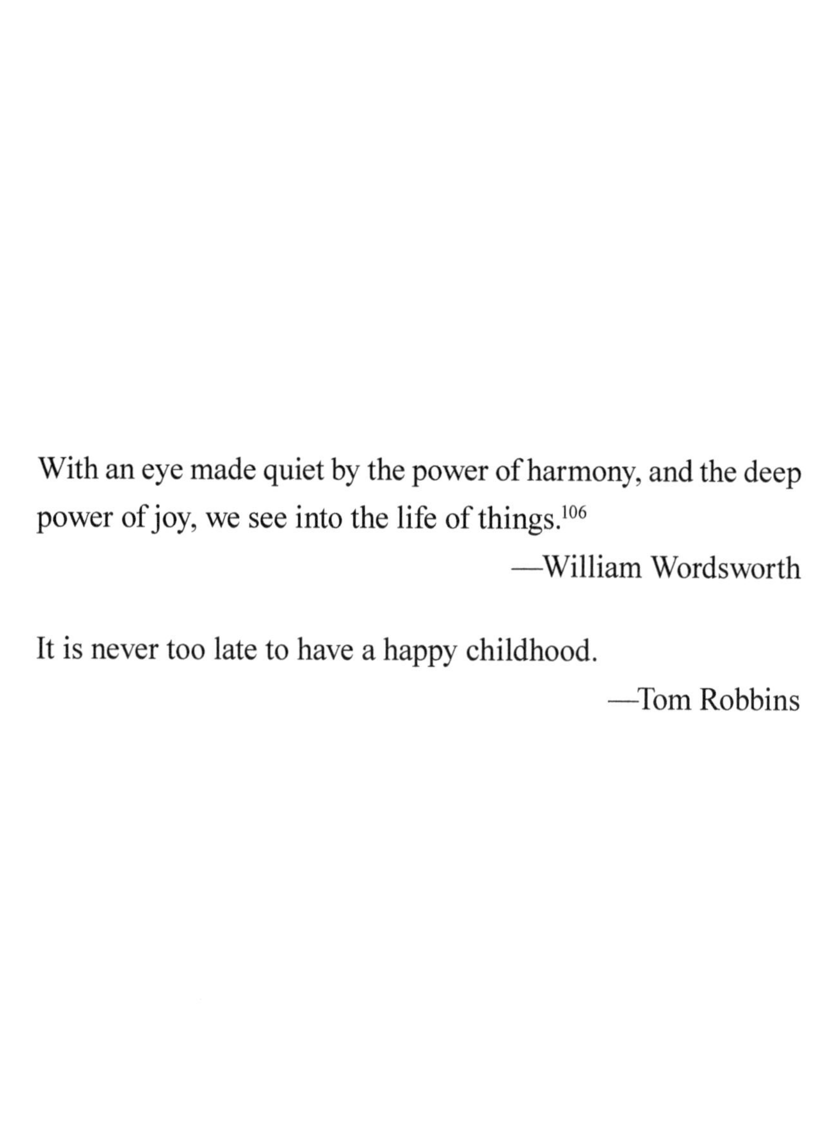

With an eye made quiet by the power of harmony, and the deep power of joy, we see into the life of things.[106]

—William Wordsworth

It is never too late to have a happy childhood.

—Tom Robbins

The Sixth Stone

Chapter 6

Wisdom as Love

Mind creates the abyss—the heart crosses it.[107]
—Nisargadatta Maharaj

Love Is All

Love is the name we have given to an indefinable, limitless experience in consciousness that has the power to transform everything it touches. Love changes us. Love changes everything. It is both the cause and the effect of our greatest achievements, our finest art, and our best life. Love is so much more than a feeling. It is conviction, decision, commitment, and courage. Love carries us across every chasm and shapes the very way we see the world. Through the eyes of love, we and everything we see are renewed.

As we learn to embody the first five steps of the seven stone path, we fall in love with the world in a new and vitalizing way. Acceptance opened the door, surrender led us through, engagement helped us find our way, allowance aligned our energy with the energies around us, and enjoyment shined like a rising sun. With all of the earlier stages embodied, we feel a deepening richness envelope our hearts and minds. It is no longer possible to feel separate from the interdependent consciousness coursing through all things. Love renders mute all our words, concepts, and theories. Without ownership or ego, we allow our hearts to open and lead us into a direct experience of the mystery beyond all thought, yet present within all things. There is no longer a conflict between egoism and altruism, between self-interest and working for the good of those around us. In this dawning awareness we become ardent and skillful caretakers of ourselves and others.

The Nature of Love

Other languages are more nuanced in their handling of the cluster of experiences that come under the heading of the English word *love*. The Greeks have four words, the Italians five. In Sanskrit, there are ninety-six words for *love*. In English, we ask one little word to do all the heavy lifting.

The ancient Greeks recognized four distinct forms of love, and in the interest of accuracy and clarity, they had a different word for each of them. *Eros* is biological attraction. It is not chosen—it chooses you. Largely a result of powerful hormones and other biochemical forces, it seems hardwired and linked primarily (but not entirely) to the reproductive imperative. Having a crush on someone, being infatuated, falling in lust—these are all various forms of eros. It is a wonderful thing, despite its obvious potential for sowing wreckage. And it is certainly different than *storge*, the innate love we have for our families. Then there is *philia*, the warmth of friendship and the bond one feels with one's hometown, culture, and tribe. And finally there is *agape*, the conscious, willful decision to be kind. Agape is not a feeling born in the heart but a decision born in the mind and enacted by the will. In fact, to practice agape, one must often override one's destructive, self-centered impulses and choose the high road of compassion. To put it simply, eros is in the loins, storge and philia are in the heart, and agape is in the head. Each has its powerful and beautiful part to play in the full range of human experience.

So is love an uncontrollable feeling or a willful decision? Is it a private passion or a public action? It depends on which form of love you mean. Let's look at each more carefully.

The Zeal of the Organs

In Greek mythology, Eros was a god, and a terrifying one at that. In one version of the myth, he emerged directly from the primordial chaos (*Kaos*) and was responsible for the first couple's union—Uranos the sky god and Gaia the earth goddess, a union from which all the other gods would emerge. Eros is the personification of primal, generative attraction.

Eros or erotic love is an impersonal love; it really doesn't matter who the other person is. We fall in lust rather easily. Someone walks into a room, and *boom*, before they've even uttered a word, an uninvited and irrational longing rises in us like mist from a bog. Joseph Campbell whimsically calls eros "the zeal of the organs for each other."[108]

In the myth, the arrows of Eros emanate from the love object itself, entering our eyes and traveling to our hearts, where they cause *theia mania*, a divine madness that casts reason and prudence to the wind. Anyone who has ever been caught in the throes of erotic love can testify to the power of that wonderful, frustrating, and consuming madness.

Erotic love is primarily visual. This, by the way, is why pornography is so wildly profitable. Eros is also not very loving. It is more concerned with possession than compassion. Erotic love seeks to own and control the object of its desire, not care for or nurture it. It is almost like we're casting an actor for a role in our own drama—a part scripted to suit our needs. The less we know about the other person, the better. Eros is also at the root of most celebrity worship and adoration. Idolization requires distance. Genuine intimacy would squash the illusion. The danger with erotic love is that it so easily becomes more about self-aggrandizement than coming to know or love the other person. We want what we want, and to hell with the rest. It turns out this is what most pop songs are about—the delightful, dangerous, and essentially self-centered dynamic of erotic attraction, and the devastating chaos of its painful aftermath. For many people, erotic love is notoriously short-lived and difficult to maintain.

In a later version of the Greek myth, we are told that Eros is the son of Aphrodite. The origin story of Aphrodite sets the tragic dynamics of Eros's passion in a haunting and heartbreaking context.

Aphrodite was born from an act of horrific revenge. The primordial mother Gaia was tired of being raped every night by her cruel and feckless husband, Uranos, and she was sick of the way he buried each of their children as soon as they were born. Gaia recruited her son Kronos, the one son she had been able to hide from Uranos, to put an end to the cycle of violence and abuse. One night, as Uranos descended onto Gaia yet again, Kronos leapt from his hiding place and castrated his father with a swift slash of his scythe. As the blood from Uranos's severed genitals drained into the sea, Aphrodite arose from the salty red froth.

With that nasty business done, Gaia was free. But her son bore the trauma of patricide into his own doomed life. He later married his sister Rhea and turned into a monster just like his father, murdering each of his children as soon as they were born. Don't look to Greek mythology for a lot of healthy role models. Like father, like son.

The son of Aphrodite, Eros came from great dysfunction, and he carried that turmoil with him. He is a fiery god, equally creative and destructive. When you are afflicted by Eros, you feel that thrilling terror in every fiber of your being.

No matter which origin myth of Eros you subscribe to, the whole thing is a bloody mess. In order to ameliorate the brutality of these earlier myths, the later Romans transformed Eros into a cute, chubby baby called Cupid, and his mother Aphrodite became the demure and alluring Venus.

It is the purpose of myth to put a face on our often hidden psychological energies, and to convey deep, archetypal truths in story form—stories that delight, inspire, caution, and teach us how to navigate the landscape of our own lives. One thing we learn from classical mythology about erotic love is this: it cannot be controlled. It controls us. To integrate this form of love into the others is going to take some doing. But it can be done.

Hearth and Home

The next two types of love in ancient Greek understanding are storge and philia.

Storge is the affection and bond that arises naturally within a family. It can also be used to describe the love and affection we have for our animal companions. It is less a function of free will and more an unconscious and innate fondness. Who among us is immune to the undeniable allure of babies and puppies? Storge is a rich, rewarding, and powerful form of love that sweetens the often difficult and harrowing lives we lead. Changing our baby's diapers and picking up after our dogs would be much more difficult were it not for the fact that they are just so darn cute.

When we turn our attention toward our love for our homeland, our ethnicity, our culture, and our dear friends, we are talking about philia. The smells of our grandmother's kitchen, the line of hills around our hometown, the familiar feel of the old neighborhood—these deep bonds connect us to a place, a way of life, and to our people. For Aristotle, philia was a kind of "brotherly love," a deep and authentic friendship where people want the best for each other. And, Aristotle taught, we cannot have philia for another until we have philia for ourselves. Self-love, not to be confused with self-obsession or narcissism, is a prerequisite for loving others because it is only when we show up whole that we can be any good for anyone else. It is worth noting that the opposite of philia is phobia, an irrational and debilitating fear. Throughout the ages, the wise have long recognized that the opposite of love is not hate. The opposite of love is fear. In fact, they cancel each other out. Where there is fear, there cannot be love, and where there is love, there cannot be fear. You have to choose which master to serve.

It can always go wrong. One pathological mutation of philia is blind patriotism and nationalism. When one's tribe is perceived as superior to other tribes, it isn't long before discrimination, resentment, violence, and war rear their ugly heads. Love and fear exist on a gradient continuum.

It takes courage and discernment to stay on the right side of the scale.

There is nothing inherently erotic about storge and philia, although the three can become confused in an addled mind. Yet in a sound mind, these three modalities of love share a common trait: none of them are freely chosen. Eros happens to us. Storge arises out of our given family connections. And the affection of philia is a function of shared interests, familiarity, and the attraction people feel around communal experiences—like fans of a sports team, the Grateful Dead, or Star Wars. Yet there is a fourth dimension of love not yet revealed in these definitions. It is not a love that chooses us; it is a love that we choose.

The Will to Love

The fourth and last type of love in Greek vocabulary is agape. Agape is not a feeling. It is not an innate biological response to favorable stimuli. Nor is it a byproduct of familial or tribal bonds. Agape is born in the mind, not the heart. It is a willful decision to work for the good of the other without consideration of what one might receive in return. Sometimes called unconditional love, agape transcends self-interest as well as tribal and ethnic affiliations. If agape is a decision, then we are free to choose compassionate loving-kindness regardless of the circumstances. But that doesn't mean it is going to be easy.

Agape begins with an act of imagination called empathy. Leaving aside self-interest, we move into the realization that we are no different from the other. We imagine that we are them—a bold and precarious act of identification. Suddenly, in the mind's eye, everything clarifies. Moral duty and right action come into focus. Our ambivalence lifts and we know what to do. We know the other because we are the other. As first-century rabbi Hillel the Elder said, "What is hateful to you, do not do to another." The tough but tender shoots of agape spring from the soil of empathy and come to fruition in loving-kindness.

It is in the Gospels that the word *agape* rose to prominence. Even though Jesus spoke Aramaic, his biographers wrote in

Greek. When Jesus commands his followers to love one another, even their enemies, *agape* was the only fit. The other Greek words for love simply wouldn't make sense in this context. How could you have friendliness or communal warmth for people you don't know, or for those who have harmed you? You couldn't, and you wouldn't. But you could choose the architecture of kindness; it is the only thing that builds bridges between strangers. The way forward out of perpetual conflict is the deliberate decision to forgive—a sheer act of will. Nothing else will do.

In the Sermon on the Mount in the Gospel of Matthew, Jesus said, "You have heard that it was said, 'Love your neighbor and hate your enemy,' but I tell you: Love your enemies."[109] With this simple shift, he transforms an ancient tribal ethos into a universal one. Instead of reserving loving-kindness for the in-group as the Torah implies, Jesus counsels us to love our enemies—a radical call for supreme inclusiveness. What "love your enemies" really means is that there are no such things as enemies, just other people temporarily at odds with us, harboring different worldviews, contrasting values, and conflicting goals. The harmful actions of others stem from their own frightened darkness and alienation; we know that only wounded people wound. As the poet Henry Wadsworth Longfellow put it, "If we could read the secret history of our enemies, we should find in each man's life sorrow and suffering enough to disarm all hostility." Empathy enables us to read those secret histories, opening the door to agape. And only agape, the willful decision to override deeply rooted animosities, has the capacity and power to deliver us into an era of empathetic peace both on the personal and political plane.

No easy task, agape is a hardheaded stance in a world of softheaded sentiment.

Deliberate loving-kindness is about as far away from mushy sentimentality as you can get. When Gandhi designed the Satyagraha, his campaign of nonviolent noncooperation against British colonial rule in India, he specifically cited the Sermon on the Mount as a daily inspiration. He loved the teachings of Jesus but was dismayed by how rarely Christians embodied them. He decided to apply Jesus's tactic of turning the other cheek as a political strategy. It worked. When you return your enemy's blows with loving-kindness, they soon put down their batons, no longer able to unilaterally mete out brutality. Your love reaches into the heart of your oppressor in a way reactive counterviolence cannot. In some mysterious way, love inculcates love. In the language of Gandhi, agape is "soul force" and far exceeds the reach of "body force," terminology that would resonate around the world through the soaring oratory and concrete actions of Dr. Martin Luther King Jr. in the American civil rights movement.

As Latin replaced Greek in the early Christian church, *agape* became *caritas*—charity. Today, charity simply means giving to those in need. But originally it meant unconditional love given freely regardless of the merit of the recipient and free from calculation of reciprocity. In this sense, love is not something you feel; it is something you do. If it is not manifested in action, then it is not really love; it is just a private, inconsequential sentiment. As one of the premier virtues taught by the early Church, charity was seen as proof of a transformed soul. When you really embody Christ's love, you see all people as equals worthy of compassion and mercy, no matter what they have done or might do later. This internal embodiment, what Paul called being in Christ, informs the actions of an illumined human being. In fact, it goes even further than that. When you see the Christ within all beings, you behold the presence of God in the other—our underlying divine unity, the holy Namaste. As Paul wrote in his letter to the Galatians, "There is neither Jew nor Greek, slave nor free, male nor female, for you are all one in Christ Jesus."[110] All categorical barriers become diaphanous and porous—the one love slips loose from its container. According to Christian theology, charity, or agape, is the highest form of love because it is the kind of love God has for us. Regardless of your theological or religious orientation, agape stands as a transformative power of enormous strength. This is what the Beatles meant when they sang, "All you need is love." They weren't talking about flirtation, infatuation, passion, or romance; they were talking about a love supreme, bold enough to dissolve all animosity and bright enough to dispel every shadow of disunity and ignorance.

Love in Action

On the other side of the world in China, five centuries before Jesus, another teacher taught the power of love in action. In chapters two and three, we discussed the Confucian concept of shu, or reciprocity. Confucius believed that in order to realize the inherent goodness of our humanity, we first have to cultivate the consciousness of empathy. By becoming aware of the impact our actions have on others, we build a solid foundation for kindness and morality.

If shu is the consciousness of empathy, then *ren* is the expression of kindness. The Chinese ideogram for ren is made up of the pictograms for "human being" and "two." This suggests the core meaning of ren: building connection and mutual support between people. But the compassion and kindness of ren are not born in the heart—they are born in the will. Much like agape, ren means working for the good of the other with no thought for oneself. Ren, as much as possible, is divorced from the vagaries and inconstancies of the emotional realm. When we practice the virtue of ren, we are an unwavering force for good. We are, in the truest sense of the word, fully human.

But cultivating shu and ren isn't enough. These shifts in consciousness must be made manifest in our actions. That's why *li* is so important. Li originally meant "sacrifice" or "ritual," but to link li solely to religious observance is to strip it of its fullest significance, because li reaches far beyond the confines of religion. In Confucian thought, all life properly lived has the quality of a ritual. Every human behavior and interaction has the capacity of sanctifying and ennobling its participants if carried out in the proper spirit of decorum and reverence. In other words, li is simply the outward manifestation of shu and ren. Empathy and kindness are made real in action. Using your car's turn signal is li. Behaving courteously despite your lousy mood is li. Silencing your cell phone in a movie theater is li. Any respectful behavior where the needs and interests of others come before our own is li. In the minutiae of our daily interactions, we have the opportunity to bring the pure potentiality of the ideal or the mandate of heaven (*T'ian*) down to earth, for it is only through human action that the ideal is realized. Human beings are the agents whose actions create the warp and weave of society. The moral quality of our culture is nothing more than the sum of the actions of its members. We bring the world into being through our choices and actions. When we behave selfishly and blindly, one world comes forth. When we behave consciously and compassionately, another very different world comes forth. In this sense, Confucianism is a humanistic philosophy. In the absence of a Western style deity (arguably missing from the ancient Chinese worldview), it is humanity that creates the moral atmosphere of society through its collective behavior. The good news? The Confucians claim that we are by nature good. The bad news? Our innate goodness, like the mandate of heaven itself, exists only as potential and needs to be cultivated and strengthened through deliberation and practice. To become a *junzi*, a virtuous person, requires a lifetime of habituation, much like becoming a violin virtuoso. This is why action is so important. You don't become good at playing violin by listening to others play, or by longing to be a violinist. You have to pick up a violin and play it again and again. In this same way, you do not become a virtuous human being without deliberately choosing to love and boldly embodying that love in your everyday actions.

The Confucian emphasis on ritualized behavior often gets a bad rap as empty conformity. In the Western emphasis on individualism and freedom of expression, any attempt to limit spontaneity is seen as counterproductive to human development. But any musician will tell you that were it not for their willful practice and disciplined habituation, no fluid flights of improvisational freedom would ever be possible.

The Shoebox Under the Bed

My parents were married in Haarlem, the Netherlands, in 1946, a few months after the end of World War II. My father had just returned from two long years in a German forced labor camp. The air was full of celebration, and everyone was glad to see the war come to an end. But their happiness was tempered by the terrible cost of Nazi occupation. The war left nothing untouched. People's lives were in shambles. Grief hung heavy. Everyone had to start over. Prospects for new families in postwar Holland were not good; the waiting list for an apartment was fourteen years. Making a new life in America seemed like the best path, even though it meant leaving behind everything they knew.

Their whole family came down to the dock to see the young couple off. Amy held her two-year-old son Eric on her hip. She was seven months pregnant. Hilbert tried to be strong and optimistic, but they knew the risks. Still, what lay ahead seemed brighter than what lay behind. They said long, tearful goodbyes to their grieving parents and siblings, not knowing if or when they would ever see each other again.

My brother John was born six weeks after they sailed into the New York harbor. I was born eight years later in West Paterson, New Jersey. Then the family moved west. While growing up in Ventura, California, it was always just the five of us—my two older brothers, my parents, and me. Every cousin, aunt, uncle, and grandparent lived on the other side of the world and spoke a different language. I saw one or two of them now and then when they would visit, but to me they were distant relations, strangers who shared my name.

Whenever my grandfather sent me a birthday gift, my mom would sit me down and make me write a thank-you card. I didn't want to. It didn't feel genuine to me, it felt phony, and anything phony is not worth doing—at least, that is the reasoning of an eight-year-old boy. Besides, I assured my mother that he knew I was thankful. Why be redundant? She listened patiently to my objections and then made me to write the card anyway. To me, it felt uncomfortable, awkward, and forced—an empty gesture. But it seemed important to her.

Eighteen years later, when my grandfather died, my mom flew home to Holland to empty out his apartment. Underneath his bed, she found a shoebox. She lifted the lid. Inside were all of my thank-you cards.

As a child, I did not understand any of this. I did not understand that the ritual of putting pen to paper, of sending a handwritten thank-you note, could be such a powerful, connective act. What to me seemed hollow and insincere was to my grandfather profoundly real. To hold in his hand tangible proof that his only daughter Amy, with whom he had survived years of Nazi occupation, was thriving in California, and that her three boys were safe and growing up in the land of milk and honey and reached out to him from time to time in tiny threads of connectivity—that box of cards was a treasure chest of immeasurable value. This is the real meaning and purpose of ritual. This is the value of ceremony. This is how love is concretized in action.

It is through the simple rituals of our lives that the spirit of love and beauty rises up out of the soul and takes form. As discussed in chapter three, action precedes internal transformation. We become loving by acting lovingly. We become generous by acting generously. We become courageous by acting courageously. Through no other way does it come. We become what we do. This is why agape or charity is the highest form of love: only it has the power to transform, elevate, ennoble, and edify both the giver and the receiver.

That is why they say, "Fake it till you make it." In the end, li, like agape, is the choreography through which the innate goodness of our humanity finds expression. Far from mindless conformity, li is the stroke of the pen through which the beauty of life is written.

One Cup of Tea

When I was a boy, I would get home from school around three o'clock in the afternoon. Fifteen minutes later, my dad would come home from his job at the *Ventura Star-Free Press*, where he was a type setter. I'd hear the whine of his Honda 50 motorcycle coming down the street and pulling into the garage. Mom would lift the whistling kettle off the stove and pour boiling water over the loose leaves in the tea pot. A few minutes later, they were both at the dining room table enjoying a cup of tea. We boys were neither invited nor interested. While in other rooms doing other things, we could hear their soft voices talking about the mysterious things married people talk about, against a backdrop of clinking teacups, saucers, and spoons. Every weekday afternoon, without fail, this ritual was repeated.

My parents were married for sixty-six years when my father died. I sometimes wonder if the success of their long and unwavering marriage had anything to do with that cup of tea. Knowing that every twenty-four hours, no matter what, they had a standing date, a still point in a life of busyness and demands, a few minutes set apart in which to look each other in the eye and really hear each other, really feel each other, really gauge each other's emotional weather systems, and simply enjoy the feeling of loving and being loved. This deep-level connection does not happen on its own—you have to make time and space for it. That is what rituals do: they make time and space for significance. After my father died, my mom did her best to keep her chin up. But he left a hole no one or nothing could fill. She died twenty months later.

For Confucius, nothing is more important than li. It is the reparative tissue that heals our relationships, and our healthy relationships are in turn the bricks that build a just and vigorous society. It is hardly an overstatement to say that without li, civilization is in jeopardy. We show our care and respect for each other by the way we interact, the way we speak, the way we behave, the way we dress, the way we show up on time, the way we listen, the way we give, the way we receive, the way we work, the way we eat, the way we drive—there is no end to it. By beginning to examine the practiced kindness of our own actions, we move into a deeper appreciation of the power of li. Again we notice the unbreakable bond between love and action. Real love manifests itself in concrete behaviors consciously chosen and shared. It is hard to believe something so important could be contained in a single cup of tea.

Lost in Translation

Because the New Testament was written in Greek, Greek philosophy and culture unavoidably shaped our understanding of the Gospels. Yet it is also true that Jesus and Paul, the two most significant voices in the New Testament, were both Jews, and as such they lived on the margins of the Greco-Roman world. They were at home in Jewish culture and literate in its theology, rituals, and traditions. Yet to us, Jesus and Paul speak Greek. It is as if the only surviving versions of Shakespeare were in Portuguese translations.

Many of the details of Jesus's life and teachings are forever lost to us. What remains is a series of often conflicting religious texts written not as objective biographies but as reverent hagiographies designed to persuade their readers of one thing—that Jesus was God. Jesus's actual sayings, spoken in his native Aramaic, are gone forever and are not coming back. It is painfully clear that the waves of temporal distortion between us and the ancient teacher from Nazareth began to alter his original wisdom sayings as soon as they were recorded. And nowhere is this unfortunate truth more apparent than in the shifting meanings of the word *love*.

As we have already seen, the Greek word *agape* is the word most commonly used by the authors of the New Testament for *love*. But in Jesus's own tongue Aramaic, the word for *love* is *hooba*, meaning "to set on fire." Hooba contains a number of connotations not present in the Greek concept of agape. Hooba is a passion born of the heart, a deep and powerful spark that, when kindled, roars into flames that transform everything it touches. It is not a conscious decision willfully imposed—at least, it does not begin that way. It is a heartfelt kindness, concern, and warmth that naturally results in caregiving and sacrifice for the other. Hooba may not be completely distinct from agape, but neither are the two concepts identical. Let's just say there is sufficient overlap. But it is problematic that no one knows whether agape rightly captures Jesus's own understanding of love. Hooba certainly seems to suggest something more passionate and irrational than agape. But the Christian tradition made its choices. The Jesus we have inherited clearly teaches in no uncertain terms and in great detail about agape.

Maybe we can turn this confusion into clarity. Integrating the passion of hooba into our understanding of Christian charity adds an important element, and it opens the door to an increasing understanding of religious love, or devotion.

All of this discussion of the various Greek and Aramaic words for *love* make one thing clear: the experience of love is not easily contained in words or concepts. Love is essentially ineffable. Yet its singular importance compels us to speak, for love exists in the space between us, in relationship, and therefore we must struggle to communicate something or die trying. That the clusters of meaning contained in the words *hooba* and *agape* overlap with each other proves the provisional nature of all names and concepts. It is best not to cling too tightly to any of them. Instead, words and concepts are most useful when they point to an experiential realm beyond thought where a wordless understanding takes shape, no matter how unverifiable that understanding may be in the realm of language and reason.

Love and Devotion

In many of the world's faiths, devotion to God or the gods is the cornerstone of religious life. Especially in the monotheistic traditions of the West, God is understood as a God of love. For billions of Christians, Muslims, and Jews all over the world, God is a personified conscious entity that loves us and longs for our love in return. Getting right with God in these traditions means opening one's heart to both receive and reciprocate God's infinite love. This raises vexing theological questions. If God is boundless and perfect, does he need our love? Does a perfect being need anything? Wouldn't perfection imply completion and wholeness? Would a great God worthy of worship be so flawed as to be pained by his lover's indifference? Perhaps it is not that God needs our love. It's something else he's after. He knows that as we cultivate the capacity to love, we are transformed from within by our own loving. This is the real fruit of devotion and worship. By becoming the embodiment of love, we let slip the ego and awaken to our deeper and more authentic nature.

If devotional religion is not your cup of tea, and if belief in a personal God seems silly to you, a word of caution is in order. Before dismissing as phony the spiritual lives of billions of your fellow human beings, it is wise to guard against the prideful tendency to denigrate worship and devotion as second-class spiritualty—a dualistic, childish anthropomorphism with simplistic patriarchal or matriarchal overtones. Perhaps there is more to worship than first meets the eye.

If loving is integral to human nature, then it is no surprise that it finds itself front and center in the endless expressions of religious experience the world over. We are called to the consciousness of loving gratitude in all of the world's faiths. Hinduism is one of many examples.

As discussed in previous chapters, beneath the surface of the various sects and practices of Hinduism, there is a single underlying principle: that all energy, consciousness, and matter are manifestations of one divine reality called Brahman. We too are expressions of this divine source, only we don't know it, caught as we are by the surface illusions of maya. The goal of Hinduism is piercing the veil of our ignorance and realizing our oneness with the divine. The method for eliminating this debilitating ignorance is yoga. In Indian understanding there are four types of people, hence, four types of yoga.

Jnana yoga is the path of understanding, employing the study of texts, philosophical inquiry, and rational discourse. Here, intellectual discernment opens the gate to a deepening realization of oneness with that underlying imperishable reality beneath the surface of transitory things.

Karma yoga is the path of selfless action, turning our everyday work into spiritual practice undertaken in the spirit of service and generosity. By learning to work without attachment to the fruits of work, we gradually loosen the binds of the ego and shift into oneness.

Raja yoga is the path of meditation where self-discipline and purification lead to the direct experience of oneness within the depths of our own consciousness. By turning within, we discover for ourselves our inherent identity with the ground of being and realize I Am That.

But bhakti yoga is different. It is not about meditation, study, or selfless service. Its focus is on the heart-centered practice of devotion and worship, and as such, is arguably more recognizable to Westerners accustomed to the devotional dynamics of the three Abrahamic faiths.

It is difficult to think of anything more central, more transformative, or more powerful in the human realm than love. Nothing surpasses the depth and breadth of the love experience. Why not harness this powerful energy in the service of God-realization?

Another distinction that sets bhakti yoga apart from the other three yogas is its dependence on dualism. Whereas jnana, karma, and raja yoga make explicit our oneness with Brahman from the outset, bhakti yoga requires an inherently dualistic distance between the devotee and the object of their devotion. Love requires relationship, and relationship requires that there be an *other.* As the bhakti yogi offers their adulation to one or more of the many personifications of the divine that crowd the Hindu pantheon, they are transformed in the flames of their own devotional passion. As the Christian existentialist philosopher Soren Kierkegaard wrote, “Prayer doesn’t change God, but it changes him who prays.”

Jnana yogis might privately complain that bhakti yogis remain snared in a web of maya—all forms, including the gods, are after all a part of maya. But in their humbler moments, they have to admit the broken-open humility of the bhakti yogi, rapt in the ecstasy of worship, is ideally raw and available for a direct experience of the Godhead beyond all forms. In fact, jnana and bhakti might not be so far apart after all. To a casual observer, the intellectual rapture of a jnana yogi mesmerized by a passage from the Upanishads would look a lot like the devotional rapture of a bhakti yogi mesmerized by their ecstatic love for Krishna or Saraswati. The mystics of all religions, jnanis and bhaktis alike, speak in uncomfortably intimate language about their union with God. If all paths lead to the summit as Ramakrishna famously proclaimed, then the differences between the various yoga paths dissolve in the final ascension. Once you get there, it doesn’t much matter how you got there.

The whole point of yoga, in all its forms, is to shatter the illusion of our isolation and separation. This makes yoga integral to religion. The word *religion* comes from the Greek and Latin root *religio*, meaning "to bind," "to join together," or "to reconnect." People gravitate toward religion in all its forms in order to rejoin the cosmic whole from which their egoic fear has isolated them. Somehow we lost our place in the Garden, we left the Mother-Womb, or we fell under the spell of maya—there are many mythic portraits to convey this primal alienation—and out of the imaginations of our storytellers, myth makers, and artists come the metaphorical scenarios in which our cosmic homecoming plays out. Unlike many faith traditions, Hinduism explicitly recognizes our individual variations and allows for many paths to the summit, depending on our temperament. One size does not fit all, and it never will. In the Hindu tradition, the humble devotee and the learned scholar each have their inroad to the divine. And love is no second-class citizen in the community of paths—it may very well encompass all the others, for what draws a student to philosophy other than love? What fuels the hard work of those who live lives of service other than love? And what steels the resolve of the yogi committed to meditation and conscious evolution other than love of the truth? Love is the longing for the real, the true, the sacred, and the whole, no matter what form the loving takes—the very meaning of the word philosophy. Love then is a breaking open of the heart, a dissolving of the ego, an annihilation of self-centeredness, a surrender and sublimation into the One.

Ecstatic love accomplishes what the intellect never can: utter and complete intimacy. As Charles Dickens wrote in *David Copperfield*, "A loving heart is better and stronger than wisdom." Indeed, a loving heart proves to be a requirement for wisdom.

The Ties That Bind

In our earlier discussion of eros, we saw that in this form of love, a certain sense of ownership and control rears its head. But any fool can see that love and selfishness make poor bedfellows. If love is real, it wants only what is best for its beloved. When you love someone in this deep sense, you long to create the conditions in which their best life can take flight. Instead of bondage, you offer freedom. In Buddhism, this is known as nonattachment.

As we saw in chapter one, the Buddha diagnosed the human condition as self-induced suffering. The Four Noble Truths describe the problem, identify the cause of the problem, and offer a path out of the problem. Suffering, dissatisfaction, anxiety, and incompletion are caused by egoic craving—we want things to be different from the way they are. We are attached to self-serving outcomes and deeply disappointed when they fail to arise. The malady, in a word, is attachment.

Attachment looks like this: craving, clinging, ego identification, self-serving expectations, demands, entitlement, possessiveness, control, past-future obsession, fear, bondage, and inevitably violence.

Nonattachment looks like this: empathy, compassion, kindness, connectedness, care, bonding, presence, acceptance, celebration of what is, joy, freedom, noncoercion, and inevitably nonviolence.

Which condition of consciousness, attachment or nonattachment, do you suppose is most capable of love?

Love withers under the conditions of attachment. Love thrives under the conditions of nonattachment. As Paul wrote in his first letter to the Corinthians, "Love is patient, love is kind. It does not envy, it does not boast, it is not proud. It is not rude, it is not self-seeking, it is not easily angered, it keeps no record of wrongs."[111] Paul's portrait of pure love bears more than a passing resemblance to the principles of Buddhist nonattachment. But Buddha takes it even further. Because of the fundamental impermanence of all things, all forms have a transitory nature. In Buddhist terminology, this is known as *shunyata*, or emptiness. Nothing is fixed or permanent. Because of the incessant arising and fading of all conditioned existence, the universe is said to be empty, as in empty of fixed forms. Within this field of emptiness, there is a dimension of conscious energy called *Dharmakaya*, or Buddha-nature. Each of the fleeting forms that arise out of it, including this cluster of phenomena we call ourselves, is as insubstantial as a candle flame. In the deepest teachings of Buddhist philosophy, not only is there nothing to grasp, but there is no one to do the grasping. This is what makes the suffering of the world so poignant.

Nearly all of our woundedness is predicated on a misunderstanding that there are separate things and separate individuals in conflict with one another. But under the Bodhi Tree, when Buddha attained enlightenment, he saw through the illusory nature of things and understood reality as it was: a single, interconnected whole where all matter, energy, and consciousness exists in a state of deep and mutual interdependency. There is nothing to crave and no one to do the craving—a bracing truth that rips away the foundation of our sad architecture of suffering. Reality is a field of boundless awareness. We are already that. And we are always home. From this perspective, the only thing there is, the only thing there ever was, is love.

The Mythology of Love

Love figures prominently in world mythology. Two examples from cultures on opposite sides of the world will serve to demonstrate love's archetypal nature: the Indian *Brihadaranyaka Upanishad* and the Mayan *Popul Vuh.*

The *Brihadaranyaka Upanishad* (c. 600 BCE) tells the story of the creation of the universe. In the beginning, there was only Purusha, the primal Person. He took form as Atman or Universal Soul, retaining his identity with Brahman, the ultimate ground of all being. At first he was afraid. The universe was a big place. Then he remembered he was alone and that nothing else had come into being yet. So what was there to be afraid of? His fear vanished. But neither was he happy or joyful. He was lonely. His loneliness was as vast as the entire cosmos.

He wanted someone to love, so he split himself in two. One

half was a man, and the other half was a woman. They became the primal mother-father pair, engendering all humankind. But the woman was troubled. She thought it was kind of creepy that her man, who produced her from his own body, was essentially mating with himself every time he mated with her. So she ran away and disguised herself as a cow. He turned into a bull and mated with her again, and from this union came all of the cows. She disguised herself as a mare, and he became a stallion. She became a female goat, he a billy goat. And so it went with all the animals, all the way down to the ants.

Then he looked around at everything he had made and realized that he was this creation—it was all an emanation of him. The created world and its source are one unbroken continuum. There is only one reality, Brahman-atman, and everything is its manifestation. Realizing this is the goal of spiritual work the world over. The technical term for this is panentheism, the view that everything pours forth from one divine reality.[112]

This ancient tale of cosmic longing puts into proper context all our longings, for every longing is the longing of God for God. Our longing to work for social justice and heal the world, our longing to write a symphony, our longing to have a family, our longing for love—it is all God-longing. Love is our word for this longing. We find it everywhere because love is what everything is. We can choose to turn our gaze outward to the myriad forms and worship any one of them, or all of them. Or we can choose to turn inward to the presence of that reality within us. In the end, it is all the same.

Say My Name

In pre-Colombian Mesoamerica, the Maya told a different tale with a powerfully similar underlying theme. First recorded by Spanish scribes during the Conquest, the *Popul Vuh* tells the story of God's all-too-human struggle with his own creation process.

At first, God existed as light, all alone in the still, dark sky and the deep, dark sea. He wanted there to be light throughout the world, and he wanted dawn and man to arise together. But first he had to make the earth with its valleys and forests and mountains and rivers. When it was finished, God was troubled by the vast silence of his newly made world.

So he created the animals and told them to speak, each in their own way. God saw that they could not speak to one another—some hissed, some snarled, some growled, and some howled. And none of them could say his name. He wanted someone to know and say his name. He wanted someone to love him.

So he made human beings. The first humans were made out of mud. They were mushy, and they could not see. When they spoke, they made no sense. When it rained, they slumped over. God saw that they were useless, so he broke them up and tried again.

God made the second version of human beings out of

wood. They could walk and talk and build houses. They had many children. But behind their expressionless faces, they had no minds or souls or hearts. They were uncaring, cruel, and incompetent. God sent a great flood to wipe them out. The few who survived scampered up into the trees and became monkeys.

Then God said, "It is time. I need men on the earth who will know my names, who will obey me and love me; and that will nourish and sustain me." With cornmeal, he made the bodies of four men, energizing them with corn liquor. They were strong and handsome. While they slept, God made four women. When they awoke, they all sang God's name and thanked him for their lives. God was pleased to have someone to love him, and to have someone to love. But God was troubled. The men and women knew too much and could see too far. They were as gods. So he took some dust and blew it into their eyes. From then on, they could only see what was right in front of them. Even the third version of humanity required a little adjustment in order to be what God really needed.[113]

In both of these creation stories, the Hindu and the Mesoamerican, the divine principle, personified as a god, reached out from his cosmic loneliness and made humanity for one simple reason: reality only exists in relationship with itself. A survey of world mythology and religion reveals the ubiquitous, archetypal nature of this foundational fact. Nothing exists except in relationship with everything else that exists. Love is that word used to describe the fundamental energy of this relationship. When you love anything, you are a channel through whom this primal energy flows. As we nourish others, we are nourished. As we feed others, we are fed. As we care for others, we are cared for. As we lift others, we are lifted. As we heal others, we are healed. As we cherish others, we are cherished. By simply opening the floodgates, we allow the one love to perform the task it was born to perform. Love simply wants to be. We need only to remove its hindrances and allow it to pour forth.

When we love, we are the universe loving itself. By loving others, we bind ourselves to ourselves, to each other, and to God. When we love, we step out of our cosmic loneliness and enter the stream of life that has no beginning and no end. Forms arise and fade, but the one love that informs them all can never be destroyed. This is why learning how to love is our single most important task. If you cannot or will not love, you remove yourself from your own fullest realization. When you withhold love from others, it is you who are impoverished. In Charles Dickens's *A Christmas Carol*, this theme is laid bare. At the end of the story, after all of those haunting visions of suffering—the world's and his own—Ebenezer Scrooge found his empathy. When he learned how to do for others, his own joy increased exponentially. As the Dalai Lama said, "If you want others to be happy, practice compassion. If you want to be happy, practice compassion."

Love at the End

I did not really want to get a dog again, but Lori did, and

when you are married, you make decisions together. You love this person, and so by definition you want what is best for them. She really wanted another dog, and who was I to get in the way of that? And deep down, I knew it would be good for me. It was time to move past the grieving.

We had lost our previous dog too soon. Farley was the dog love of my life, a chocolate Lab with deep brown eyes and a stalwart heart. For a lot of complicated reasons, he simply was not long for this world. Putting him down at the age of four was the hardest thing I have ever done. So when we drove out to pick up Boone, a three-year-old Brittany spaniel, I was reluctant to say the least. He jumped up in the truck seat between us. It was not love at first sight; we were both a little tentative. But Lori had a feeling, and I have come to trust her feelings.

The first few years were a little rough. Both Boone and I had some adjusting to do. He tore out a couple of window screens and chewed up the drapes. He ran away a few times but always came back. At some point, he simply settled down and made peace with the world around him.

We walked him every day and taught him the simple tricks that make any dog easier to live with—sit, stay, heel, down, come, that sort of thing. He loved hiking in the mountains with us, and because he was a sporting dog, he dutifully pointed out every squirrel, rabbit, and bird, lifting a foreleg and standing still as a statue.

His long, wispy, white and russet coat waved in the wind and shone in the sun. His tawny eyes, the color of rabbit fur, never missed anything. His mind was keen. You could tell he was always thinking, not like some dogs with their vacuous stares and shallow interests. He was a philosopher dog.

He was cautious around other dogs, never the life of the party, always hanging back. He did not like dog parks where everyone lets their dogs run off leash. It was all a bit much for him, all that rushing around and thoughtless, brash disregard for personal space. He preferred a more civilized, formal decorum. But he was never unkind to any dog or person. He did not have a cold bone in his body. He loved what he loved deeply and without reservation. He simply kept to himself, which is kind of how Lori and I are, so it was a good fit.

We had twelve years with Boone. Toward the end, his kidneys started failing. Then other organs. Then he started falling down. We put rugs all over our wood and tiled floors so he would not have to struggle so much to stand up and walk.

Then he stopped eating. He would look up at us as if to say, *I'm tired, and I just can't do it anymore*. The light had gone out of his eyes. He was receding. In the last days, his breathing became so labored that he lay on the ground with his muzzle pointed up toward the ceiling, trying to open his air passage. We called the vet and made an appointment for the following afternoon. I lay with him on the floor that night and held him—that final, expansive, heartbreaking night.

The next day, Lori and I loaded him into the back seat of the car and drove him to the vet. A series of lasts—his last meal, his last pee, his last swaying meander through the backyard, his last nuzzle with each of the cats, his last sight of our home fading in the rear window as we drove toward our impossible errand.

The three of us walked into the examination room. Simon, the vet tech and our frequent pet sitter, came in and greeted us with a kind half smile. I thought of how many times he must have had to do this, to be with families in this awful moment. What a strong and loving heart he has. He brought out a warm blanket for Boone to lay on. Lori and I sat on the floor with him. Simon said we could have as much time as we needed. Boone was barely breathing, his muzzle up, his throat outstretched, gasping. "Let's do it," I said.

Dr. Massey came in and sat on the floor with all of us, setting a large, pink syringe on the blanket. "We can take as long as you need," she said. "There's absolutely no rush." Simon and Dr. Massey were both so kind and generous; I don't know how to describe it. Despite the dire nature of our gathering, it was one of the most loving moments I have ever experienced. Death wiped away all pretense. There was nothing left but honesty. Death will do that. The room was filled with a vibrant immediacy, a potent intimacy, and a startling clarity—every word a jewel, every gesture grace.

My eyes met Dr. Massey's eyes, and I nodded. She reached for his right foreleg, where there was still an IV in place from some earlier blood work. She aligned the needle with the shunt. Lori and I had our hands on Boone. Through the tears, we felt the love moving us forward.

Euthanasia is not killing; it is loving. Death is a fact—it

was already happening with or without us. We were simply lifting our friend out of a pit of misery. Death is inevitable, but suffering is optional.

We had to do this. We owed him this. This was the deal we made the day he jumped into my truck twelve years earlier. We were going to be together the whole way, right to the end, through thick and thin, through the ripped screens and the torn curtains and the long walks through the autumn leaves and the boundless love and the utter and complete acceptance and the way his laughing smile pulled me back from the sadness of my tenacious self-obsession and the way his love was a safe harbor from the storms of life.

Dr. Massey slipped the needle into the shunt.

Boone turned to look at me. With our eyes, we said it all: Thank you, thank you, thank you.

Then the injection. He took one last breath. His neck relaxed, his eyes closed, his head went down, and he was gone.

That is how love is, and that is where it takes you—all along the skittering edge of life, and down into its deepest abysses. It does not solve problems or answer questions; it lifts you past the place where problems and questions have power, and in love's swift flight, you watch them recede until they appear small and insignificant. But love only comes to those who say yes, to those who risk comfort, fortune, safety, and self-interest.

Love does not stop time or freeze your account balances. None of us owns any of this, even our own lives. It is all borrowed, and we must give it all back. All forms arise and all forms fade, said the Buddha. And just like all the poets, prophets, and songwriters say, love is the only thing that lasts. It is the only thing that is real. It is the nameless energy that shimmers around us and between us and within us, sweetening our lives and making all the pain mean something. Without love we are nothing. With love, we are everything. Boone is gone. So is Farley before him. So are my mom and dad. And so many others. I will be gone one day too, as will my new dog, a rescued Irish terrier mix named Cooper. But the love we all share has no beginning and no end. It just is. And the blessing of our lives is that we came to know love and are known in love.

Love is a glimpse of eternity. It is a clear window through which we see past each other's imperfections and behold each other's infinite value, and in this way we find the long road home to the realization of our own infinite value.

Love is the flight we take through the clouds of our unknowing.

Love is a poem we write with invisible ink on paper that is slipping through our hands. Love, like water, flows around obstacles and finds a way.

Love never stops.

Loves accepts what is. Love surrenders to the currents of life. Love engages in kindness and affection. Love allows itself to be led into deeper and deeper realizations of itself. Love enjoys the pleasures and beauties that arise in the course of a well-lived life. Love harbors all boats, fuels all fires, and soothes all weary travelers. Love is the home we left home to find.

A Wise Person

Awash in the serenity of acceptance, surrendered to the beauties and vicissitudes of life, committed to and engaged with the work that is theirs to do, allowing and harmonizing with the energies of life around them, and with an open heart receiving the enjoyment of a life well lived, the wise person opens their eyes, their mind, and their heart to the love that is always flowing around us and holding us up the way water holds a boat afloat. Love is not the goal—it is the natural by-product of a commitment to the consciousness of acceptance, surrender, engagement, allowance, and enjoyment.

A wise person understands and celebrates the value of eros (primal, physical love), philia (friendly, community love), storge (family love), and agape (willful compassion) and integrates these forms of love into a unified whole. They recognize that each of these modes of love bears its own gifts and draws us closer to the realization of our beatific oneness.

A wise person knows that analytically dividing love into four subcategories is an intellectual game—at once worthwhile and superfluous. Love, like life itself, defies our ham-fisted attempts to sort it into categories. In fact, our efforts to analyze love threaten to destroy the very thing we seek to understand. As the poet Wordsworth wrote, "We murder to dissect."[114]

A wise person knows that love is not just emotion or sentiment—it must be moved by the will and concretized in action. Love is not what we feel; it is what we do. Only when love is manifested in the field of action are its fruits fully realized. This means that we must choose love, even when our heart runs away from it.

A wise person choreographs their lives in such a way that their love is apparent in every gesture. Every door held open, every restraint of tongue and pen, every unearned gift given, every humble deference, and every shimmering act of beauty offered is another shard of love made real by the engine of intention and action.

A wise person allows devotional energy into their life. It may be for a god, or it may be for any number of other forms. In the Bhagavad Gita, Krishna says that whatever we devote ourselves to whole-heartedly leads us to him. Our prayers do not change God—they change us. It is in our broken-openness that we are made whole. We are never more powerful than when we are on our knees, the sacred yes on our lips.

A wise person loves what they love, fully and without apology, knowing that it is in the energies of love itself that our transformation is made real. In the self-sacrifice of love, our self-obsession unravels revealing the vibrant core of our transcendent aliveness.

A wise person knows that in love, one never seeks to control the other. Love is the allowance of the fullest freedom. Love never fears or demands. Love never hoards or withholds. Love does not hold grudges or keep score. Love does not resent or envy. Instead, love liberates and moves both the lover and the loved into a boundless field where all is forgiven, all is cherished, and all is enlarged in the magnifying lens of loving-kindness. As Thich Nhat Hanh said, "You must love in such a way that the person you love feels free..."[115]

A wise person knows that love does not protect us from pain

or solve all of our problems. But it does enable us to weather our pain and address our problems in a way that honors what is best in ourselves and in others.

A wise person knows that when they love fully and without reservation, they tap into an infinite well of being that goes far beyond the categories of our understanding. In love, we move into the ineffable. This is why the poets say the heart understands what the head never can. And as the Hindus teach, when we practice love, we move into deep and intimate contact with our own essential, infinite sacred self, our Sat-Chit-Ananda, our true being, true consciousness, and true bliss, where all the contradictions and paradoxes that plagued our intellect are transcended leaving us aloft in a sacred knowing beyond the veil.

Closing Meditation

We have come so far, and we are nearing the end of our journey. We have stepped across the stream using the stones of acceptance, surrender, engagement, allowance, enjoyment, and love as our path. Let us pause as we have at the end of each of the previous chapters to allow these new realizations to settle into place and take root.

Find a quiet place to sit still. Close your eyes if you are listening, or soften your gaze if you are reading. Without straining, lift your head slightly to lengthen your spine, and let your shoulders fall and relax. Allow a focused yet relaxed alertness to move through your body. Take a deep breath, then another, allowing your breathing to find its own natural rhythm.

Allow all of the tension to drain out of your face, your neck, your chest, your stomach, your hips, your thighs, your calves, and your feet. Allow all of your busyness and worry to slip through the soles of your feet, down into the floor, and into the earth beneath the floor, which can bear all. Feel yourself held and supported by an infinitely abundant universe and a beautiful, beautiful planet. Know that everything you need has already been provided. Feel peace arising.

Imagine that you are in a beautiful meadow surrounded by a ring of trees. There is no one around—you are alone. But you feel safe, welcome, and alive. The sun warms your skin. There are flowers—columbine, lavender, poppies, and deep blue irises. A soft breeze mingles the scents of the meadow flowers with cedar, fir, pine, and the warm loam of the earth, and you feel in your heart a rich and profound sense of belonging. This is your home. You absolutely belong here. You are embraced, known, and loved. In the stillness, you can feel the subtle movement of the earth as it spins on its axis, soaring through space on its long journey around the sun.

Now imagine that you are drifting upward, over the meadow and high above the earth. You can see the valleys below, the meadows, the mountains, and the rivers that wind toward the sea shining in the distance. You see the towns and the people on their errands, struggling to get through the difficult terrain of their cravings and fears, and bravely willing to love anyway. Your heart breaks open in loving-kindness for all of them, realizing in an instant your oneness with every stranger you will never meet. And as this boundless love washes over you, you feel and know your own infinite value, your own simple perfection. You know with a certainty you have never allowed yourself to feel before that despite your woundedness and imperfection, you are embraced by the loving that encircles the entire sphere of being, and there is nothing you need to do, or be, or achieve, or attain—you simply are this loving-kindness. You are the love of God embodied. You are the love from which all the gods took form. You are the love that arches over all thoughts and forms.

In this expanded consciousness, you see with new eyes the path that brought you here.

You know that it began in acceptance, the willingness to say yes to the conditions around us. You are grateful for the ability to surrender, even though it felt at first like a dangerous misstep. And you see now that your engagement, your actions in the world, bore fruit only when they were informed by the consciousness of acceptance and surrender. With the eyes of love, you see that the wisdom of allowance moved you into accord with the deepest, most constituent elements of your sacred calling. By letting go and allowing what was moving around you and through you to carry you where it was going, you found a way of life that your thought-addled mind could never have found on its own. And you see that your joy is only now beginning to dawn.

You see with increasing clarity that the richness of love in all its forms radiates from every single object in the universe, from every sentient being around you, and from the very core of your own being. It is in love that we meet. Love is simply the space where we gather when we are free enough to drop the hindrances that hold us back from this reckoning. Love allows us to know what we can never understand. These tears are washing away the lie that we are alone, that we don't matter, that we are unlovable because of the things we have done. In this love, we are forgiven, we are whole, we are free, and we are carried home to the place where we and all that is are joined in an unbreakable bond. Love is the reminder of our oneness—a oneness we had forgotten in the busyness of our lives. Love is a message from the infinitely real—We Are That, and there is no place where we do not belong, no time when we do not exist, and no hardship we cannot endure.

We know now that wisdom has little to do with the mind and its concepts. We know now that wisdom is a word for the consciousness of loving, a consciousness where healing and belonging take flight from the ground of our own being. From our place among these stars, we see the whole of existence as an expression of loving. This is why the God of the *Popul Vuh* wanted someone to say his name. In our loving, we are all, always, saying each other's names.

Breathe deeply into the reality of your own loving. Inhale love. Exhale love. Slowly, graciously, gently bring your mind back into your body—your lovely, warm, and beautiful body—and begin to move your head and your neck. Stretch your arms and your hands and your fingers. Feel the aliveness of each of your organs, in accord with all of your other organs, in harmonious and fully conscious engagement with all of the energy systems of your aliveness. How can you be anything but utterly, totally, and head over heels in love with this miraculous aliveness?

We are grateful, and humble, and unbound, and unlimited. We go forth from this place, from this moment, and vow to bring into each of our actions, our convictions, our intentions, and our commitments the echoes of this loving-kindness. It is not always going to be easy. We will forget. But we know that we always have within us this bottomless well of love that is available in all of the challenges ahead. And we know that we are walking alongside all of these other beautiful, humble, gracious, and willing beings, each with their own wounds, each with their own visions and intentions and concepts and capacities and gifts and limitations, and that together we create the world. There is always hope no matter how dark it gets because in this next now moment, someone will be willing to take a breath and start again with an open heart, an open mind, and open hands, and open eyes, and their example will enflame another, and another, until the tipping point of love moves us all closer to the ideal. The kingdom of heaven is among us, in the fabric of our loving. Our intentions are the threads, our fate the frame, our actions the weaver's hands. We weave this world from the loom of our loving. That is proof enough that we matter and that each of us is infinitely significant. But it is also true that when one of us falls, the love goes on. Death has no power over love. We are no longer paralyzed by these contradictions. We know now how to move into the field where all paradox is integrated into a wordless knowing called love. The heart sees unity where the mind saw only separation.

We are ready now for the wisdom of integration, the final stage of the seven stone path. We have cut loose enough of the dead weight of our misunderstanding to be lifted into the space where all polarities are once again reunited, where all labels, categories, and concepts fade away, or in the words of Hafiz, are "turned to ash."

I Have Learned So Much

I have learned so much from God
that I can no longer call myself a Christian,
a Hindu, a Muslim, a Buddhist, a Jew.

The truth has shared so much of itself with me
that I can no longer call myself a man, a woman,
or even a pure soul.

Love has befriended Hafiz so completely
it has turned to ash and freed me of
every concept and image
my mind has ever known.[116]

—Hafiz (c. 1315–1390)

The Seventh Stone

Chapter 7

Wisdom as Integration

Do I contradict myself? Very well then, I contradict myself. I am large. I contain multitudes.[117]
—Walt Whitman

Becoming One

In any inquiry, including this one, the tendency is to divide the whole of reality into parts, thinking that if we name and describe enough of the parts, we will know something about the whole. There is some truth to that. But it is also true that as we burrow deeper and deeper into the minutiae of the conceptual world, we turn our eyes away from the wider horizon of the mystery in which we find ourselves. Our burgeoning knowledge blinds us to simple awareness. As Laozi put it in the *Dao De Jing*, "The more you know, the less you understand."[118]

Concepts refer to reality the way a map refers to a place. Reality, in and of itself, eludes conceptual categorization. The map is not the place. Description falls short of experience. There is something beyond the reach of the mind. That's what we're really after.

As we have worked to understand the first six stones, we have made progress on the task of identifying and understanding the essential insights of the world's wisdom traditions—no small thing. But there is one final step to take: putting it all back together into an insoluble whole. As the ancient Rig Veda attests: the truth is one—the wise call it by many names. All of our names for God, all of our conflicting ideologies, and all of our never-ending disputes are testaments to our imprisonment in the field of inherently partial concepts. Part of us, the deepest part of us, longs to heal the scars from this immemorial battle.

The word *integrate* literally means "to make whole." Wholeness, or integration, is our ancient dream, as old as the moment we emerged as separate entities from the mother-womb of creation. We long to realize our oneness with wisdom, with each other, and with all matter, energy, and consciousness. We yearn to weave the disparate aspects of ourselves into a seamless whole. We want to move beyond the field of paradox and opposition, where the oneness of reality bifurcated into dualistically opposed propositions, the way white light splits into colors as it passes through a prism. On the long journey of evolution, the human mind has been a prism through which the oneness of reality split into separate and conflicting concepts. How can we get back home?

Two Truths

As college professors, my colleagues and I often talk shop, swap stories, and share strategies. Sometimes we sit in each other's classes to pick up a few tips. We are always looking for ways to address the perennial concerns of classroom management. And ask any teacher—one of the most vexing of these age-old challenges is tardiness.

It is an early sign of trouble. Chronic tardiness is a treacherous first step on a greased chute that leads right off campus and out of the middle class. Success in college, and in life, is impossible without good time management, personal responsibility, and the conscious recognition that our actions impact others. The repeated disruption to delicate classroom dynamics created by a steady stream of late students pouring through the door one by one for the first half hour of class is distracting and annoying for everyone in the room.

On a more fundamental level, it is a broken promise. It is difficult to respect people who routinely and flippantly break promises.

Some of my colleagues take a hard line. When a student arrives late, they are made to stand at the doorway until they are acknowledged by the lecturer and granted permission to enter—a very long and awkward moment. I suppose the rationale is that this embarrassing ritual, witnessed by all, will send waves of aversion through the entire room. No one would want to have to go through that—the college classroom equivalent of sticking your puppy's nose in his mistakes.

These somewhat hardline professors are respected colleagues, brilliant academics, and excellent teachers. Each of them has legions of devoted students who love them and credit them with awakening their fascination and hardening their resolve. Yet some of these hardline professors have high fail and dropout rates; by the end of the semester, their classrooms are nearly empty. They see themselves as gatekeepers, the guardians of the citadel of higher education, keeping the undisciplined and underprepared from wasting their own time, the professor's time, and draining energy from the entire room. High-level academic work and meticulous time management are not for everyone.

For some students, this stern approach to tardiness works. But I just can't bring myself to do it. To me, it seems like little more than ritualized shaming. I take a different approach. In my mind, my students are my colleagues in a learning process, and I certainly do not chastise my colleagues when they arrive late for a meeting, an all-too-common occurrence. I give them the benefit of the doubt and assume they have a good reason that is fundamentally none of my business. I look past occasional lateness, unless it becomes chronic. Then I have a private conversation with the repeat offender and try to get at the root of the problem. I respectfully lead the student to a deepening awareness of the deleterious effects tardiness has both on their own immersion in the process and on the other students in the classroom. A great majority of them modify their behavior and begin arriving on time, or at least closer to it. I try not to let perfection be the enemy of the good.

There are so many legitimate reasons a student might be late—the city bus was too full and passed by their bus stop, they were delayed at the international border (my college is eleven miles from Mexico, where many of our students reside), legitimate family emergencies, childcare issues, and so on. So many of our community college students are working poor, struggling to manage a tight work and school schedule. They may not have ready access to childcare, transportation options, and the other perks of domestic stability that affluence affords.

A large percentage of our working class students feel ostracized and marginalized from mainstream society. If they are brave enough to even enroll at all, their college classrooms are a place where they work closely with educated, accomplished adults whose profession it is to train and integrate them into their own best lives. Our students are vulnerable and take enormous personal risks every time they step on campus. Many of them are the first person in their family to attend college. From our side of the lectern, we see college as an unmitigated good. From their side, college is a hostile and alien environment, a place that draws them further and further away from their home, their family, their friends, and their culture. They are looking for a reason, any reason, to walk away. Why hand it to them?

On the downside, my more lenient, flexible approach sends a misleading message that punctuality is merely a suggestion: *You don't owe the professor or any of the other students in the room anything. Go ahead and do whatever you want.* This approach, like the more rigid approach, is far from perfect.

So which of these two approaches to student tardiness—the hard line or the soft touch—is the right one?

It is not that simple. We are both right.

Students need to be challenged and held to high standards. Old habits need to be broken, and old fears need to be stripped away, sometimes brusquely. Stern measures can be effective means of transformation.

But classrooms must also be safe harbors, sanctuaries of compassion in an already hostile and hazardous world, a place where students are honored and welcomed, not humiliated and shamed and made to feel like flawed outsiders.

Both approaches have their weaknesses. Both approaches have their strengths. Both approaches can be effective. Both approaches can fail.

How can two contradictory truths both be true at the same time? Doesn't one cancel the other one out?

The Paradoxical Nature of Truth

"The early bird catches the worm."

"All good things come to those who wait."

So which is it? Should I assertively rush forward and grab what is mine, or hold back and wait for things to come to me? The truth is both of these aphorisms are correct in different ways, at different times, and under different circumstances. And therein lies the problem with any truth-claim: they are almost always provisional, incomplete, and specific to a particular context. Something that is true now may not be true later. Truth-claims are snapshots. After the camera's shutter opens and closes, the world keeps moving.

Ralph Waldo Emerson had his critics. He was often accused of claiming one thing in one essay and then saying something different in another. He was, and still is, hard to pin down.

His critics branded him as inconsistent, a fatal flaw in any thinker, or so they said. In his most famous essay, *Self Reliance*, Emerson responded to his critics.

> A foolish consistency is the hobgoblin of little minds, adored by little statesmen and philosophers and divines. With consistency a great soul has simply nothing to do. He may as well concern himself with his shadow on the wall. Speak what you think now in hard words, and tomorrow speak what tomorrow thinks in hard words again, though it contradict everything you said today.—"Ah, so you shall be sure to be misunderstood."—Is it so bad, then, to be misunderstood? Pythagoras was misunderstood, and Socrates, and Jesus, and Luther, and Copernicus, and Galileo, and Newton, and every pure and wise spirit that ever took flesh. To be great is to be misunderstood.[119]

To be a great soul, Emerson believed, was to practice nonattachment to one's former utterances. Our stated positions are little more than the shadows we cast against a wall. In this spirit, every sentence is an exploration, not a declaration. If we are to use language properly, we must allow it to propel us forward, not hold us back. Why remain beholden to some prior formulation that no longer tells enough of the truth of what we have now come to understand? It is not that what we said yesterday has now become false; rather, it is that what we said yesterday was yesterday's best attempt at articulating the truth. Today we've got something better. We have changed. The world has changed. And our truth-statements must change with it.

By the way, what is a hobgoblin, and why is Emerson wielding it as an insult? A hobgoblin is a folklore creature whose task it is to interfere with us, confound us, bind us up in meaningless confusion, and lead us down false paths. So too slavish devotion to the false god consistency holds us back from our ever-deepening realization of wisdom. If clarity and truth are your goals, unyielding consistency is not your friend. Hobgoblins have got to go.

The word *paradox* literally means "two truths"—two contradictory statements that cannot coexist without negating each other. In the world of Aristotelean logic, paradox violates the law of noncontradiction, which states that a thing cannot be both true and false at the same time. For example, something cannot be both wet and dry; it's one or the other. If you claim that something is both wet and dry, you are, by Aristotle's standards, being incoherent, and to be incoherent is to be irrational. You might as well be gobbling like a turkey. He has a point. All language and thought would degenerate into gibberish were it not for this fundamental law of rationality. But like all laws, it was made to be broken.

On one level, it makes perfect sense to insist that concepts remain distinct from one another, and that real differences ought not to be overlooked. Up is not down, and red is not blue.

Words like *wet* and *dry* should have simple, clear, and unambiguous meaning. But on another level, as we have seen, language is itself an imperfect tool riddled with approximations and partiality. Let's not pretend that a word, a sentence, or a paragraph is a monolithic, one-dimensional reality. Language points at reality the way a finger points at the moon—and anyone can see that a finger is not the moon. We need to find a way to honor language's ability to show us the way toward understanding while not being bound by its partial portraits of reality.

Transcending the Ordinary

Second-century Buddhist philosopher Nagarjuna proposed a possible solution to this conundrum. He argued that there are two levels of knowing: ordinary knowledge and transcendent knowledge, or *prajna*.

Ordinary knowledge is comprised of concepts, rational sequences, and logical analysis of empirical evidence. Ordinary knowledge relies on analogical comparisons. We compare new perceptions and experiences to previous perceptions and experiences stored in memory. While walking through the forest at twilight, we see a long, thin shape laying across the path. Neural circuits alight in our brain as we seek to identify the object. Because we are a little afraid of snakes, we see a snake. But as we draw nearer, we see that it is only a piece of rope.

We seek to understand new experiences by cataloging them in a grid of our existing conceptual framework. We scan the horizon and categorize everything we see into a hierarchical, organizational structure. This structure is built on a foundation of prior experiences, existing paradigms, widely-accepted cultural norms, unconscious prejudices, fear, hope, and our best guesses. It is not all bad—in fact, it is quite wondrous. It is, after all, ordinary knowledge that makes possible heart transplants, Mars landings, and the microchip. But there is more. There are things ordinary knowledge just cannot grasp.

Transcendent knowledge, or prajna, is an entirely different way of apprehending reality. Prajna is nonconceptual, intuitive, mystical awareness beyond the reach of conceptual thinking. If ordinary knowledge is the thought-stream, then prajna is the boundless stillness beneath the flow of the thought-stream.

Prajna is a level of awareness unbound from the categories of understanding. It is not composed of concepts; in fact, it is understood to be empty, as in empty of fixed forms. The problem with prajna is that it is ineffable. It is impossible to talk about for one simple reason: language and thought exist only at the level of ordinary knowledge. Language and thought turn to dust as they pass into prajna. In prajna, words fail us because here we apprehend a level of reality where all categories dissolve, and without categories, there isn't much to talk about. Old epistemologies fail. Prajna is not something we know; it is something we are. We cannot think it, but we can experience it.

By making this distinction, Nagarjuna was attempting to resolve the vexing problem of the paradoxical nature of all truth claims. At the level of ordinary knowledge, it is entirely valid to insist on conceptual clarity—something cannot be both wet and dry at the same time. God cannot at once exist and not exist. But at the level of prajna, concepts such as wet and dry or existence and nonexistence, and even the concept of God itself, dissolve into indeterminacy.

In the Western philosophical tradition, there is an intriguing parallel to this approach to truth. In his masterpiece *The Republic*, Plato argues that there are four levels of knowing, each higher and more refined that the last. The lowest level is the perception of images. It isn't really knowledge per se because the images are themselves only approximations of sensory objects. The photograph of a tiger is not an actual tiger. Plato likens this level of knowledge to viewing shadows on a wall and mistaking them for real things. The second level of knowledge is empirical or sensory data—seeing the actual tiger. This is better than the previous level where we were locked into a realm of pure imagery. But this second level is still is only perception. No real thinking is taking place.

For Plato, the first two levels are not really knowledge at all. They are nothing more than beliefs or opinions. The fact that many people remain at these impoverished levels of "knowledge" and cannot or will not move higher results in a lot of chaos and darkness in the world. As we will see, knowledge requires a more objective and verifiable foundation than mere perception.

The third level is rational thought, and this is where real knowledge begins. Here, says Plato, we use the rational mind to analyze the data gleaned in the lower sensory realm. We propose hypotheses, design experiments to test those hypotheses, and establish theories. Most human knowledge is built upon this process. Rational knowledge is superior to mere perception or belief because it is supported by substantiated logical processes—claims are made that can be independently verified by anyone with a sound mind. This is the realm of science and mathematics. But there is still a fourth and final level of knowledge beyond the rational stage.

At the top of Plato's epistemological hierarchy is the level of knowing called *noesis*. Like Nagarjuna's prajna, noesis leaves behind the perceptual field, the conceptual field, language, thought, and all rational processes. It is a kind of mystical, intuitive, experiential knowing more akin to embodiment than logical certainty. For Plato, this highest level of knowing, what Vedanta calls *vidya* or realization, transcends rational thought and can never be explained using concepts, language, or the processes of reason. This means that the insights of noesis, vidya, or prajna can never be described with words or concepts to anyone's satisfaction. This leaves these highest realizations open to endless ridicule. For people who believe that rational knowledge is the highest form of knowledge, all truth-claims made from the level of noesis or prajna are derided as nonsense. Plato, like mystics the world over, was well aware of this, and he knew that there was nothing you could do about it. It is just the way it has to be. Now you know why Buddha has that sly, enigmatic smile on his face.

Here is the most important part: when you drag the integral insights of noesis or prajna down into the level of discursive thought, they shatter into paradoxical, contradictory truth-claims, like white light through a prism. That's why "Those who know don't talk. Those who talk don't know."[120]

The Cloud of Unknowing

This is why meditation and contemplation are such essential practices in the world's wisdom traditions. Thinking only gets you so far. At some point, you have to leap into the cloud of unknowing, a place where all the polarities are integrated. Meditation and contemplation are simply the most direct way to slip beneath the waves of the thought-stream and enter the boundless space within, a realm Krishna in the Bhagavad Gita calls the "Knower," or the "Inner Witness." From the vantage point of the inner witness, we calmly observe our thoughts, reactions, judgments, fears, and cravings without getting caught up in any of them. Inner witness is, of course, just another name for the nameless ground of being beyond all categories, concepts, and definitions. But it'll do.

This is why all of the arguments about the existence and nature of God are so tiresome and unsolvable: we are jousting with concepts that are, by their very nature, partial, incomplete, and doomed to insufficiency. Whatever ultimate reality is, it is beyond even the concept of ultimate reality. As we discussed in chapter two, any idea of ultimate reality is a mask made in our own likeness. Masks are concepts, and concepts are useful because they indicate partial truths. But in the end, concepts distort and obscure the very reality they attempt to portray. If you want to know God, you have to forget everything you know about God.

At the level of prajna, all paradox and contradiction is in a way resolved. As the Heart Sutra attests, "Form is emptiness.

Emptiness is form." In transcendent awareness, these apparently contradictory claims are both true, or at least true enough. They only seem contradictory at the level of ordinary knowledge. In prajna, one moves into the realization that both truth-claims in any contradictory pair have something to offer. Both of them indicate something partially true about ultimate reality, but ultimate reality is wholly contained by neither of them. A finger pointing at the moon is not the moon, the map is not the place, and the menu is not the food.

In this way, integration is the fine art of loosening the grasp of the conceptual mind without relinquishing it entirely. We still know what we know, but at the same time, we are not bound by any of it. In a word, we are free. We playfully inhabit a middle ground. As the Zen master Huang Po described, "The enlightened ones are neither attached to nor detached from their senses and thoughts."

Bud, Blossom, Fruit

In German philosophy, Georg Wilhelm Friedrich Hegel (1770–1831) was working on a similar problem. In his towering work *The Phenomenology of Spirt*, Hegel argued that truth evolved throughout human history in a dialectical process. Earlier assumptions, principles, theories, and understandings gave way to better ones. Someone asserted a truth-claim or thesis. Then someone else challenged that truth-claim by offering an opposing truth-claim—an antithesis. At this stage of the process, these two truth claims constitute a paradox, a contradiction. Hegel called the tension between these two incomplete truth-claims negation. Negation may sound like a bad word, but for Hegel, negation is a good thing because it is the engine that drives the dialectic. Out of the tension of negation comes a third formulation of truth called a synthesis. A synthesis takes the best aspects of the partial truths of both the thesis and the antithesis up into a higher, fuller, and more complete expression of truth. By taking the best and leaving the rest, the synthesis is truer and more complete than either the thesis or antithesis were. But it does not end there. Each synthesis becomes a thesis in a new triad, spawning its own antithesis, and so on. Our entire journey as a human species from ignorance to wisdom has unfolded in this way.

In the preface to *The Phenomenology of Spirit*, Hegel offered a helpful metaphor.[121] He wrote that the dialectical process develops like fruit on the branch of a tree. First comes the bud (the thesis), followed by the blossom (the antithesis), which is in turn followed by the fruit (the synthesis). Each of the three stages are plainly interconnected in significant ways. No stage exists apart from the others. In fact, each stage depends on all of the other stages for its existence. Yet the birth of a stage spells the death of the earlier stages. When the blossom emerges, the bud no longer exists.

And here is the unexpected part: the bud contained its own negation. The blossom came from nowhere other than the bud. By giving birth to the next stage, each stage generates its own destruction. So it is that every truth-claim contains its own contradiction. When you sit long enough with any truth-claim, it begins to corrode from within. The center cannot hold.

Which stage is the highest truth of the fruit tree, the best expression of its essence? The bud? The blossom? The fruit? We are asking the wrong question. You cannot have any of the stages without all of the stages. Truth has always proceeded in this way. The history of our collective human consciousness and the developmental evolution of a single person's worldview both conform to this dialectical pattern.

For Hegel, mere propositions are never a sufficient endpoint. Instead, the purpose of any linguistic expression is to move us forward toward ever increasing insight and clarity. It would be foolish to stop short anywhere along the way and miss out on what is next. Statements like "God exists" or "God does not exist" are dialectically important, each serving to negate the other. But the exciting part lay just beyond their rudimentary duality—the openness these statements provoke in us is so much more valuable than the stale and static nature of the statements themselves. Our work is never done. The task of wisdom seeking is not to plant your flag on an island and stay put, but to sail on to ever brighter harbors. "A conclusion," wrote Martin Henry Fischer, "is the place where you got tired of thinking."

In the Hegelian dialectic, it is never either/or but always both/and. Instead of choosing sides in a paradox, we draw confidence from the fact that the partial truths contained by both statements help buoy us forward across the open waters ahead.

Finding the Rudder

With Hegel's dialectic in mind, it now becomes possible to more artfully navigate the sea of contradiction in which we find ourselves. It is no longer necessary for us to cling to any particular proclamation, doctrine, or ideology. In fact, we feel the rudder of dialectical discernment guiding our boat through wave after wave of assertion and counter-assertion. Nor is it any longer necessary for us to vigorously attack any counterpoint to our current understanding; in fact, criticisms of our current position might be just the sort of negation we need to move us off of our comfortable stasis and out into open water again.

In Herman Melville's *Moby Dick*, Captain Ahab's longing for the hunt carries him far from shore. In the grand metaphor of this quintessentially American masterpiece, the sea is a realm of great and potent indeterminacy, and the shore stands as an image of stultifying safety. In Ishmael's words, "…[A]ll deep, earnest thinking is but the intrepid effort of the soul to keep the open independence of her sea, while the wildest winds of heaven and earth conspire to cast her on the treacherous, slavish shore."[122] Melville perfectly captures the spirit of the dialectical path to truth—it is in our fluidity that our aliveness is ensured. The moment we hit ground, we are trapped in an impoverished partiality. The wild, stormy, unfathomable mystery of the sea stands as a cipher for God, and the land represents the pedestrian realm of confinement in a given conceptual framework. "…[I]n landlessness alone resides the highest truth…"[123]

The mark of wisdom, then, is the ability to hold two conflicting truths aloft at the same time without being bound to either of them. The fluidity and totality of the sea is always preferable to the partiality of the fixed shore.

Let's look at two opposing truths as an illustration of this idea.

It is true that our life is the result of our choices. Our freely chosen thoughts, words, and actions shape us. But it is also true that we are indelibly shaped by our genetic traits and the countless elements of our environment that we did not choose—our parents, our family, our century, our race, our body type, our gender, our sexual orientation, our inherent cognitive traits, our culture, the value system into which we was born, and the myriad events in our lives that came to us unbidden.

Are we utterly free to invent ourselves through our choices as the existentialists claim, or is the general tone of our life set by forces beyond our control? Both views are undeniably true. A simple mind would dwell on their apparent mutual exclusion. A subtler mind allows both truths to remain aloft while moving freely in the tension between them. As Laozi wrote in the *Dao De Jing*, "The mark of a moderate man is freedom from his own ideas."[124]

True intelligence requires that we remain light on our feet. Seeing the errors in our own thinking and the strengths in our opponent's thinking frees us from the mistake of digging in our heels and making a fool of ourselves. The dialectical model of truth helps us do this. In his book *The Crack-Up*, F. Scott Fitzgerald wrote, "[T]he test of a first-rate intelligence is the ability to hold two opposed ideas in the mind at the same time, and still retain the ability to function."[125]

In fact, slavish attachment to our current ideology not only is deleterious to our well-being but also threatens the whole world. In his essay "The Triumph of Stupidity," Bertrand Russell wrote that the problem with the modern world was that "the stupid are cocksure while the intelligent are full of doubt."[126] Fundamentalists, zealots, and ideologues of all stripes plant their flag in a given explanation of the world and declare war on all other truth-claims. Their purported certainty ignores and defies the dialectical nature of truth. In Melville's metaphor, their ships have run entirely aground.

The River Raft

In the Buddhist tradition, truth is likened to a ferry at a river crossing. The teachings of the Buddha are seen as a raft whose purpose it is to carry us from one side of the river to the other. The Four Noble Truths, the Noble Eightfold Path, and all of the other insights and practices of Buddhism have tremendous instrumental value; that is, they function as powerful transformative tools. We are changed by them. But they are not the end—they are only the means.

If you are on a long journey through the jungle and come to a deep, wide river, you need a raft to get across. Once you reach the other shore, only a fool would hoist the waterlogged raft onto their back and drag it down the road. You would leave the raft behind at the river. Likewise, the teachings and practices of Buddhism or any ideology are not to be clung to or claimed as possessions. And they are most certainly not to be used as instruments of self-aggrandizement, setting your tribe above the whole of humanity in a false hierarchy.

Buddhism counsels nonattachment to all forms, including ideas, teachings, and ideological identities. As the young Zen monk demonstrated in the story shared in the introduction of this book, attachment to doctrines can inhibit empathy and compassionate action, thereby violating the underlying principles that led to the doctrines in the first place. When he and his fellow monk saw the geisha attempting to cross the stream, his slavish attachment to the monastic rule of chastity blinded him to a simple opportunity to be kind.

Attachment to doctrines, texts, and ideologies sometimes goes by the name fundamentalism. Scholars disagree about whether or not that is the right word to use for this phenomenon, but it will do. Fundamentalists, no matter their religious or ideological affiliation, share several common traits. They tend to read their own sacred literature in a narrow and literal way, condemning any attempt to interpret passages metaphorically or to even acknowledge textual contradictions or errors. For this reason they are also known as literalists.

Fundamentalists also share the view that the modern world is a fallen and corrupt place to be avoided and condemned. They often speak of the world being in moral decline. They lament the alleged decadence of contemporary culture and long for a return to an earlier, purer time—a utopian fantasy of a past that never actually existed. Hence they seek to live apart either literally or symbolically, adopting unique and identifying manners of dress and behavior. Although they believe in an all-powerful God, their all-powerful God has evidently lost control of the world—a slip-up not possible for an omnipotent being, one would think. Some sects even argue that Satan himself runs the world, in flagrant defiance of the all-powerful God. Critics of fundamentalism of course have a field day with these theological inconsistencies. Yet fundamentalism persists, capturing the imagination and loyalty of vast swaths of humanity.

Fundamentalism is in many ways a fairly recent development. Its rise coincides with the scientific age. When the Renaissance lifted European consciousness out of the medieval period, many thinkers began to see the world differently, not as a divine mystery of unexplainable magic but as a machine governed by knowable laws and thereby predictable and subject to human influence and control. With the publication of Isaac Newton's *Principia* in 1632, this worldview was codified, ushering in the Age of Reason or the European Enlightenment. Facts were valued more highly than anything else—facts that could be demonstrated with empirical evidence, replicated in experiments, and supported by rational, mathematical, and peer-reviewed processes. A new, fact-based worldview began to emerge replacing magic and faith with knowledge. From the scientific perspective, this shift was greeted with great optimism and fanfare, but in religious circles, this shift was seen as an assault on Church authority. But even religion could not escape the long reach of the Enlightenment.

In the seventeenth and eighteenth centuries, a new scientific initiative in biblical studies, particularly in Germany and France, sparked a reimagining of what it meant to be a Christian. A hunger arose to view the Bible not as a faith-text but as a fact-text. Soon, doctrines like creationism clothed themselves in the garb of science, hoping to compete with the naturalistic philosophies of Darwin and others. Western religion found itself at a crossroads: should it continue to read its own sacred literature as powerful repositories of spiritual wisdom, or should it read its sacred literature as scientific documentation? The die was cast, and today we are living in the wake of this upheaval.

In all three of the Abrahamic religions—Judaism, Christianity, and Islam—fundamentalist forces fought for control of the mainstream. In the camps of the hardliners, belief became doctrine, doctrine became dogma, dogma bred fanaticism, and fanaticism led to horror. In Buddhist terms, they had carried the raft deep into the forest, claiming that their raft was the only raft, and that anyone who did not climb onto their raft was lost forever and cut off from God. More liberal and inclusive voices within the Abrahamic faiths could only watch as their religion, once a refuge of love and sanity in a difficult world, became a hammer used to wield power, crush dissent, and elicit fear.

Despite these unfortunate developments, there is something behind the facade of religion worth saving. The mythic forms, rituals, and ethical ideals of the world's religions call us to our higher selves, enflame our loving-kindness, and draw us into community. If we read them correctly, religious scriptures lead us toward freedom and authenticity. But how?

The Power of Myth

Mythology is the collective story humanity tells itself about itself. Myths are portraits of the mystery of existence, drawn from the ordinary things around us. Domestic objects become sacred talismans, nature's powers get personified as gods and goddesses, and ordinary humans become heroes of surprising courage, nobility, and grace. We're caught in the grip of these mythic scenarios, narrative arcs, and compelling personalities because they bring us into direct contact with the essential mystery of our own existence in a way facts and literal declarations never can.

At the root of mythology's power is the metaphor. A metaphor takes a familiar idea and lays it over the top of an unfamiliar idea, in order to increase our understanding of the unfamiliar idea. For example, in Christianity, the familiar idea of father is laid over the top of the mysterious sacred source of all existence. By calling ultimate reality "Father," Christians are performing a simple act of communication and connection. We know what a father is, but the mysterious source of existence eludes our conceptual grasp. The metaphor comes to the rescue and at least gives us a handle to hold.

All myth, therefore, is best read metaphorically. Yet it is a common error to read myths literally. Mistaking the metaphor with that to which it refers is like mistaking the map for the destination or the menu for the food—it is purely a cognitive error. It might be a small thing were it not for its dire consequences. All over the world and throughout history, incalculable suffering has been generated by the fact that warring tribes have different metaphors for the same overarching mystery. For Joseph Campbell and others, this is the vexing challenge of mythology and religion: the constant struggle to stay awake to the fact that mythology is only vibrantly alive and useful to us when it is properly read as metaphor. As Campbell writes in *The Hero with a Thousand Faces*, "Wherever the poetry of myth is interpreted as biography, history, or science, it is killed… [I]t is never difficult to demonstrate that as science and history mythology is absurd. When a civilization begins to interpret its mythology in this way, the life goes out of it."[127]

With this assertion, Campbell is directly challenging fundamentalist literalism, Christian or otherwise. The creation account of Genesis, the virgin birth of Jesus, the miracles, the resurrection—according to Campbell, these are all to be properly read as metaphors. He goes even further by asserting that when we don't, we destroy the very truth these myths convey. For Campbell, fundamentalists and literalists only think they are cleaving close to the true meaning of texts, but in fact their approach does the opposite, wreaking harm to the very texts they claim to revere. By turning richly metaphorical scripture rife with psychological insight into dry, dusty "facts," we lose the opportunity to gain the wisdom they might otherwise convey. As Campbell writes, "Mythology…is psychology misread as biography, history, and cosmology."[128]

Myth, properly read, throws us out of the field of ordinary knowledge and into the transcendent knowledge of prajna. The true purpose and power of myth is to lift us into the transcendent realm beyond conceptual knowing. That's why it employs symbolism, metaphor, and fantasy to suggest, not contain, ultimate truth. Again, it's provocation, not denotation we're after.

And who creates myth? Throughout millennia, it is artists who create the symbolic language and imagery of mythology. By writing and performing music, choreographing dances, painting caves, crafting rituals and liturgy, designing buildings, planning cities, and writing plays, poems, songs, novels, and screenplays, artists of every stripe craft metaphorical portraits of the mystery drawn from the ordinary objects all around us. The value of mythology is never the image itself but what the image incites in us. As Campbell writes,

> The function of myth and ritual is to make possible, and then to facilitate, the jump—by analogy. Forms and conceptions that the mind and its senses can comprehend are presented and arranged in such a way as to suggest a truth or openness beyond. And then, the conditions for mediation having been provided, the individual is left alone. Myth is but the penultimate; the ultimate is openness—that void, or being, beyond the categories—into which the mind must plunge alone and be dissolved. Therefore, God and the gods are only convenient means—themselves of the nature of the world of names and forms, though eloquent of, and

> ultimately conducive to, the ineffable. They are mere symbols to move and awaken the mind, and to call it past themselves.[129]

Myths, properly read, cast us into the openness of integrated consciousness in a way facts and literal meaning never can. This is the ultimate power of myth. Art has a way of tearing aside our carefully maintained facades and drawing us into the immediate presence of our deepest, most important truths—truths that can never be spoken or even conceptualized. That's what Beethoven meant when he said, "Music is a higher revelation than wisdom and philosophy."

Making Peace

Any attempt to cultivate the consciousness of integration has at its core the renunciation of attachment to all ideologies. This means when you find yourself in conflict with someone, you begin by dropping your allegiance to any thought-system that contributes to the conflict, moving instead into the realization that our shared humanity is a higher truth than the doctrines that divide us.

And here is the surprise: it is not necessary for the other party to participate in the peacemaking. This shift is a wholly internal and absolutely unilateral one. The pouting stance "I'll make peace when *they* make peace" is passive aggression to the *n*th degree. If you want to perpetuate violence and conflict forever, there's your plan.

The key word is humility. By avoiding arrogance, superiority, and other ego pitfalls, we leave room for the realization of oneness to rise up through the cracks of our embittered self-obsession. If our goal is genuine reconciliation, we must see the other as an extension of ourselves. When our enemy feels our loving-kindness, they are disarmed, or at least open to persuasion in a way they were not before. As Martin Luther King Jr. wrote, "You can have no influence over those for whom you have underlying contempt."

In our families, in our communities, and in the larger world, we have an opportunity to build peaceful relations, even with those who stand in ideological opposition to us. As we demonstrate our softening grasp on our ideology through humor, empathy, loving-kindness, and humility, we send a subtle but powerful message: you too can be free of this endless conflict consciousness by loosening your grip on your ideology. The universal longing for peace and reconciliation is a powerful one. You can count on it resting in the core of every human being. Oneness is our underlying nature. You do not have to argue for it or create it from scratch. Oneness is what we are. Therefore, it is enough to just suggest it or leave room for it. It is gained more effectively by allowance than by coercion. In his startling portrait of integrated consciousness, Rumi suggests, "Out beyond ideas of wrongdoing and rightdoing,/ there is a field. I'll meet you there.// When the soul lies down in that grass,/ the world is too full to talk about./ Ideas, language, even the phrase *each other/* doesn't make any sense."[130]

Peace, then, is not an endpoint to be achieved only after we have resolved all our conflicts. It is allowed when we walk together toward a place where our conflicts no longer have the same grip on us they used to have. Peace is not something that happens in the future; it is a presence. Peace is not a destination; it is a way of being in the world here and now. As Thich Nhat Hanh wrote, "It is my conviction that there is no way to peace—peace *is* the way."[131]

Gandhi taught that in any political transformation, the means are more important than the ends. Because *Satya* (Being or Truth) is all there is, we needn't worry about achieving it or creating it. It is already the foundation of all existence. We need only ensure that our means, that is, our words and actions, are in alignment with nonviolence, empathy, and compassion. As we renounce or release our list of grievances and resolve to begin again, this time unburdened by the past, we arrive together in the present moment, a field of infinite possibility, what Rumi called the field beyond all ideas of wrongdoing and rightdoing.

As we shift into the consciousness of integration, we embody the oneness that is our essential nature. Instead of criticizing others, we trust them to find their own way. If, as Ramakrishna attests, "There are many paths to the summit," then it is essential to cultivate the humility of letting others take their own paths. When we catch ourselves in the consciousness of criticism, inwardly ridiculing the beliefs of another, we are engaging in violence. Instead, choose nonviolence.

Peace means falling out of love with our own ideas. Peace means letting go of this formulation or that ideology, no matter how elegant or moving or meaningful it used to be.

St. Thomas Aquinas was one of the most important and influential theologians of the Christian tradition. His writings changed the course of not only the Christian Church but also Western history. While saying mass on December 6, 1273, Aquinas had a life-changing mystical experience. Despite his fame and influence as an author, he put down his pen and never wrote another word. When his friend implored him to continue writing, he said, "All that I have written seems like straw compared to what has now been revealed to me." Words matter to those with little or no experience, but to those with experience, words lose their allure. Like morning dew in the noonday sun, formulaic beliefs disappear in the heat and light of love.

Why Religion?

For many people, religion can be an effective way of moving into the consciousness of integration. Religion, at its best, offers deep and vivid opportunities for meaningful relationship with mythic frameworks that help us understand the world around us as an interconnected whole. Learning to live within a power larger and more encompassing than our own egos—whether we call that power God, Brahman, Shakti, Allah, or Dao—helps us move into accord with the interdependent field of matter, energy, and consciousness in which our strange and mysterious lives play out.

In his book *Modern Man in Search of a Soul*, Carl Jung pushes back on the materialism of his colleague Sigmund Freud when he asserts that religion at its best often serves as a healing modality. With the decline in religion, he writes, a deep need is going unmet.

> [E]verywhere the mental state of European man shows an alarming lack of balance. We are living undeniably in a period of the greatest restlessness, nervous tension, confusion and disorientation of outlook….It seems to me, that, side by side with the decline of religious life, the neuroses grow noticeably more frequent…. Man has always stood in need of the spiritual help which each individual's own religion held out to him…. Healing may be called a religious problem…. Man is never helped in his suffering by what he thinks for himself, but only by revelations of a wisdom greater than his own. It is this which lifts him out of his distress."[132]

Jung then argues that the psychoanalyst and the clergyman must forge new alliances in an attempt to heal the individual and collective neuroses of modernity through a thoughtful analysis of the psyche and its interrelationship with the archetypes of the collective unconscious. This is not a call to get back the old time religion—this is a bold recognition that we have neglected the deep waters of our own souls, a stream tended for millennia by shamans, priestesses, priests and the mystical heart of our own sacred natures.

As we've seen before, the word *religion* comes from *religare*, meaning to link back or to connect. At its core, religion is a means of reintegration. People turn to religion to come in out of the alienation and loneliness of their current belief system, the one that tells them they are a single, solitary entity cast adrift in a cold and meaningless universe. As belief systems go, that one doesn't bear much fruit, nor is it particularly accurate. Seeing with one's own eyes and one's own heart the interconnectedness of all things, and finding a group of people with whom one can share this experiential knowing, is a great homecoming. This is why we gather in mosques, churches, synagogues, temples, ashrams, monasteries, sweat lodges, and cathedrals. This is why we fall to our knees in awe. This is why we raise our voices in hymnal song. This is why we meditate and pray. This is why we unleash the God-longing in us, a longing the mystics tell us is simply God-within-us longing for Itself. As thirteenth-century Christian mystic Meister Eckhart wrote, "...[W]e must abandon the God we have in our thinking and believing for God's sake, so that we might come to know God as God truly is—who never left us, beyond knowing, in a single oneness and pure union."[133] We feel in our bones a great belonging, a belonging that precedes our religious and spiritual practices, yet we honor that belonging with our rituals, liturgies, and sacred service.

In integrated spiritual and religious consciousness, we have moved beyond slavish attachment to concepts and ideologies. We are no longer enthralled by doctrinal debate. We honor conflicting opinions and belief systems because we now understand: all concepts and beliefs are provisional, partial, and incomplete. We are no longer interested in doctrinal accuracy; we have gone beyond words and concepts to the field where words and concepts cannot go. And when we meet each other in that field, we no longer ask each other, "By which path did you come?" We're simply glad to be together.

The Method of No-Method

One of the ways the consciousness of integration manifests itself is through the unadorned simplicity of our actions. After all the preparation and thinking is done, when we show up in this now moment fully awake and free of hindrances, ready and willing to allow effortless-effort to unfold of its own accord, we realize mastery. In Daoism, this is called wu-wei. Nowhere is it more artfully described than in Thomas Merton's translation of Zhuangzi's "Cutting Up an Ox."

> Prince Wen Hui's cook was cutting up an ox. Out went a hand, down went a shoulder, he planted a foot, he pressed with a knee, the ox fell apart with a whisper. The bright cleaver murmured like a gentle wind. Rhythm! Timing! Like a sacred dance, like "The Mulberry Grove," like ancient harmonies!
>
> "Good work!" the Prince exclaimed, "Your method is faultless!"
>
> "Method?" said the cook laying aside his cleaver, "What I follow is Tao beyond all methods!
>
> "When I first began to cut up an oxen I would see before me the whole ox all in one mass. After three years I no longer saw this mass. I saw the distinctions. But now, I see nothing with the eye. My whole being apprehends. My senses are idle. The spirit free to work without plan follows its own instinct, guided by natural line, by the secret opening, the hidden space, my cleaver finds its own way. I cut through no joint, chop no bone.

> "A good cook needs a new chopper once a year—he cuts. A poor cook needs a new one every month—he hacks! I have used this same cleaver nineteen years. It has cut up a thousand oxen. Its edge is as keen as if newly sharpened. There are spaces in the joints; the blade is thin and keen: when this thinness finds that space there is all the room you need! It goes like a breeze! Hence I have this cleaver nineteen years as if newly sharpened!
>
> "True, there are sometimes tough joints. I feel them coming, I slow down, I watch closely, hold back, barely move the blade, and whump! The part falls away landing like a clod of earth. Then I withdraw the blade, I stand still and let the joy of the work sink in. I clean the blade and put it away."
>
> Prince Wan Hui said, "This is it! My cook has shown me how I ought to live my own life!"[134]

In Zhuangzi's ancient parable, the cook's mastery is portrayed as fluid action so in harmony with existing conditions that plans, thoughts, and effort are no longer needed—in fact, they would hinder the flow. Perhaps most useful is the cook's description of the two preliminary stages that precede mastery. The first stage is characterized by an utter lack of discernment. Having no experience, the cook saw the ox as a blur; he could not identify the parts or understand their interrelationships. After a lot of instruction, practice, trial, and error, he reached the second stage, learning the parts of the ox and the way they joined together. But the third and highest stage was reached only when the cook left behind the analytical thinking that perceived the ox as a collection of parts. Only when he transcended mere perception and analysis and instead apprehended the ox with his whole being did his most effective and most effortless action arise. This is the power of integrated consciousness.

Personal Integration

In the groundbreaking psychology of Carl Jung, the theme of integration looms large. For Jung, personal integration was an essential component of what he called individuation. Individuation means leaving behind the immature psyche and growing into a deeper, more fully realized state where all of the elements of consciousness, both surface awareness and the deeper collective unconscious, are integrated into a harmonious whole. It means no longer simply playing out the program of your acculturation, following the herd, and kowtowing to your fears; it means really, truly, finally becoming an individual. As we learn to leave behind the conflicted fragmentation of the underdeveloped psyche, we become more balanced, more insightful, more compassionate, and healthier. Individuation, then, is Jung's word for finally become who we really are, and this is no small thing. As Emerson wrote, "To be yourself in a world that is constantly trying to make you something else is the greatest accomplishment."

Integration means not only acknowledging all of the different aspects of ourselves but also making peace with them. If we are shy, then we are shy. If we are ambitious, then we are ambitious. If we are loud and outgoing, then we are loud and outgoing. If we are reclusive, then we are reclusive. If we are a little rough around the edges, then we are a little rough around the edges. When we deny the so-called negative aspects of ourselves, what Jung called our shadow, we court danger. Our psyche will not bear compartmentalization. We thrive only when we acknowledge, embrace, and even celebrate all of the disparate aspects of our messy selves. Weakness comes from fragmentation. Strength comes from integration.

A few years ago, I had the pleasure of attending a workshop with the late, great Debbie Ford, known for her work with the Jungian concept of the shadow. I'll never forget an exercise she had us do. She told us to draw a vertical line down the middle of a sheet of paper. Then she said, "Bring to mind the most difficult person in your life, an enemy, a person you just can't stand. Write a list of all of their qualities on the left side of the page."

Someone immediately came to mind. It was a former colleague who really rubbed me the wrong way. In many ways I loved the man, but every time we had to interact, I found myself bristling with anger, which for the sake of collegiality, I suppressed. As I thought about him, I wrote down words like arrogant, obnoxious, opinionated, pompous, conceited, dogmatic, loud, cruel, insensitive, and temperamental.

Then Debbie Ford told us to bring to mind a hero, someone we really admired, and to write down a list of their qualities on the right side of the page. Several of my idols came to mind, bold and brilliant leaders who have inspired me. I wrote down words like compassionate, bright, humble, courageous, principled, articulate, wise, sensitive, funny, insightful, flexible, kind, peaceful, and creative.

The she dropped the bomb.

"Take a good long look at both lists," she said. "*All* of those qualities are *your* qualities. Both lists. You just described yourself."

At first I thought she was crazy, wrong, or both. "This is stupid," I thought to myself. "I don't have any of these negative qualities—I *hate* these qualities." But as she continued to explain, it made sense. The positive qualities on the right side of the page were our ideals, our latent potentials ready to be realized. Sometimes we even embodied and displayed them. The negative qualities on the left side of the page were our shadow, that part of ourselves we deny and suppress. Then when we meet someone in the world who exhibits those same negative qualities, an immediate aversion for that person flares up like a wildfire, often out of proportion with their actual offense. The reason for our sudden animosity is that we have come face-to-face with our own shadow, that part of us we have struggled to deny and suppress. We don't like what we see because we're seeing an unflattering manifestation of our own worst qualities. Our hatred of them is, in the end, self-hatred, which creates enormous psychic upheaval. In our unawakened state, we blame the other person for our distress, completely unaware that we are generating all of it ourselves. Instead, Ford taught, this is a great opportunity. As Jung wrote, "Everything that irritates us about others can lead to an understanding of ourselves." Those qualities we most dislike in others are the same qualities within ourselves that we have yet to make peace with.

The good news is as soon as we become aware of this dynamic, integration begins. And just as importantly, forgiveness for others, and even for ourselves, becomes possible. We realize that our contempt for this difficult person had very little to do with them or their behavior. For the first time, we become capable of owning our anger, and when we own and acknowledge our anger, we can let it go. Suddenly we see our enemy as they really are: a quirky, wounded, needy person who doesn't always say or do the right things, just like us. With this shift, our relationships are healed, and more importantly, the chasm of suffering within our fragmented psyche begins to mend as well. No longer will our submerged negative qualities eat at us from the dark. We make a place for them at the table, where we can keep an eye on them. Self-awareness is the beginning of freedom.

In this sense, integration means no longer compartmentalizing your various attributes, idealizing some and denigrating others. We come to love and accept all of our energies, aspects, and tendencies, even our shadow. We accept our imperfection as we renounce our attachment to a fantasy about who we are and how we are supposed to be. We let go of our illusions and learn to love the whole truth and nothing but the truth.

By making peace with our shadow, we move into wholeness. We are no longer caught by a shameful denial of crucial aspects of ourselves, or trapped in self-made conflict between our apparent contradictions. We begin to heal. And when we see the world with new eyes, we see a new world.

Integration also means renouncing the confusion of overthinking, coming out of the complexity of conceptualization, and coming back into natural harmony with our unmediated being. Time spent in nature helps us do this, and so does meditation, because it helps us shift from the thought-stream with its compartmentalized concepts to the boundlessness of awareness. This is why the wisdom of integration is such an essential stage. For thousands of years, philosophers, seers, sages, and mystics have tried to understand what consciousness is and how conscious works. But trying to understand consciousness is like trying to see your own eyes—you can't, because you use your eyes to see. Thinking about thinking is hamstrung by bias, subjectivity, partiality, distortion, and incompletion. We cannot understand the mystery of consciousness. We can only be the mystery of consciousness.

American philosopher and psychologist William James said that trying to understand consciousness by thinking about it is like trying to understand darkness by turning on a light: what you seek to understand is obliterated by the act of observation. How can we use an act of thinking to examine an act of thinking? A better approach would be to practice what the Zen Buddhists call no-thinking. Holistic awareness, quite apart from intellectual conceptualization, has a better shot at knowing the mystery than all the rational discourse in the world. As Jung put it, "…[T]he greatest and most important problems of life are fundamentally insoluble. They must be so, for they express the necessary polarity inherent in every self-regulating system. They can never be solved, but only outgrown."[135] And growth does not come from the mind but from the soul; the mind is only a tool we wield. As we outgrow our fragmentation and leave behind the problems it creates, we move deeper and deeper into the wisdom of integration.

In this same way, as we look back over the seven stones we have studied—acceptance, surrender, engagement, allowance, enjoyment, love, and now integration—we see the same dynamic in play. We see a new way of framing the process of personal integration.

As we have seen, there were contradictions between the seven stones. At the level of thought, contradictions always remain contradictions. How can we practice acceptance, for example, when there are things in the world we should never accept—child abuse, slavery, rape, racism, and genocide? How can we surrender in the face of these horrors? How can we practice the acquiescence of acceptance and surrender while still engaging deeply and energetically with the wounded world around us? On the surface, these paradoxes and contradictions stop us in our tracks. One could be forgiven for thinking that none of this makes any sense. This is why it is essential to view these stones or stages dialectically, that is, as evolutionary steps. As we saw in our earlier discussion of Hegel, from a distance, these so-called contradictions appear as they truly are: interlinked phases of a single, dynamic process. If you stay stuck in the insistence that contradictions are deal breakers, you rob yourself of the life-giving nourishment of the process as a whole. The wisdom of integration comes only after we release our slavish attachment to any particular iteration of truth and move instead into an appreciation of the whole sweeping landscape of truth before us. This shift requires not only a new, more dialectical approach at the level of thought but also a renewed commitment to the practice of meditation, because in meditation we leave the shore of conceptual, ordinary knowledge and swim with the current toward prajna or transcendent awareness, a realm of consciousness free of the grid of rigid conceptualization and rich with the unquantifiable aliveness of being itself.

Truth Is a Pathless Land

Even though this entire book has been predicated on the image of a path, the path metaphor is yet another concept we need to abandon in order to fully embody wisdom. The wisdom of integration requires the renunciation of attachment to all concepts, doctrines, and ideologies—even the concept of philosophical and spiritual awakening as a path. It was a useful metaphor, but metaphors have a shelf life. They grow stale. They calcify into hardened monoliths, weighing us down and inhibiting the fluid unfolding of our awakening. In the end, there is no path before us, only behind us. As Krishnamurti said, "…[T]ruth is a pathless land, and you can't approach it by any path whatsoever…"[136]

A path is just a route that many others have taken. Their traveling trammeled down the grass and wore a groove in the ground. If we are to honor our authentic individuation, we cannot follow in the footsteps of others because we do not see what they see, feel what they feel, or know what they know. Nor could they possibly embody the experiential knowing we possess. We must march to the beat of our own drummer and honor the unique authority of our own inner voice. As Matsuo Basho wrote, “Don’t follow in the footsteps of the old poets, seek what they sought.”[137]

Even the very concept of seeking is, in the end, a burdensome distortion. Seeking implies that who we are now is wrong, and until we abandon who we are and move toward a projected ideal, we can never be right. Seeking implies that we cannot awaken *here*, but only *over there*, and that *over there* is infinitely better than *here*. Sadly, much of what passes for spiritual work is shaped by this unfortunate construct.

In the nondualistic philosophies of Vedanta and Buddhism, there is nothing to seek because we are already one with the ultimate. We have only to awaken to our innate oneness. There is nowhere to go and nothing to become. We are already That. If anything, we awaken not by becoming something different, but by becoming more authentically who we already are. As thirteenth-century Christian mystic Meister Eckhart put it, “God is not attained by a process of addition of anything to the soul, but by a process of subtraction.” Only when we remove hindrances and layers of illusion will our inherent wisdom rise to the surface. The only place any of that happens is here and now. And that is why the whole process of seeking is suspect.

When the ninth-century Muslim scholar Abu Yazid al-Bistami said truth “can never be found by seeking, yet only seekers find it,"[138] he was expressing this same idea. On the surface, his statement is a paradox. It contradicts itself. But upon deeper reflection, we see that *seeking* changes meaning from the first usage to the second. In the first usage, al-Bistami is criticizing the fear-based, self-centered craving that characterizes so much of our religious longing. Like the Buddha, al-Bistami is pointing to the futility of egoic grasping and attachment. Then in the second usage, he acknowledges the simple truth that the consciousness of seeking has its benefits, namely, the fact that without a basic openness and willingness, no depth experience is possible. In a clever way, al-Bistami's statement is its own dialectic, containing both thesis and antithesis. It is for us to rise from the tension of this springboard into the clarity of our own synthesis. Living in the question is preferable to dwelling on an answer. Seeking doesn't find anything, but it puts us in a state of broken-open humility in which the seeds of wisdom can take root. By moving us toward emptiness, seeking leaves room for what is to come. It makes wisdom and enlightenment a priority, authorizing us to jettison any excess baggage that holds us back. As Laozi wrote in the *Dao De Jing*, "In the pursuit of knowledge, every day something is added. In the practice of the Dao, every day something is dropped."[139]

Drunk on Teachings

Teachers, texts, and doctrines help, just as maps are useful to any traveler. But the danger of attachment is very real. We fall in love with our gurus, ministers, rabbis, imams, therapists, and teachers, mistaking the messenger for the message. We trade in the wonder of the wilderness for the comfort of a cage, preferring the safety of our confinement to the perceived risks of life out in the open. As we begin to experience our own innate joy emerging throughout the awakening process, we mistakenly credit our teachers for the transformation. It's understandable. But they were not the source of the dawn—they were simply shaking us awake.

In the Gospel of Thomas, Jesus was certainly aware of this problematic student-teacher dynamic. In order to test his student's spiritual maturity, the master teacher gave them an oral exam:

> Jesus said to his followers, "Compare me to something and tell me what I am like," he said.
>
> Simon Peter said to him, "You are like a just messenger."
>
> Matthew said to him, "You are like a wise philosopher."
>
> Thomas said to him, "Teacher, my mouth is utterly unable to say what you are like."
>
> Jesus said, "I am not your teacher. Because you have drunk, you have become intoxicated from the bubbling spring I have tended."
>
> And he took him, and withdrew, and spoke three sayings to him.
>
> When Thomas came back to his friends, they asked him, "What did Jesus say to you?"

> Thomas said to them, "If I tell you one of the sayings he spoke to me, you will pick up rocks and stone me, and fire will comes from the rocks and consume you."[140]

By prompting his students to "Tell me what I am like," Jesus was measuring the depth of his disciple's insight. Was their understanding of him superficial or deep? Were they simply drawn to his charisma, or were they seeing past the surface into the ineffable reality of Christ-consciousness? Were they quick to label him? Or were they cognizant of the indefinable nature of this walking, talking manifestation of the awakened divine? By acknowledging the indefinable mystery of Jesus, only Thomas gave a satisfactory answer. And for this he was rewarded by being pulled aside for an even deeper, more esoteric teaching—a teaching so secret, it's not even in the text.

When Jesus said, "I am not your teacher," we see in plain words the archetypal idea that wisdom can never been handed from one person to another. The best any teacher can do is provoke the truth in us through the artfulness of their words, the power of their example, the spark in their eye, and the kindness of their unwavering faith in us. According to Jesus, the danger of misunderstanding the student-teacher relationship is real. When Jesus said, "I am not your teacher … you have become intoxicated from the bubbling spring I have tended," he made it clear that he is not the message—he is simply tending the spring. It is the spring we thirst for, and it is from the spring we must drink with our own lips, and even then, only in moderation.

So it is that teachers, doctrines, methods, and theories only pave the road, a road we must walk with our own two feet. The hazards along the way are many—attachment, arrogance, rigidity, overthinking, fear, and sloth, to name a few. It is our loving that pulls us onward—love for our teachers; love for ideas, books, community, and practices; and all of the other passageways that lead us deeper into our own freedom and joy. We should be grateful for those who went before us and left us their maps. But it is only in the furnace of our own experience that the elements they left for us are forged into the steel of our convictions, virtues, and realization.

We are grateful for our teachers, but they walk alongside us, not before us. We do not follow them; we walk with them. We look where they are pointing, but can never see what they see, nor can they can see what we see. Yet with the right discipline, a trusting stance, and an open, grace-filled heart, we encourage each other toward our most fully realized life. As Ram Dass often said, "We are all just walking each other home."

Simplicity, Patience, and Compassion

One of the hallmarks of the wisdom of integration is simplicity. As we integrate the formerly fragmented pieces of our psyches and worldviews, we leave behind the dry complexity of the conceptual grid and slip into the open waters of awareness. We grow less interested in debate and more interested in unity. Fighting for ground on the ideological battlefield seems futile, almost funny to us now. We have to laugh when we see how simple it all is. We have let go of a lot of baggage, and it feels good. As the Zen saying goes, "How refreshing, the whinny of a pack horse unburdened of everything."

Near the end of the *Dao De Jing*, Laozi distills his profound and nuanced teachings down to three words: simplicity, patience, and compassion.

> Some say that my teaching is nonsense.
> Others call it lofty but impractical.
> But to those who have looked inside themselves,
> this nonsense makes perfect sense.
> And to those who put it into practice,
> this loftiness has roots that go deep.
>
> I have just three things to teach:
> Simplicity, patience, compassion.
> These three are your greatest treasures.
> Simple in actions and in thoughts,
> you return to the source of being.
> Patient with both friends and enemies,
> you accord with the way things are.
> Compassionate toward yourself,
> you reconcile all beings in the world.[141]

Simplicity means moving past the notion that life is a struggle and instead embodying the consciousness of peace. Patience means learning how to wait and making peace with incompletion. Compassion means allowing the boundaries between everyone and everything to become porous, and making empathy the platform upon which we build our lives together. In this state, contradictions no longer vex us because we see them as necessary stages in a dialectical unfolding. Through the eyes of the wisdom of integration, we see the unification of all oppositions.

Words are insufficient, but we use and honor them anyway. Reason, logic, and science are powerful tools that lead us out of darkness and confusion, but they also confine us to a portrait of reality that leaves so much unsaid. Doctrines help us codify, express, and convey important insights and truths, but we must always see them provisionally and be willing to abandon them when they no longer serve our humanity. As in Zhuangzi's parable of cutting up an ox, when contradictions appear, we slow down, soften our stance, and feel our way through, releasing old methods and understandings that no longer serve us.

We are firm in our virtues but flexible in our willingness to learn and be led. We trust in the generative nature of the universe but work diligently to cocreate our own best lives and a world that works for everyone. We know we are shaped by large forces around us, but we retain our free will in the face of them. We recognize that nature is endlessly adaptive, resilient, and knows best how to right itself, but we never stop deliberating about how human activity harms nature's processes to the detriment of us all. We reach out to help others in need but stop short of controlling them, condemning them, or imposing our values on them. We abandon either/or thinking in favor of both/and. As Soren Kierkegaard put it, "Life is not a problem to be solved, but a reality to be experienced." In the wisdom of integration, we see problems as openings and set-backs as sacred pauses. Even our suffering takes on new significance.

The Poisonous Tree

In his book *After the Ecstasy, the Laundry* Jack Kornfield recounts the Buddhist image of the poisonous tree, an eloquent expression of the wisdom of integration. The poisonous tree represents all of the suffering of the world. In the early stages of our spiritual maturation, we seek to cut down the tree and remove it from the world so no one will suffer. We conceptualize the world as a dualistic battlefield of pure and impure, sacred and profane, or good and evil, and we work to root out everything that is impure, profane, and evil. Suffering is bad, and we have to get rid of it. We want to chop down and uproot the poisonous tree. At this stage, our spiritual work is little more than hedonism—we simply want to feel better by pretending that there is no suffering. In our limited understanding, our highest good is feeling good.

As we grow wiser and more compassionate, we come to understand that the tree of suffering is part of the interconnected web of being, and as such it cannot be evil. We understand that suffering has a place in the grand scheme of things, but we're not sure what. We still see the tree as harmful and repugnant, so we fence it off and steer others away from it. We praise the virtues of mercy, compassion, and respect. But beneath our spiritual veneer, we fear suffering—in ourselves and others—and are left exhausted and confused by its overwhelming power. We are ready for the third phase. Kornfield writes,

> Finally, as our wisdom deepens, we understand that our very problems and poisons are our best teachers. It is said that the wisest beings will come looking for this poisonous tree to use its fruit as medicine to transform the sufferings of the world. The energies of passion and desire, anger and confusion become transformed into the ardor, strength, and clarity that bring awakening. We understand that it is through facing the very sufferings of the world that the deepest freedom and compassion arise. What we once named poison is now recognized as an ally in our practice.[142]

The three phases of the process act like the thesis-antithesis-synthesis of the Hegelian triad. The incomplete truth of each stage is taken up into the next phase, and the apparent contradictions find integration in the synthesis. As we move into the wisdom of integration, we come to see the world with all its ugliness and beauty as a unified whole. We reassess our suffering and our enemies as instruments of our awakening. Like a round river stone, we lose our rough edges only when we are ground smooth by the process of tumbling along life's watercourse way. Our inner beauty is revealed only after our outer protective shell is scoured away by our suffering. This is what we come to understand in the wisdom of integration.

Final Integration

In his book *Contemplation in a World of Action,* Trappist monk, author, and theologian Thomas Merton worked hard to integrate his Christian mysticism with the mysticism of the Indian traditions, especially Buddhism. His interfaith dialogue with Buddhist monks left an indelible mark on the field of world religions and on the Roman Catholic Church. Merton embodied integration and expressed it in powerful ways.

> Again, the state of insight which is final integration implies an "openness," a "poverty" similar to those described in such detail not only by the Rhenish mystics, by St. John of the Cross, by the early Franciscans, but also by the Sufis, the early Taoist masters and Zen Buddhists. Final integration implies the void, poverty and nonaction which leave one entirely docile to the "Spirit" and hence a potential instrument for unusual creativity. The person who has attained final integration is no longer limited by the culture in which he has grown up … He accepts not only his own community, his own society, his own friends, his own culture, but all humankind. He does not remain bound to one limited set of values in such a way that he opposes them aggressively or defensively to others … He has a unified vision and experience of the one truth shining out in all its various manifestations, some clearer than others, some more definite and more certain than others. He does not set these partial views up in opposition to each

> other, but unifies them in a dialectic or an insight of complementarity.[143]

For Merton, the wisdom of integration means emptying out and moving from the busy mind with its endless conceptual attachments toward an openness, serenity, and freedom. This shift shatters our provincial notions of self and dissolves our boundaries. Oneness is no longer a poetic ideal; it is a lived reality. Integrated wisdom means embodying the consciousness of loving-kindness for all sentient beings, each with their own limited and limiting perspective and tiny, but delicious slice of the pie.

We accept what is. We surrender to life with all its contradictions. We engage bravely and humbly in the field of action. We allow ourselves to align with the energies around us and work cooperatively for the greater good. We enjoy the beauty of our lives, the beauty of the world, and the beauty of one another. We love without fear, ownership, or control. And we integrate all of these stages into a final state of wholeness that is perfect in its imperfection, harmonious in its disharmony, and rhythmic in its arrhythmia.

All is well. There is nothing we need. There is nothing we lack. We see our problems as opportunities. We show up ready and unafraid. We take on the work that is ours to do without arrogance or groveling. We sing our song, tell our story, carve our place, and stand tall in the middle of the field where we are planted. We say, I am just one, but together we are many, and together we embody the collective wisdom of the sacred source in our hearts. Let us encourage each other to be bold. Let us lift those who have lost their strength. And when the time comes, let us allow ourselves to be lifted.

We did not create this world, but we must learn how to live in it. Philosophy, the love of wisdom, must be at the core of everything we do. We turn to the ancient masters of all the world's wisdom traditions for guidance and inspiration. We study the art, religion, philosophy, science, and mythology of our ancestors, and we support the artists among us who cast the ancient archetypes into ever new forms.

The word *universe* means "one song." There is only one song, and we are all singing. No matter who you are, let your voice be heard. Let your voice take its rightful place in the music of the spheres. When you speak out lovingly, humbly, and authentically, you are as much the voice of God as any prophet, any Buddha, or any angel. When you dare to sing out in your own uniquely powerful voice, you will hear the music of your own infinite value, and you will feel the uncluttered simplicity of your authentic being. Others will hear your voice, and it will inspire them to find their own. Who are you to impoverish the one-song by your absence?

A Wise Person

A wise person feels the draw of integration, following its thread through the thicket of contradiction and paradox.

A wise person recognizes that all truth-claims are partial and incomplete, and they look for the truth hidden behind its many imperfect expressions.

A wise person understands that ordinary knowledge and transcendent knowledge are two distinct realms each with their own set of evidentiary rules. They know that what constitutes proof in one realm does not constitute proof in the other. Ordinary knowledge is rooted in reason, evidence, and logic, whereas transcendent knowledge is rooted in intuition, awareness, and mystical insight.

A wise person realizes that arguments at the level of ordinary knowledge are sometimes unresolvable, but when those same unresolved contradictions are viewed from the perspective of transcendent knowledge, paradox dissolves.

A wise person perceives the dialectical nature of truth—namely, that it moves through discreet stages of thesis, antithesis, and synthesis, and that like the stages of a bud, blossom, and fruit, they are all part of one unfolding.

A wise person knows that dogged attachment to a single ideology leads one further away from truth, not toward it. If all doctrines and concepts are viewed as partial expressions in a dialectical process, then stopping anywhere along the way is a mistake.

A wise person understands that reading mythology as literal fact destroys its power, beauty, and meaning. Myth is metaphor, and its power lies in its ability to throw us into direct experience of the ineffable, a realm beyond reason, science, and fact.

A wise person knows that our shared humanity is a higher truth than the doctrines that divide us, and that peace is only possible when we renounce attachment to ideologies. By seeing all positions and truth-claims as provisional, the way to resolution through negotiation becomes clear.

The wise person understands that even if it is not for them, religion plays a vital role in most people's lives. It provides community and a shared narrative encompassing both the suffering and the grace of the world. Religion, like art and mythology, is one of the many valid ways of moving beyond the surface of things and touching the eternal.

The wise person understands that their actions achieve an effortless mastery when they see themselves and their work as one inseparable whole.

A wise person understands that when they view all of the fragmented aspects of their psyche as an integrated whole, even their shadow—those least pleasant aspects of themselves—they move from confusion into clarity, from partiality into wholeness, and from debilitation into empowerment.

A wise person knows that action has to be taken to further our deepening into the consciousness of integration. It isn't enough just to read about it or think about it. You have to embody it. Meditation is an excellent way to move toward embodiment, as is time spent in nature.

A wise person realizes that truth is a pathless land. They also know that though teachings and teachers are important, we must not become attached to them. Strengthened by the examples and suggestions of others, yet knowing that they are going where others have not gone, the wise person moves through the waters of indeterminacy with gratitude and courage. A sailboat was not built for the harbor.

A wise person puts above all else these three principles: simplicity, patience, and compassion. They favor clarity over clutter. They know how to wait. And they stay open-hearted, no matter what it costs.

A wise person knows that the suffering of the world is, in the end, to be integrated along with everything else. Our enemies, our struggles, and our unmet needs are the hands that shape our lives, the way a potter's hands shape clay on the wheel. We are made by our adversity. Yes, it hurts, but it is childish to wish it away and pine for a pain-free world. Wisdom finds a way forward through the ravages of suffering by the light of compassion.

A wise person moves from the partiality of choosing sides toward a unified vision of the world. They come to see all things as interconnected and mutually dependent. Everything causes everything else, and all energy, matter, and consciousness exist in a continuum of interdependence.

Closing Meditation

In our final guided meditation, let's bring all of the elements of the seven stone path together into one integrated whole.

We've done a lot of thinking. We've done all the thinking we need to do for now. Let's go into the stillness and allow the things we've come to understand to take root in embodiment.

If you are reading this, soften your gaze. If you are listening to this, close your eyes if you can. Sit back in your chair and place both feet flat on the floor. Let your hands rest in your lap. Take a big, deep cleansing breath. And another. Allow your breathing to resume its natural rhythm.

Subtly lift the crown of your head so that your spine lengthens slightly, without straining or stretching. Allow your shoulders to drop, and let a softness come over your face, relaxing all of the muscles around your eyes and your mouth. Let all of the tension of the day slip away. Feel a deep relaxation slowly filling your body with peace.

Allow the tension and stress that you normally hold in your neck and shoulders to soften and slip away. Bring your attention to your chest and allow gratitude to bathe your heart, your lungs, and all of your other organs with healing energy. Bring your attention to your abdomen, your stomach, and your entire digestive system. Gratefully acknowledge the miraculous work they perform every hour of every day, turning the energy of food, which is the energy of the sun, into the energy of your body-mind. We are made of light from a nearby star.

As you become more relaxed, you feel the last remnants of tension slip down through your legs, out through the soles of your feet, and into the earth, which is strong enough to hold all of it. Feel yourself supported, embraced, and buoyed by the strength of our Mother.

Now gently bring your attention to your thoughts. Notice how they come and go without your consent. They flow continually unbidden. The mind's nature is activity. Instead of trying to still the mind, simply let it do what it does without interference. No struggle, no strain.

Allow yourself this realization: the very fact that you can witness your thoughts arise and fade means that there is a part of you that is not your thoughts. This one simple idea is the most important shift in the entire meditation process—the realization that we are not our thoughts. We have operated under a mistaken and unexamined assumption all these years; we identified with our thoughts. We thought our thoughts were us. It was a simple mistake, and it is simply corrected. In fact, we have already corrected it. Simply noticing that we can witness our thoughts means that we are not our thoughts—we are their witness. All of the immeasurable benefits of meditation flow from this one realization.

Now gently turn your attention toward that part of you that is witnessing your thoughts, what Krishna in the Bhagavad Gita called the inner witness or the Knower. Our goal here is not to generate more thoughts about this, but to leave the realm of thought behind. Simply continue witnessing your thoughts with the same nonattachment with which you would watch passing traffic from your second-story hotel room in a foreign city. The cars come and go. You don't try to control them. They have nothing to do with you. You just watch. You are only their witness. You are free.

As we slip further into this realization, we feel a deep and expanding spaciousness. Here there are no thoughts, no concepts, no impressions, no sensations, no opinions, no reactions, and no resistance. Some people describe it as a field of light, others as a vast and empty sky. Avoiding the temptation to name it or describe it, simply be in this nameless spaciousness and notice the way it feels. Don't think about it. Don't form an opinion about it. Simply experience it. Allow it. Be it.

If thoughts or sensations arise, notice them come and go, without resisting or clinging to any of them. We are in a place of stillness and freedom, of boundlessness beyond all concepts, a place of pure awareness and radiant love.

Stay a while in the silence.

Now, one at a time, let us bring into the spaciousness of our awareness the seven stones, not as concepts but as embodied, experiential realities.

Feel the freedom that comes when we embrace the wisdom of acceptance.

Taste the serenity of the wisdom of surrender.

Be emboldened by the wisdom of engagement.

Feel how the wisdom of allowance draws you into alignment with all of the energies coursing through and around you.

Like a child, allow the wisdom of enjoyment to well up and fill your heart.

Fall into the wisdom of love as you embrace the wonderful, painful, imperfect world and all of the wounded souls who walk alongside you.

Feel yourself moving out of the confusion of fragmentation and into the wisdom of integration as you let the beauty of the world take your breath away. Take solace in the knowledge that just beneath the surface of the foreground lies a deeply harmonious background of interdependence and interconnectedness, and that we are safely held and supported by the sacred web of being that manifests itself as all things.

We see that our being does not end at our fingertips but extends throughout all forms, dimensions, and fields of awareness. Everything is integrated with everything else.

We are awakening from the dream of separateness.

All is well. As we witness the arising and fading of all body-mind states, we rest easy in the heart of awareness, knowing that this embodied wisdom is not part of the transient world of forms, but is the Witness of them all. We are one with the God-principle that gives rise to every form, just as the sea gives rise to every wave. We are beyond doctrine, beyond belief, beyond opinion, beyond fact, and deep in a star-filled sky of awareness.

We will not forget this boundless knowing. We know now that we are this awareness. As we gradually and gently bring our attention back to this room, this space, our body, this chair, these hands, and this miraculous body-mind temple, we open our eyes, stretch, and allow the lingering inner light to bathe the remains of this day, the day after, and the day after that. We carry this light into everything we do. We vow to be the presence of compassion and wisdom as best we can in the challenges that lay ahead. We do not burden ourselves with complexities. We celebrate the possible. We do better. And we take refuge in the wisdom we have become.

We allow our loving to show us where to go, and how to get there.

This is what it means to walk the seven stone path.

Afterword

All the way to heaven is heaven.
—St. Catherine of Siena

We've come to the end of our study of the seven stone path. Now what?

Here's what. Let's put it into practice.

A book like this only matters if it results in real change. Who doesn't love the beautiful ideas of the world's wisdom traditions? But just as dots and lines on a page don't become music until we play them, the principles and practices in this book don't become wisdom until we embody them.

How do we "play" the music of this book?

Here are a few suggestions. First, begin paying attention to your own thoughts and actions. Self-examination and self-knowledge are where all philosophy begins. If we are not conscious of the processes by which we arrive at our assumptions, conclusions, convictions, positions, opinions, and worldview, then we too easily fall prey to error.

Challenge yourself to deepen into each of the seven stages in the course of your everyday life at work, in your family, in your relationships, in your art, in your service, and in your play.

But don't try to do it all alone. Buddha called the community the *sangha*, and he deemed it an essential part of the awakening process. Whether you join together in formal communities, neighborhood circles, or friendships, find a way to come out of your isolation. Study this book in a book club. Build a workshop around it. Create exercises. Journal together about it. See if you can adapt some or all of the ideas in this book to your own community's unique needs, perspectives, and purposes.

Also, get serious about your meditation practice. Yes, it is important to work in collaboration with others, but equally important is your inner work. Commit to at least five minutes a day of meditation, then ten, then twenty. Meditate when you don't feel like it—especially when you don't feel like it. Commit to sit every day, even if it isn't "working"—especially when it isn't working. Soon the struggle will soften and the sweetness will arise. Wait for it. It always does. You can count on it. And if you're new to meditation, there are countless teachers online, and maybe even in your town, who can help. You can read and think about these ideas all you want, but there is no substitute for the depth insight meditation affords. As we've seen in this book, thinking only gets you so far. To make the final passage, we must let go of the realm of thought in order to swim across deep water to the realm of awareness. Meditation is that passage.

Ultimately, spiritual or philosophical transformation is not a process of becoming something new. It is not a rejection of a broken version of yourself. Awakening or realization is a process of moving past all definitions of self and into simple, boundless awareness. Enlightenment is not a private experience, and neither is it a possession or an achievement. As many teachers say, there are no enlightened persons; there is only enlightenment. When enlightenment happens, there is no one there to claim it. All the mystical traditions teach the same thing: that the final realization is a homecoming into oneness, like a raindrop falling into the sea and realizing that it was the sea all along. It only thought it was a raindrop.

There is inevitable disruption when old modes of thinking and old ways of being fall away. It is not always comfortable to learn and grow. Pain is what growth feels like. But ultimately there is no struggle, no striving, no ardent seeking, and no loneliness, because we are not becoming something we are not—we are awakening to what we have always been. Wisdom is homecoming.

Wisdom as Acceptance

Wisdom begins with acceptance of what is. Acceptance is the decision to stop resisting current conditions. When we move out of resistance and into acceptance, when we unclench our hearts and minds and fists, the foundation for right action is established, and doors open through which wisdom can begin moving in and out of our lives. Without this first essential step, none of the other steps are possible.

Wisdom as Surrender

If acceptance means acknowledging the river is flowing, surrender means falling in. The last remnants of our resistance wash away, leaving us in state of readiness unlike anything we have ever experienced before. By relinquishing strident seeking and combative assertions, we leave room for wider and deeper awareness.

Wisdom as Engagement

Now that we have deepened into the consciousness of acceptance and surrender, we are ready to stand tall and engage with the world in the field of action without attachment to outcomes. Here we engage in action not as a personal act but as an act of service. We acknowledge that real transformation, on the individual level as well as globally, cannot occur without conscious, vigorous, compassionate action.

Wisdom as Allowance

We've accepted current conditions, surrendered the ego to our larger purpose, and engaged with life in the field of action. Now we move into deeper accord with the generative intelligence of the universe through allowance. Allowance means aligning, cooperating, and cocreating at the deepest level with the energies already moving around us. We embrace the paradox of action in the midst of inaction, mastering the practice of creative letting-be.

Wisdom as Enjoyment

When the first four steps are in full practice, we move into enjoyment, making peace with the material world and genuinely embracing the beauty and pleasure of life. Through laughter and aesthetic rapture, we continue to emerge from our egoic shell and enter the wider world. We are at play in the field of forms without attachment to any of them.

Wisdom as Love

As we learn to embody the first five steps, we fall in love with the world in a new and vitalizing way. Without ownership or ego, we allow our heart to open and lead us into a direct experience of the mystery beyond all thought, present within all things. Here we experience the collapse of the apparent conflict between egoism and altruism. We become ardent and skillful caretakers of ourselves and others.

Wisdom as Integration

In the end, it all comes together. No longer torn by paradoxes, bound by rules, or confined to doctrines, we transcend all dualities and emerge in a field of pure awareness characterized by serenity and loving-kindness. We recognize that the world's religions and wisdom traditions are all viable maps to this experiential awareness, a mode of consciousness bound by none of them. We return to childlike simplicity and humbly show up in our own lives unburdened, willing, and joyfully alert. By artfully embodying all seven stages, we have transcended conflicts and unified dichotomies into a seamless whole beyond the reach of the conceptual mind, which is forever reliant on dualistic thought systems predicated on opposition and conflict. We have not achieved wisdom—we have become wisdom.

Acknowledgments

With the creation of any book, there are countless people to acknowledge and thank for their priceless contributions.

First in line is my wife, Lori Bolland, who held a vision of the possibility of this book longer and better than I have. We've been together since 1983 when I was just a wee twenty-five-year-old. She has always been the source of my courage and the inspirer of my willingness to take risks in all areas of my life. She knew it would work, she knew it would be all right, and she knew I would always find my feet, no matter how far I fell. She has been my first reader, editor, and proofreader, always willing to say kindly and quietly, "This passage doesn't make any sense," or, "I don't know what you mean here." This has proven essential. As a writer, the last thing you need is a yes-man. I can count on Lori for the truth. Although it sounds overly dramatic, it is quite plainly true that were it not for her, this book, and most of the rest of the work I do, would never have happened.

After Lori, it is tempting to go back in time and acknowledge every friend, family member, teacher, colleague, collaborator, author, artist, and fateful stranger who ever helped me, held me in kind regard, or showed me something I had missed. But that would be an endless list and a bore to read. Once I start down that road, I would never come back. Instead, I am simply reminded of Meister Eckhart's line: "If the only prayer you ever say in your entire life is 'Thank you,' it will be enough." I have to believe that. I wake up every morning and fall asleep every evening with those holy words on my lips. To everyone and everything, and the spirit that unites us all, thank you.

Focusing strictly on the production of this book, I want to thank my friend, trusted ally, and former student Ammar Campa-Najjar, who brought his considerable skill as a writer, thinker, and communications expert to bear on the task of reading early drafts of this book and offering invaluable advice. He helped me pull the fuzzy parts into sharper focus.

Once the book was finished, I imposed on six trusted friends to read it and offer their invaluable insights and suggestions: Joan Borysenko, Richard Louv, Oriah Mountain Dreamer, Wendy Craig-Purcell, Chip Franklin, Maggy Whitehouse, and Dr. Sheila Patel, each one of them accomplished professionals, brilliant communicators, experienced teachers, and generous mentors.

These are just a few of the many hands that helped build this book. But if there are things about *The Seven Stone Path* that bother you or seem flawed, I assure you the fault for those is entirely mine.

And a hearty thank-you to everyone at Balboa Press who shepherded me through the daunting task of book publishing, from editing to design, to marketing, to distribution. In their capable hands, the impossible became not only possible, it became downright easy. The only thing in the way, as usual, was myself.

Endnotes

[1] Nisargadatta Maharaj, *I Am That,* trans. Maurice Frydman, ed. Sudhakar S. Dikshit (Durham: Acorn, 1982), 534.

[2] Confucius, *The Analects of Confucius*, trans. Arthur Waley (New York: Vintage Books, 1989), 2:17, 91.

[3] Nisargadatta Maharaj, *I Am That*, 384.

[4] Plato, "The Apology," in *The Last Days of Socrates*, trans. Hugh Tredennick (London: Penguin Books, 1969), 49.

[5] Lao Tzu, *Tao Te Ching*, trans. Stephen Mitchell (New York: HarperCollins, 1988), 1. In the body of this book I have converted all Wade-Giles transliterations of Chinese words into the more contemporary (and more accurate) Pinyin transliterations, so that Lao Tzu becomes Laozi, *Tao Te Ching* becomes *Dao De Jing*, and so on. Preferred worldwide by scholars of Chinese history, philosophy, and language, Pinyin is rapidly eclipsing the older and less precise Wade-Giles system. Here in the endnotes, however, I have retained the Wade-Giles renderings out of respect for my sources and their transliteration preferences.

[6] Lao Tzu, *Tao Te Ching*, 56.

[7] Matthew, 7:6 (NIV).

[8] Krishnamurti, "Truth is a Pathless Land—The Dissolution of the Order of the Star," in *Krishnamurti: 100 Years*, Evelyne Blau (New York: Stewart, Tabori & Chang, 1995), 85.

[9] Henry David Thoreau, *Walden and Other Writings* (New York: Bantam, 1982), 343.

[10] Dogen, "The Manifestation of the Truth," in *The Enlightened Mind*, ed. Stephen Mitchell (New York: HarperCollins, 1993), 101.

[11] Jim Dreaver, "Release Attachment to Outcomes," quoted in Trish Scott's blog *Breathing,* May 27, 2018, https://scottfree2b.wordpress.com/category/j-krishnamurti/.

[12] Lao Tzu, *Tao Te Ching*, 50.

[13] Albert Einstein, "Correspondence," quoted in Freeman Dyson's *Disturbing the Universe* (New York: Basic Books, 1979), 193.

[14] *The Gospel of Thomas: The Hidden Sayings of Jesus*, trans. Marvin Meyer (New York: HarperCollins, 1979), verse 51.

[15] Luke 17:20–21 (NIV).

[16] *The Qur'an*, 50:16, January 9, 2023, https://quran.com/50/16

[17] Dogen, in *The Enlightened Mind*, 99.

[18] Matthew 4:17 (NIV).

[19] Ibid. 6:25–29 (NIV).

[20] Ibid. 6:33 (NIV).

[21] Lao Tzu, *Tao Te Ching*, 51.

[22] Epictetus, *The Art of Living: The Classic Manual on Virtue, Happiness, and Effectiveness—A New Interpretation by Sharon Lebell* (New York: HarperCollins, 1995), 17.

[23] Marcus Aurelius, *Meditations*, trans. Gregory Hays (New York: Random House, 2003), 60.

[24] Ibid. 34.

[25] Epictetus, *The Art of Living*, 7.

[26] Ralph Waldo Emerson, "Spiritual Laws," in *The Essential Writings of Ralph Waldo Emerson*, ed. Brooks Atkinson (New York: Modern Library, 2000), 188.

[27] Reinhold Niebhur, "Serenity Prayer," in *Twelve Steps and Twelve Traditions* (New York: Alcoholics Anonymous World Services, 1981), 41.

[28] *Bhagavad Gita*, trans. Eknath Easwaran (Tomales, CA: Nilgiri Press, 2007), 3:33, 108.

[29] Rudyard Kipling, "If," public domain on Poets.org, accessed 1/24/23, https://poets.org/poem/if

[30] Epictetus, *The Art of Living*, 21.

[31] Eckhart Tolle, *Stillness Speaks*, (Novato, CA: New World Library, 2003), 103.

[32] Carl Jung, *Modern Man in Search of a Soul*, trans. W. S. Dell and Cary F. Baynes (Oxon, UK: Routledge, 2001), 240.

[33] Adyashanti, *The End of Your World: Uncensored Straight Talk on the Nature of Enlightenment*, ed. Tami Simon (Boulder: Sounds True, 2008), 149.

[34] Lao Tzu, *Tao Te Ching*, 50.

[35] Ibid. 29.

[36] *Bhagavad Gita*, 4:18, 118.

[37] Matthew 11:30 (NIV).

[38] John 12:24 (NIV).

[39] Friedrich Nietzsche, *The Gay Science,* in *The Portable Nietzsche*, trans. and ed. Walter Kaufmann (New York: Viking Press, 1966), 95.

[40] Chuang Tzu, *The Way of Chuang Tzu*, trans. Thomas Merton (New York: New Directions, 1997), 154.

[41] John 14:10 (NIV).

[42] Luke 17:21 (NIV).

[43] *The Rig Veda*, trans.Wendy Doniger (London: Penguin, 1981), 1.164.46, 80.

[44] Nisargadatta Maharaj, *I Am That*, 229.

[45] Abu Yazid al-Bistami, in *The Enlightened Mind*, 76.

[46] Meister Eckhart, in *The Enlightened Mind*, 114.

[47] Ramana Maharshi, quoted in "Spiritual…But Not Religious" (Bhuddini blog), accessed 1/14/23, http://spiritualnotreligious.blogspot.com/2011/04/ramani-maharshi-surrender-self-enquiry.html.

[48] Adyashanti, *True Meditation: Discover the Freedom of Pure Awareness,* ed. Tami Simon (Boulder, CO: Sounds True, 2006), 45.

[49] Epictetus, *The Art of Living*, 107.

[50] *Twelve Steps and Twelve Traditions* (New York: Alcoholics Anonymous World Services, 1981), 5.

[51] Lao Tzu, *Tao Te Ching*, 38.

[52] Ibid. 78.

[53] *Bhagavad Gita*, 6:5-6, 140.

[54] Lao Tzu, *Tao Te Ching*, 58.

[55] *Twelve Steps and Twelve Traditions* (New York: Alcoholics Anonymous World Services, 1999), 99.

[56] Epictetus, *The Art of Living*, 65.

[57] Rumi, "Each Note," *The Essential Rumi*, 103. Used with permission.

[58] Epictetus, *The Art of Living*, 24.

[59] Buddha, *The Dhammapada*, trans. Eknath Easwaran (Tomales: CA, Nilgiri Press, 2007), verse 145.

[60] *Bhagavad Gita*, 2:16-18, 90.

[61] Ibid. 2:12, 89.

[62] Ibid. 3:15, 106.

[63] Ibid. 3:25, 107.

[64] Luke 23:34 (NIV).

[65] *Bhagavad Gita*, 18:48, 262.

[66] Barre Toelken, "Seeing with a Native Eye: How Many Sheep Will It Hold" in *Seeing with a Native Eye: Essays on Native American Religion*, ed. Walter Holden Capps (New York: Harper & Row, 1976), 21-22.

[67] *The Indians' Book: An Offering by the American Indians of Indian Lore, Musical and Narrative, To Form a Record of the Songs and Legends of Their Race*, recorded and edited by Natalie Curtis Burlin (New York: Harper and Brothers, 1907) 11, online facsimile accessed through Open Library on 1/19/23, https://openlibrary.org/books/OL7043663M/The_Indians%27_book at https://archive.org/details/offeringindianlore00burlrich/page/11/mode/1up?ref=ol&view=theater.

[68] Matthew 5:44 (NIV).

[69] Nisargadatta Maharaj, *I Am That*, 490.

[70] Galatians 6:7 (NIV).

[71] Albert Camus, "The Myth of Sisyphus," in *The Myth of Sisyphus and Other Essays* (New York: Random House, 1955), 88-91.

[72] Camus, "The Myth of Sisyphus," 90-91.

[73] Buddha, *The Dhamapada*, verse 1.

[74] Nisargadatta Maharaj, *I Am That*, 492.

[75] Malcolm Gladwell, "The 10,000 Rule: In Hamburg We Had to Play for Eight Hours" in *Outliers*: *The Story of Success* (New York: Little, Brown and Company, 2008), 35-68.

[76] Nisargadatta Maharaj, *I Am That*, 513.

[77] Joseph Campbell, *The Hero With a Thousand Faces*, 3rd ed. (Novato, CA: New World Library, 2008).

[78] Epictetus, *The Art of Living*, 25.

[79] Epictetus, *The Art of Living*, 113.

[80] Deepak Chopra, Twitter, February 7, 2012, 4:48 PM. https://twitter.com/deepakchopra/status/167047109793685505

[81] George Lucas, *Star Wars Episode IV: A New Hope* (Twentieth Century Fox, 1977)

[82] Lao Tzu, *Tao Te Ching*, 64.

[83] Philip Novak, *The World's Wisdom* (New York: HarperCollins, 1994), 152.

[84] Lao Tzu, *Tao Te Ching*, 48.

[85] Ibid.

[86] Ibid. 27.

[87] Ibid. 15.

[88] Ibid. 78.

[89] Eknath Easwaran, *The Compassionate Universe: The Power of the Individual to Heal the Environment* (Tomales, CA, Nilgiri Press, 1989), 54.

[90] Matthew 11:28–30 (NIV)

[91] Mitchell, Stephen, *The Gospel of Jesus* (New York: HarperCollins, 1991), 75.

[92] Henry David Thoreau, *Walden and Other Writings*, ed. Joseph Wood Krutch (New York: Bantam Books, 1962), 343.

[93] *Bhagavad Gita*, 4:18, 118.

[94] Epictetus, *The Art of Living*, 35.

[95] Ibid. 44.

[96] Dogen, in *The Enlightened Mind*, 100.

[97] *Bhagavad Gita*, 5:8, 128.

[98] John 14:10-12 (NIV)

[99] *The Gospel of Thomas*, verse 70.

[100] Epictetus, *The Art of Living*, 46.

[101] Judith Boss, *Ethics for Life: A Text with Readings*, 6th ed. (New York: McGraw Hill, 2014), 308-313.

[102] Ralph Waldo Emerson, "Merlin's Song," *The Complete Works of Ralph Waldo Emerson*, Volume IX, Poems (Boston and New York: Houghton, Mifflin & Company, 1904), and (New York: Bartleby.com, 2013), 219.

[103] Mohandas K. Gandhi, as quoted in the introduction to the Isha Upanishad, in *The Upanishads*, 2nd. ed., trans. Eknath Easwaran (Tomales, CA: Nilgiri Press, 2007), 53.

[104] Matsuo Basho, *The Essential Haiku: Versions of Basho, Busson and Issa*, ed. and trans. Robert Hass (New York: Ecco, 1994), 11

[105] Joseph Campbell, with Bill Moyers, "Episode VI: Masks o Eternity," from *The Power of Myth*, (Mystic Fire Video, 1988)

[106] William Wordsworth, "Lines Composed a Few Miles Abov Tintern Abbey, on Revisiting the Banks of the Wye During a Tour, July 13, 1798," in *The Norton Anthology of English Literature*, 5th ed. Vol. 2, ed. M. H. Abrams (New York: W. W Norton & Company, 1986), 152.

[107] Nisargadatta Maharaj, *I Am That*, 8.

[108] Joseph Campbell, with Bill Moyers, "Episode V: Love and the Goddess," from *The Power of Myth*, (Mystic Fire Video, 1988)

[109] Matthew 5:43–44 (NIV)

[110] Galatians 3:28 (NIV)

[111] 1 Corinthians 13:4–5 (NIV)

[112] *Hindu Myths*, trans. Wendy Doniger O'Flaherty (New York Penguin, 1975), 34-35, as quoted in *The World of Myth*, ed. David Adams Leeming (New York: Oxford University Press, 1990), 31

[113] Paul Jordan Smith, "In the Very Beginning," *Parabola*, 2, no. 2 (Spring 1977), 41-43, as quoted in *The World of Myth*, ed. David Adams Leeming (New York: Oxford University Press, 1990) 60-62.

[114] William Wordsworth, "The Tables Turned," in *The Norton Anthology of English Literature*, 151.

[115] Thich Nhat Hanh, *True Love: A Practice for Awakening the Heart* (Boulder, CO: Shambhala, 2009), 4.

[116] "I Have Learned So Much," from *The Gift: Poems By Hafiz*, trans. Daniel Ladinsky (New York: Penguin, 1999), 32. Used with permission.

[117] Walt Whitman, "Song of Myself," from *Leaves of Grass*, in *The Norton Anthology of Modern Poetry*, 2nd ed., ed. Richard Ellmann and Robert O'Clair (New York, W. W. Norton & Company, 1973), 53.

[118] Lao Tzu, *Tao Te Ching*, 47.

[119] Ralph Waldo Emerson, "Self Reliance," in *The Essential Writings of Ralph Waldo Emerson*, ed. Brooks Atkinson (New York: Modern Library, 2000), 138.

[120] Lao Tzu, *Tao Te Ching*, 56.

[121] Georg Wilhelm Friedrich Hegel, *Phenomenology of Spirit*, trans. A. V. Miller (Oxford: Oxford University Press, 1977), 2.

[122] Herman Melville, *Moby Dick or the White Whale*, (Boston: The Saint Botolph Society, 1892), 104.

[123] Ibid.

[124] Lao Tzu, *Tao Te Ching*, 59.

[125] F. Scott Fitzgerald, *The Crack Up*, (Richmond, UK: Alma, 2018), 58.

[126] Bertrand Russell, "The Triumph of Stupidity," in *Mortals and Others: Bertrand Russell's American Essays, 1931-1935*, v. 2, ed. H. Ruja, (Oxon, UK: Routledge, 1998), 28.

[127] Joseph Campbell, *The Hero With a Thousand Faces* (Novato, CA: New World Library, 2008), 213

[128] Ibid. 219.

[129] Ibid. 221-222.

[130] Rumi, "A Great Wagon," *The Essential Rumi*, 36. Used with permission.

[131] Thich Nhat Hanh, *The Art of Power* (New York: HarperOne, 2007), 163.

[132] Carl Jung, *Modern Man in Search of a Soul*, 236, 242, 246.

[133] Meister Eckhart, *Book of the Heart: Meditations for the Restless Soul*, trans. Jon M. Sweeney and Mark S. Burrows (Charolttesville, VA: Hampton Roads Publishing, 2017), 59.

[134] Chuang Tzu, *The Way of Chuang Tzu*, trans. Thomas Merton (New York: New Directions, 1997), 45.

[135] Carl Gustav Jung, "Commentary on *The Secret of the Golden Flower: A Chinese Book of Life*," In *Jung on Active Imagination*, ed. Joan Chodorow (Princeton, NJ: Princeton University Press, 1997), 75.

[136] Krishnamurti, in *Krishnamurti: 100 Years*, 85.

[137] Matsuo Basho, "Basho on Poetry—Learn From the Pine," in *The Essential Haiku: Versions of Basho, Buson, & Issa*, 233.

[138] Abu Yazid al-Bistami, in *The Enlightened Mind*, 76.

[139] Lao Tzu, *Tao Te Ching*, 48.

[140] *The Gospel of Thomas,* verse 13.

[141] Lao Tzu, *Tao Te Ching*, 67.

[142] Jack Kornfield, *After the Ecstasy, the Laundry* (New York: Bantam Books, 2000), 166.

[143] Thomas Merton, *Contemplation in a World of Action* (Notre Dame: Notre Dame Press, 1998), 206-207.

Milton Keynes UK
Ingram Content Group UK Ltd.
UKHW040633090224
437425UK00003B/53

9 798765 240